THE
CAN'T-IDATES

Running For President When
Nobody Knows Your Name

Craig Tomashoff

bobtimystic
BOOKS

The Can't-idates: Running For President When Nobody Knows Your Name
is another Bobtimystic Books project.

Design & editing:
Bob Makela

ISBN-13: 978-0692606377
ISBN-10: 0692606378

Manufactured in the United States of America
First Edition
Eighth Printing

To order this book or to contact the publisher go to:

www.BobtimysticBooks.com

Suggested retail price: $20.00

For Roman and Chiara,
who will prove that all good things are possible.

"Those who stand for nothing
fall for anything."

~Alexander Hamilton

"I don't make jokes. I just watch the government
and report the facts."

~Will Rogers

table of contents

Acknowledgements

Okay, this is hard. Ordinarily, I'm the sort of person who dispenses "thank yous" as if they were CDs from the '90s offering 800 free hours of AOL. It's cool at first, but gets unnecessary very quickly. I can't help it, though. My mom taught me ages ago that if you want to make an impression, always show gratitude for anything and everything someone does for you. I suppose that in a way, this cheapens the gratitude since it is so freely dispersed. And I probably go overboard thanking people who are simply doing what they're supposed to do, like the gym front desk attendant who scans my pass or the driver who doesn't speed through the crosswalk as I enter it.

Given that this is such a key part of my personality, it's crazy to think I can cram into a page or two my thank yous regarding my first book. Still...here goes. And if you hear play-off music from the orchestra in the background, I'm sorry I didn't get to your name. For those I have gotten to, please realize how grateful I am for your contributions. Thanks go out to:

- Rove McManus, the world's best talk show host, who let me book a vampire/pro wrestler presidential candidate on his show and got me fixated on citizen candidates.

- Allison and Joe Dubois, who have always believed in me far more than I believed in me.

- Chris Hardwick, whose Nerdist podcasts kept me company during my 10,000-mile road trip. Those interviews also made me realize that pursuing my own ideas isn't crazy. It's the natural way of things.

- Tom Lennon, Brian Grazer, Ron Howard and other guys who I will never actually meet, but who spoke on those Nerdist podcasts about rejection and how to kick its ass.

- The late, great Jackie Collins, who always told me I could do this if I really tried. And if she were still with us, she'd make one helluva president!

- Queen Latifah, because nobody has ever been a better example for me of how to live life to its best and fullest.

- Todd Yasui, who kept me going with two simple words— "keep writing."

- Sherrie Smith, who had to listen to these interviews even more than I did as she transcribed.

- Craig Thomas, who kept this story politically correct—in a good way.

- Stephanie Storey, who first read all this and told me it might not completely suck.

- Mae Massad, who was the second to read all this and tell me it might not completely suck.

- Marlo Bernier, who talked me down from at least 284 ledges.

- Warren Littlefield, whose encouragement and advice proved that nice guys can finish wherever the hell they want.

- Chris Carmiol, whose editing assured me this might not suck.

- Ian Birch, my mentor and sounding board, who has always made me feel like I knew what I was doing, even if I didn't know it.

- Shari Kaufman, who has inspired me as long as I've known her, so it's no surprise she was there when this idea first came to be.

- AARP, for every discount that helped me travel 10,000 miles cheaply.

- Budget Rent A Car, for the sweet deal on the Nissan.

- Wendy's, for the multiple strawberry salads and Asiago ranch chicken clubs that kept me from starving.

- Black Cherry Kickstart, which kept me completely and totally awake on 14-hour drives.

- Motel 6, my home with an ice machine away from home.

- The staff—as well as the double cheeseburgers and vanilla shakes—at Dyer's Burgers on Beale Street in Memphis, all of which made for the best dining experience I had along those 10,000 long miles.

- Bob Makela, whose interest in this project has made what you're holding in your hands (virtually or otherwise) possible.

- Judy Santos, who told me to go for this and supported my efforts all the way along—even though it meant more time monitoring those pesky kids of ours.

- Those meddling kids, Roman and Chiara. The book really is, ultimately, a story of the good and bad things that families do for us. And you two are the best family a hack journalist could ask for. Roman, you make me proud every day and I hope I can return the favor. Chiara, you make me smile every day just

8

knowing that you're out there in the world.

- David Duchovny, who flexed his massive and extremely manly Twitter muscles before we even had the book in our hands.

- My brothers Chris and Curtis, who along the way offered plenty of words of wisdom and encouragement and suggestions on where to go for really cool minor league baseball shirts.

- My parents, Walt and Barbara, whose financial and moral support was unflagging as I embarked on this insane idea. I was maybe a bit too honest at certain points in these pages, and you may not love it all, but trust me when I say I can't thank you enough for the good things you've done over the years to make me believe all things are possible.

- The friends and families of the Can't-idates. First, for your generosity in talking to me. And second, because your role in all this isn't easy and you deserve some appreciation for hanging in there too.

- The Can't-idates, whose stories compelled me to meet you and whose passion and kindness made all that time sitting on my ass in a rental car the most meaningful journalistic experience of my life. While you also may not like everything you read here, understand that I couldn't have done this without you. The enthusiasm you had for both me and your campaigns continues to inspire me.

- Everybody who told me no when I mentioned this idea. I have no idea how any of this turns out, but without your insistence that I was wasting my time, I'd probably never have tried any of this. And you may be right in the long run, but I don't regret a minute of this project. However, dwelling on regrets is like worrying how Samuel L. Jackson is going to get rid of all those blankety-blank snakes on that blankety-blank plane. Both situations are over. Finished. Gone. Look forward to what's to come, not what's already done. Just like all these Can't-idates and their campaigns.

Introduction

As much as we love our children, the cold, hard fact is that we frequently lie to them in order to give them hope, which, in this world, is often in short supply. As far as I'm concerned, that's totally fine. Adults recognize the harshness of a world that seems determined to discourage the next generation, so we manufacture comforting fiction to soften the blow and keep them in line (at least somewhat). How else do you explain countless fantastical tales throughout history, from stories of Greek gods to the annual appearance of Santa Claus to certain beliefs about what will cause hair to grow on your palms?

Most of these stories are innocent and well-intentioned. They tend to achieve the desired effect of keeping our kids believing in the unbelievable and living the good lives we want them to live. There is, however, one complete and total lie we have spun for years that may be doing far more harm than good. It has wreaked havoc on our entire democratic system. We tell America's future leaders that if they work and study hard, any of them, no matter where they came from, can one day be President of the United States.

Presidential candidates want you to believe in this fiction because it humanizes them. They spend huge chunks of their

10

day trying to portray themselves as men and women "from Main Street and not from Wall Street," each one attempting to out-ordinary the next by sharing everything from stories of immigrant parents to childhood newspaper routes to their favorite barbecue recipes. However, claiming they truly feel the plight of average Americans is like hearing them say they're connoisseurs of Mexican cuisine because they've sampled the late night menu at Taco Bell. It's pretty hollow reasoning and produces nothing but a lot of hot air. I'm reasonably certain this was not quite what the Founding Fathers had in mind when they set this whole democracy thing in motion. In fact, they took great pains to keep the requirements for leading this nation as minimal as possible. It's more complicated to get a Costco membership card than it is to make a run at the presidency. Article II, Section 1 of the Constitution specifically states: "No Person except a natural born Citizen, or a Citizen of the United States at the time of the Adoption of this Constitution, shall be eligible to the Office of President; neither shall any Person be eligible to that Office who shall not have attained to the Age of thirty five Years, and been fourteen Years a Resident within the United States."

And that's it. Turn 21 and you can drink. Turn 25 and you get a better rate on your auto insurance. Turn 35 and you can be the Commander in Chief. It all seems so simple. Which is maybe why we constantly remind our kids that someday it could be them. It really does seem that almost no one is ruled out of this race. At least, that's how it feels if you spend three minutes viewing any cable news outlet once the election cycle starts spinning. I could swear that at one point, the only person not running for the Republican presidential nomination was that crazy old guy you see arguing with cashiers at the grocery store. And even he would have filed if he weren't so busy watching Clint Eastwood movies and telling the neighborhood kids to get off his lawn.

If you look closely at the candidates who get all the coverage, you will soon learn that your presidential odds greatly decrease if you fail to meet at least one of the following conditions:

- You are a Democrat or a Republican.
- Your last name is Bush or Clinton.
- You have an Ivy League degree. (The last four presidents hail from Yale or Harvard.)
- The most recent job on your resume is "Governor." (Four of the last six presidents were their home state's chief executive prior to becoming *the* chief executive.)
- You settled in the past for being a U.S. Senator. (Barack Obama and John F. Kennedy are two of the 16 Commanders in Chief who served in the Senate.)
- You were a war hero. (This used to be somewhat of a prerequisite for the job, going all the way back to George Washington and continuing on through Ulysses S. Grant, Andrew Jackson and Dwight D. Eisenhower.)
- You have a few hundred million dollars to spare. (In 2012, Barack Obama raised $1.123 billion to get re-elected. His challenger, Mitt Romney, came up with another million $1.109 billion.)
- You own a cable TV network or a local television station. (In 2012, the candidates and their political action committees spent nearly $3 billion total on TV spots, up 38% from 2008.)

It's virtually unheard of for an unknown, untested, uninhibited, un-wealthy candidate to even make it into the primary process, let alone put up a fight in a general election. In the 2012 battle, the best vote total for a non-establishment party candidate was .99% for former New Mexico governor Gary Johnson (Libertarian), followed by the Green Party's Jill Stein at .36%. Miscellaneous write-in candidates racked up another 11% of the vote. In 2008, the also-rans were even less of a challenge: Ralph Nader got .56% for the Green Party, Bob Barr got .4% for the Libertarians and the write-ins came up with .09% of the vote.

The signature requirements for an upstart presidential candidate to get on all 50 state ballots increased tenfold between 1930 and 1980. In 2016, independent and minority party candidates must accumulate at least 675,000 signatures, 26 times the number needed by an established Democratic candidate. Some states, like New Hampshire, simply require a payment of $1,000 to get your name on their ballot. Most others are far more discriminating. There are also other ways to garner enough attention to become, at the very least, a write-in candidate. Get into one of the many pre-primary debates before a primary, for instance. That'll get the word out about who you are and where you stand on the issues, and do it more cheaply than buying a local TV ad.

There's just one problem. You'll need to be considered a "viable" candidate in order to make it into even the lowliest of debates. And there is no standard political definition for what is considered "viable," since it usually takes being in a debate to be considered viable in the first place. Add it all up and it becomes pretty clear—with very few exceptions, most of us stand a better chance of marrying a Kardashian than we do of becoming president. (It's debatable as to which is the more difficult job.)

This brings us to the 2016 election, which is unlike any other I can remember in my lifetime. In theory, it's a wide-open race in terms of likely winners, since there's no incumbent running. (Although the anointing of Hillary Clinton on the Democratic side of things comes close.) During the early stages of the campaign season, the Republicans were all trying to take advantage of this fact, with varying degrees of success. Jeb Bush. Chris Christie. Ted Cruz. Donald Trump. Rand Paul. Marco Rubio. Rick Perry. Scott Walker. Carly Fiorina. Lindsey Graham. Rick Santorum. John Kasich. Ben Carson. If you've ever referred to Barack Obama as a tyrant and/or have a vowel somewhere in your first or last name, odds are you've at least formed an exploratory committee.

Too many choices can make most candidates seem indistinguishable from one another. So it all becomes reminiscent of barking dogs or crying children, where your attention is just diverted to the loudest one. But it doesn't mean you necessarily like that option. You just notice it more. In turn, this inevitably leads to record voter apathy—right at the moment when we have the most choice. We the people aren't the only ones to blame for this. There's some irony here: the media spends hours shaming candidates for their personal and professional failures, and then shames voters for not showing up at the polls. If you tell us these people suck, you can't be surprised that we don't want to cast our votes for any of them.

Sure, it's sad that the turnout for the 2014 mid-term elections, in what the brochure says is the greatest democracy in history, was the worst in 72 years. Barely a third of registered voters showed up to vote for politicians they liked (or at least tolerated). Presidential elections are a different story. We feel like there's more at stake—thanks once again to the 24-hour news cycle—so more of us show up to vote. In 2012, it was 55%. The numbers for other recent elections are pretty similar—58% in 2008, 57% in 2004, 51% in 2000. Those figures are embarrassing when compared to the turnout during the 1800s, which were typically in the 70% range. Then again, there was no MSNBC, CNN or Fox News to publicly flog candidates and drive away voters back then.

Poll after poll makes it clear that most people haven't exactly been thrilled with their presidential options for 2016, no matter who the eventual nominees are. If you don't believe it, just start up a conversation about the election the next time you're at a dinner party and see what happens. Odds are bringing up the DMV or jury duty would elicit less grimacing. It's hardly surprising that a 2014 Gallup poll found that 60% of the country wanted to have a major party alternative to the Democrats and Republicans.

As I write this in late-2015, we're a year away from the presidential election. Still, a *Washington Post* survey discovered that the shark from Jaws, Darth Vader and the Terminator all had better favorability numbers than any mainstream candidate while six of them—Huckabee, Cruz, Bush, Santorum, Christie and Trump—ranked slightly lower than Lord Voldemort from the *Harry Potter* series.

I've always wondered if mainstream, big-name presidential candidates are at least honest with themselves, if not with the people whose votes they crave. They have to know that their shot at earning the Commander in Chief job is slim, and that what they're really campaigning for is a cabinet job with the eventual victor—or, even better, a gig as a cable news commentator. Running for president has become the ultimate photo op if you're in politics; the chance for everybody to know your name perhaps even more than what you stand for. It's not surprising that every four years, dozens of semi-well known political characters looking to enhance their media profile decide to race for the White House as well. It helped Mike Huckabee get his own Fox News show.

Sometimes the allegedly independent candidates create legitimacy to get exactly the attention they're after. They generate enough buzz running against the establishment to capture the public's imagination and, at times, their votes. The plan certainly gave Bernie Sanders his moment in the early days of the 2016 campaign. In 2000, consumer advocate Ralph Nader ran as the Green Party candidate for president and won nearly 3% of the popular vote. In 1992, billionaire fast-talker Ross Perot started and stopped and started his campaign, capturing close to 20%.

Exploiting the ignorance and anger of segregationist Southerners, South Carolina Gov. Strom Thurmond became

Craig Tomashoff

notorious with his presidential bid in 1948, as did Gov. George
Wallace in 1968, 1972 and 1976. Even a beloved former president,
Theodore Roosevelt, tried to run a third time by creating his
own Bull Moose Party, and ended up with almost a third of
the popular vote.

Then there are those candidates who offer decidedly
less political experience—but far more intrigue. You are never going to vote for any of these people, although they do make for an
entertaining 30-second, end-of-the-local-news human interest
story for the anchors to make fun of. They are the Carrot Tops
of the political process, people whose very presence makes you
laugh—but not in a good way. They are the misfits who asked
every inane question in your college psych classes just so they
could hear themselves speak. We need these people. They're part
of our national heritage. The notion of political gadflies tweaking
the system to make a point, even it's a self-serving one, is part of
our long electoral history.

In 1872, for example, Victoria Woodhull ran for president representing the Equal Rights Party. On the plus side, she'd
worked as a stockbroker, a profession few women attempted in
those days, so she supported women's suffrage long before it became the law of the land. On the minus side—at least in the eyes
of some people—she also happened to be a clairvoyant, as well as
a major proponent of prostitution and free love. Despite the pop-
ularity of those final two activities, or perhaps because of them,
Woodhull's campaign never quite took off.

Slightly more than a century later—specifically 1992,
1996 and 2000—Iowa doctor-turned-presidential candidate John
Hagelin and his Natural Law Party felt the answer to all the
problems that bedeviled the country was teaching the citizens of
America transcendental mediation. On a somewhat less spiritual
note, Minnesotan Jack Shepard ran his 2008 campaign from Rome,

Italy, where he'd fled 25 years earlier to avoid the warrant for his arrest on arson charges. In 2012, Keith Judd shelled out the $2,500 it takes to get on the primary ballot in West Virginia and even captured 40% of the vote from his Democratic opponent, Barack Obama. The irony there is that Judd also happened to be in a Texas prison at the time, serving a 210-month sentence for extortion. That same year saw professional wrestler/vampire Jonathan "The Impaler" Sharkey give the campaign trail a go. And we won't soon forget the bearded, be-gloved New Yorker Jimmy McMillan and his "Rent Is Too Damn High" protest during the Republican primaries.

My favorite recent candidate, though, was probably Jill Reed. She was the 2012 nominee of the Twelve Visions Party. What exactly are those dozen visions, you might ask? Well, they include the following words to live by:

- Become the person you were meant to be
- Live the life you were meant to live
- Feel extraordinary every day
- Slow down aging permanently
- Land the job of your passions
- Build the business of your passions
- Experience the love of your life
- Have the body you always envied
- Become a genius of society
- Have everything you ever wanted
- Ride a prosperity wave to rich
- Enjoy nearly-perfect health

If you paid $100 for a ticket to hear Tony Robbins tell you all this, you'd convince yourself you'd just heard something brilliant and inspiring. When it comes from a Casper, Wyoming daughter of a Sunday school teacher, though, it has the resonance of advice from a state fair psychic. Like pretty much everyone else, I was so ready to see Reed as the perfect comic relief in yet another election that was depressing on many levels. That's why stories about crazy fringe candidates are as much a presidential election tradition as a Gary Hart-Bill Clinton-John Edwards sex scandal. We love to view these people as being cluelessly foolish, while mainstream candidates speak happily of castrating pigs and trot out gospel choirs to sing Eminem songs to announce their presence.

The real question is: Who is the true punchline here—a misguided but genuine believer in New Age philosophy or a cynical politician who figures wearing horn-rimmed glasses will eradicate the image of him as a bumbling idiot who forgets his own positions on the issues? "Real people" running for president are simply enjoying the ultimate privilege that comes with living in our democracy. They are asserting a Constitutional right most of us ignore, and doing it free of the thick cloud of cynicism that emanates from every major candidate's campaign.

Sure, there are some fringe candidates who seem more like they're stuck in the last SNL sketch of the night. The International Parliament Group, for example, is looking to create a committee of presidents rather than leave the job to just one person. The 1960 candidate for the Universal Party, Gabriel Green, probably doomed his campaign by claiming his alien contacts could prevent "[making] robots of all of us." Still, despite the likelihood of national ridicule and complete rejection, hundreds of wannabe presidents file paperwork with the Federal Election Commission every four years, hoping to be the inspiring alternative for voters dissatisfied with their better-known presidential options.

Exactly one year before the 2016 Super Tuesday primaries—March 1, 2015—there were 193 folks you've never heard of who had registered with the FEC. Weeks before any U.S.

Senator or governor had officially jumped into the race, computer programmers and ranchers and housewives and even a topless dancer had thrown their hats (or pasties) into the ring. Hillary Clinton teased her candidacy for months while regular folk candidates were holding fund-raising bake sales and having their seven-year-old daughters create campaign buttons. They're no doubt the sort of "everyday Americans" Clinton was referring to when she finally announced her candidacy in April 2015.

Her first "surprise" campaign appearance was the perfect example of the Everest-sized gap between well-known candidates lives and those of the people whose votes they want. Shortly after making her campaign official, Clinton slipped into a van and stopped at a Toledo, Ohio Chipotle, where she went in to order her own chicken burrito bowl. This "spontaneous" photo op was surely the product of many hours and dollars spent on consultants eager to prove she's a real "woman of the people." Look, Hillary eats fast food like the rest of us!

She hasn't exactly cornered the market on this "I'm Just Like You" approach to campaigning. Mike Huckabee has explained that he'd "like to be the kind of president that's more concerned about the people on Main Street, not just the folks on Wall Street." Rand Paul speaks of "people who work for the people who own businesses." Marco Rubio insists he's the man to help "the millions and millions who *aren't* rich." Soak up these quotes while absorbing the net worth of each of these candidates: $15 million (Clinton), $5 million (Huckabee), $1.3 million (Paul) and $500,000 (Rubio). There's certainly nothing wrong with having all that money. We can all agree it certainly beats the alternative. However, it also seems a bit disingenuous to hear a candidate who hosts $500,000-a-plate fundraising dinners boast about his parents' immigrant upbringing and how happy he was that no bureaucrat said "let me give you a check and make you dependent on government." (I'm looking at you, Ted Cruz.)

So what are voters to do? We're stuck between a rock and some head cases. On one hand, we all say we want a leader who can personally relate to the struggles of low- and middle-income Americans. On the other hand, we don't want to waste our votes on candidates who can't win. I'm not gullible enough to fall for the aforementioned lie that any of us can grow up to be president. Still, wouldn't it be nice to at least find some candidates you'd enjoy having a beer and burger with? There has to be somebody out there running for president with the compassion of FDR, the folksiness of Will Rogers, the intellect of Stephen Hawking and the straight talk of your college roommate.

Here's the thing. If you want to hire somebody to fix your back porch, you interview contractors until you find the person who shows the most enthusiasm for the job. If you want the best pizza in your neighborhood, you go to each pizza joint until you come across a winner. So if you want to hire somebody to fix your country, why not consider the people who were so enthusiastic that they committed to the gig before any "established" candidates?

With that theory as a starting point, I wrote letters to all 193 people who had filled out their FEC paperwork by March 2015. In my note, I told each candidate I wanted to hear about them and their campaigns. I wanted to understand what motivates their candidacy and (provided they weren't totally nuts) then share their views with as many readers as possible.

Within a few days of sending the letters out, I started getting calls from candidates at all hours of the day and night— and immediately regretted undertaking this project. It wasn't so much that the people I was talking to were conspiracy-believing crazies. Rather, most seemed like either incarnations of Reese Witherspoon's overachieving Tracy Flick from *Election* or every guy who ever called an AM talk radio show.

The citizen candidate stereotypes we've all come to know from those five-paragraph news stories that crop up every election cycle seemed horribly true. There was the aerospace engineer in Kansas who lives on his disability income while trying to interpret the meaning of the chance encounters he's had with Barack Obama. Or the former record store clerk in Phoenix whose family wanted him committed when he declared he'd be running for president and would see if Michael Jackson could be his running mate. Meanwhile, a handful of 20-somethings—from the ex-soldier in New Jersey to the former sorority girl—were completely unaware that they weren't old enough to run for president. A computer engineer explained that he opted to run only after becoming convinced his Lyme disease was the result of governmental biological warfare.

Initially, it was all very discouraging. Then again, what job interviews don't have their share of disappointments? I spent the better part of a month talking to every one of these candidates who got back to me, which amounted to nearly 100 people. (Some never got in touch, while roughly two dozen of my letters came back as undeliverable. I somehow knew the guy whose address was a Washington, D.C. motel wasn't going to call back.)

Gradually, several of them began to convince me that maybe they weren't completely crazy. Scott Cole, a middle school teacher in North Carolina, was running as a way of teaching his history students about the mess politics had become. Vermont ex-cop John Wood decided to give the presidency a shot after his 7-year-old daughter asked one night while he read a bedtime story, "Daddy, do people have to be rich to run for president?" Bishop John Lewis recounted what it was like growing up African-American in rural Texas and how he has kept faith in the

U.S.—even though he spent his childhood ordering hamburgers from the back door of restaurants that wouldn't let minorities in. I would probably never vote for computer programmer John Dummett, who proudly claims to be the first candidate to have sued Barack Obama for not being born in America. At the same time, I was totally captivated by his story about taking up politics after encountering a very encouraging Ronald Reagan while on a middle school field trip back in the '60s.

Some people even came perilously close to convincing me to sign on for their campaigns. Dr. Brian Ari Cole, for instance. Take the name off the top of his resumé and you'd swear he was a presidential frontrunner:

- His grandfather worked with the NAACP in the 1960s and went to jail for protesting Jim Crow laws
- He grew up all around the world, with both his dad and step-dad being in the Air Force
- He studied medicine at Boston University
- He ran for Congress while living in Hawaii in 2003
- He graduated from Harvard's Kennedy School of Government in 2009
- As an emergency room physician, he's had personal experience with the needs of drug addicts and the underclass
- Through the Kennedy School, he's befriended the likes of Sen. John McCain, Newt Gingrich and Republican National Committee Chairman Reince Priebus
- He's a fiscally conservative African-American Republican

Most impressive of all, the soft-spoken yet strikingly thoughtful Dr. Cole is more realistic than most of his 2016 candidate peers. "People within the Republican party have said privately that they feel lucky to have me. The Republicans are funny—they've also said they're not looking for a centrist," he told me over the phone. He understood that nobody in America knew his name. Nonetheless, he had high hopes that his intellect and passion would eventually get him noticed. This was a candidate who convinced me he had plenty of the right answers, without all of Ben Carson's questionable ramblings. It turns out there was just one problem he couldn't solve, the same one that eventually stops every candidate you will never hear about.

"I haven't been able to generate the kind of interest I need to be a viable candidate, so I'm suspending my campaign," he told me a couple of weeks after we first spoke. "I hope something changes, but for now I'm no longer running."

For the first time since I'd undertaken this project, I had indisputable evidence of the flaws embedded in our system for picking a president. Good people—people who don't need to visit a Chipotle or an Iowa pig castrator's barbecue to prove they are in touch with Middle America—have very little incentive other than their own personal motivations to get involved in politics. The process of running for president is apparently like walking into the *Cheers* bar. It's only a good time when everybody knows your name. So I shifted my approach and began looking for just one thing: candidates with the most intriguing personal stories. I wanted people who have somehow decided that the best way to give their existence meaning is to run for president. I'd love to give every single person running the chance to speak their mind.

However, given the limits of my time and the public's patience, this seemed to be the best and only way to go.

From the dozens upon dozens of citizen politicians I spoke with, I found a group of 15 ordinary people with extraordinary personal stories that set them on their political path. Some seemed silly on the surface. Like the Las Vegas man who was inspired to be Commander in Chief after failing the bar exam four times and seeing few other career options. Or the Massachusetts prankster who advocates free ponies for all and government-mandated tooth brushing—all while wearing a boot on his head. Or the biker in Boise who said he would hold his campaign kick-off fundraiser in my honor at his group's local hangout, a bar called The Busted Shovel.

Some people were mysterious, like the Sydneys Voluptuous Buttocks Committee in Buffalo that refused to put Sydney on the phone. A South Dakota martial arts expert overwhelmed me with his excitement about his run for the presidency, then got me a little teary when he mentioned he was doing this to show his son anything is possible in America. That same passion poured from my multiple conversations with the minister in the poorer neighborhoods of Cleveland, who spent our first 20 minutes on the phone telling me how she grew up in a well-to-do African-American family, but left it all behind to spend her days attending civil rights protests on a daily basis.

Then there were the candidates whose lives had taken one tragic turn after another, to the point where running for president had, in their minds, become a plausible answer to their problems: the ex-corporate exec from a broken little Michigan town, who began his campaign after his son developed a drug addiction and he himself had a near-death experience; the reluctantly-closeted Arkansas mom with an 18-year-old severely autistic son, who needed to work to get federal assistance—yet *couldn't* work because she had no money for childcare; and the Vietnam vet who saw many friends either drenched in Agent Orange or blown up in combat, then years later saw many more die waiting for medical help at the VA hospital.

Is there the slightest chance that any of these people will get on any state's primary ballots, let alone make it to a debate or hear a national news anchor speak their names? Probably not. Does it matter? Not really. They realize, for the most part anyway, that the deck is stacked against them. But they're running anyway. We all complain about the lack of good candidates we can relate to. Everyone says they want someone real, someone authentic, to run for president. You don't get much more real than the small-town father of four who has seen his entire city's economy vanish or the lesbian who has to hide her true self because she lives in the Bible Belt.

With very few exceptions, they're also doing this despite the fact that everyone dismisses their dream as completely crazy. One of the candidates I talked to told me he was put on psychiatric leave at his high-tech firm after telling them he'd filed his FEC paperwork. A South Carolina realtor explained that his son-in-law—a Manhattan stockbroker—told his daughter to cut ties with him as long as he ran for president, because it would make the son-in-law look crazy by association. A guy who worked in a nuclear plant lost his security clearance when he told a co-worker he was running.

So where exactly is the upside in all of this? I honestly couldn't understand why anyone would want to be president in the first place, let alone want to run for the office when the mere mention of that ambition could drive a wedge between you and the rest of the world. I've done some pretty self-destructive things in my life: showing up hung over to a scholarship interview that could have paid for my entire graduate degree, mocking a former boss to the person who turned out to be his best friend, joining online dating websites more than once. Still, an ordinary person running for president? The only thing nearly that insane is *writing* about ordinary people running for president.

At least that's the sense I got as I started explaining my plan to people. Reactions ranged from acceptance to significant eye rolling and heavy sighing to complete mocking. I'll never forget going to a job interview with the editor of a major Hollywood news website, who asked if I could start right away were she to hire me. I mentioned that I might be going out of town for a few weeks to work on a book proposal. She leaned forward, looking genuinely interested in me for the first time since I'd sat down in her office. She asked what the book was about. I told her I was traveling cross-country to meet presidential candidates that nobody will most likely ever hear of or vote for. The sour-milk expression on her face said I might as well have told her I was off to write a new *Transformers* sequel.

My instinct after such an encounter would ordinarily be to call the people I'd wanted to meet and postpone my trip indefinitely. That would have been the safe and sane thing to do. Then I got two messages that changed my mind. The first was from Harley Brown, the Boise biker running for president. It seems his campaign had run into some financial difficulties. Since he wasn't able to raise any money, it looked like he had no choice but to shut things down. After a brief email conversation, though, he decided to hang in there until I came up to see him. Because you never know...maybe what I was doing might at least get his ideas out to the American public. From there, maybe something good could happen.

This meant a couple of important things. First, what might seem like a joke to the outside world was very serious to him. Secondly, he needed my help. Like it or not, I was part of a political process now. It still would have been easy enough to shirk that responsibility, until I got the other message. It was an email from my son's high school, laying out plans for his graduation ceremony that would be taking place three days after I'd be back from this proposed presidential road trip. If you haven't been through the emotional hurricane that is having your eldest child take this big step, let me just say the only thing that's been equally life-shaking was that initial slow-motion ride home from the maternity ward 17 years earlier.

I freely admit that on more than one occasion over the past

several years, I'd Googled phrases like "teenager + sell + chemical experiments." However, now my boy was moving to the city I once lived in (Boston) to study the same thing I studied in college (journalism). This realization presented me with a mix of pride—he was following in my footsteps—and fear—have I truly prepared the kid for life? When it comes to Father of the Year voting, I rank somewhere between Darth Vader and Homer Simpson.

Not only had I divorced his mom, but I actually moved out of the house on his ninth birthday. When it came time to have the birds-and-bees conversation, I succumbed to my own nervousness by explaining sex while playing a game of Madden so we'd have a distraction. I can't count the number of times I'd complain about his weight, then take him and his sister out for cheeseburgers and milkshakes.

Now that he was leaving for his own life, I wanted to do better. I had to teach him the value of being his own person, following his own instincts, doing what he felt was right no matter who told him he was nuts to try it. In other words, the unexpected truth was I wanted him to be more like these citizen candidates I'd been talking to. I had to go on this trip to support those people, but also to give my son a graduation present that would hopefully last longer than a new baseball mitt or video game. Which is how I ended up driving 10,000 miles across America in 21 days. To interview 15 brave citizens running for president while enduring four tick bites.

I knew that none of these people would ever get elected. Still, that wasn't the point. The point was just to try. If we're also going to stick with that other great political lie—that every vote is important—I was really just doing what we all fantasize we'd do if we could. I was going to find the best person to hand my vote over to, regardless of what the outcome might be. Somebody has to, right? It's fun to complain about our broken political system.

But if the final answer is to vote for the most likely winner, that's not the best path toward any change. The only way to make a difference is to search for somebody capable of making a difference, regardless of what school they went to or how much money they have or what they order at Chipotle. We need candidates who are told they can't do this.

So I went in search of the Can't-idates.

Doug Shreffler

Maybe it's the Virgo in me. Or perhaps it's the result of growing up in the sort of WASPy heritage where, let's just say, life was something to be endured rather than enjoyed. Whatever the reason, I'm an overly cautious person by nature. This isn't something I'm proud of, but it takes forever and a weekend for me to commit to most things. And once I do, I can find 57 reasons to bail out on that commitment.

This applies to the simplest of tasks. More than once, I've spent three hours in a bookstore carrying two different novels I'm trying to decide between, only to leave without buying anything, because I'm certain I'd only end up making the wrong choice. I've gone hungry while traveling because I couldn't summon the nerve to try an unfamiliar place for dinner, yet also couldn't stand the liberal health guilt of eating at a familiar fast food joint. It takes a lot of convincing just to get me out on a first date, and I spend so much time worrying about whether or not to ask for a second that third dates are virtually unheard of.

Given this constant surrender to uncertainty, I decided to make Doug Shreffler the first stop on my presidential journey. He only lived an hour away from me, in Port Hueneme, California, so if things went horribly wrong for any reason, I wouldn't have invested too much time or money in my plan to meet the Can't-idates. We'd talked for about 15 minutes on the phone a week earlier, and Shreffler came across as rather grandfatherly, even though he had only turned 56 three months earlier. (The same age I'd be turning four months later.) The conversation started off innocuously enough. He talked about how seeing Barack Obama's 2008 win inspired him to the point where he felt anyone could run and win if they tried hard enough. Shreffler also talked about growing up in the Midwest, about wanting to be a fighter pilot when he was a kid, and about being tired of the two-party system in an era when we needed new options; which was all interesting, though not earth-shaking.

But when I asked what he did for a living, Shreffler hesitated for a moment before shifting suddenly into a hushed voice. He explained that he'd done some "work" for the CIA in the late '70s and throughout the '80s. His first mission: deliver clemency papers to G. Gordon Liddy, Watergate mastermind/international man of mystery. Crazy claims of covert conspiracies? Now *this* was the raw meat the press corps usually devours when it came to fringe candidates. I asked him to tell me more. He hesitated.

"It's probably better if we talk in person," he explained. "You never know who might be listening."

On one hand, there was no reason I shouldn't drive the hour to Port Hueneme to at least meet Doug Shreffler. His secret CIA backstory was pretty provocative. An entire cinematic and literary universe, along with a large percentage of AM talk radio, have been built on that very storyline. On the other hand, I was deliberately trying to avoid the stereotypical conspiracy theorists and otherwise loony people we usually think of as "alternative" candidates. But I wanted to take a chance with my vote in the same way these people were taking chances, so it made sense to at least connect with him and see where it led.

I'd been to Port Hueneme a handful of times, but these weren't trips I cared to repeat. The tiny beachside city along the California coast used to be known for its seafood and surfing—until Jan. 31, 2000. That's when Alaska Airlines Flight 261 crashed into the Pacific Ocean a few miles away. As it turned out, I knew a couple of people on that flight. They were the parents of a college friend in Seattle. Over the next few years, my friend spent time traveling to Point Hueneme to make peace with the tragedy, and to help create a memorial to all the victims. I'd head out there to see her when I could, which was often enough for me to start thinking of it as the Little Town of Death. That explained the dark mood on my drive to Shreffler's apartment, which turned out to be just a few blocks from a sundial monument, built in tribute to the passengers of Flight 261.

Across the street from his apartment, kids screamed and ran around an elementary school playground. Just down the road, uniformed soldiers rambled around a naval base. And then there was Shreffler, so eager to discuss his campaign that he called twice while I was driving to make sure I was on my way. He stood in front of a one-story building the color of stained teeth, only with slightly less character. An American flag hung by the front window next to some old red, white and blue bunting. Shreffler practically bounced over to shake my hand. He looked a lot like your favorite uncle—grey hair, globe-shaped belly, stiff dark blue jeans that most likely had never been worn before, and a long-sleeved gray dress shirt adorned with an American flag pin on the right collar. Moving briskly and happily, he led me into his one-bedroom apartment, and for a minute it felt like I'd wandered into an episode of *Hoarders*.

The living room had a Salvation Army showroom vibe, with all kinds of worn and mismatched furniture. On the far wall, he'd hung several photos of what looked to be a happy family on a fishing vacation, which, Shreffler explained, were all shots he'd taken of his brother, sister-in-law and niece. Much of the rest of the living room was filled with half a dozen computer monitors, a guitar, an amp and an electronic keyboard. Noticing me staring at all this, Shreffler eagerly sat down, picked up the electric guitar, and launched into Lynyrd Skynyrd's "Gimme Three Steps."

"I can play everything, even drums," he boasted. "I actually had a music career in between working assignments for the government."

Shreffler abruptly ended the mini-concert, and I followed him over to a tiny dining room table, next to a kitchen that appeared to have been hit by an earthquake. Open cupboards spilled most of their contents onto the counters and into the sink; except there had been no earthquake for several months now.

Shreffler saw me peeking into the kitchen and nervously volunteered that he loves to cook—soufflés, steak, salmon—and has friends over for dinner on many Thursday nights. It was a Thursday afternoon, so I thought ever so briefly about sticking around just to have the full experience. Then I looked back at the foot-high pile of dirty plates in the sink and the thought quickly passed.

"I know it doesn't look like the neatest house," Shreffler explained, looking down at his shoes as if he expected them to walk away on their own. "I'm always self-conscious, particularly with my bathroom. I'm used to living much nicer than this. I grew up in a very wealthy part of St. Louis. My dad had a nice place for us in Michigan and Mom was left very well-to-do when he died."

We sat down at the tiny dining table and, before I could ask Shreffler about his qualifications to run the country, he launched a preemptive strike: "You've had an interesting career," he said. "I've done quite a lot of research on your background. I figured you already knew so much about me, I wanted to research you." He paused for dramatic effect. "Of everything you've done, was working on *Saturday Night Live* your favorite?"

I've had many jobs in my lifetime, from washing dishes in a nursing home kitchen, to trying to make Jesse Ventura seem coherent on television. But one thing I've never done is work at *Saturday Night Live*. Still, the eager look on Shreffler's face reminded me of that moment when my puppy realizes he's getting a walk. He beamed with pride that he'd unearthed this fact about me and couldn't wait to hear my answer. He seemed so pleased that I couldn't bear to tell him the truth. So I went with a lie and told him *SNL* was great—it's where I got introduced to my secret wife, Kristen Wiig.

I said this as a joke, assuming there was no way anyone with Internet access would believe me. But judging by his satisfied grin, I didn't get the sense Shreffler was going to fact check me. He seemed happy enough to simply be sharing conversation. Although, I have to say, his willingness to so easily accept my misinformation called into question a major part of Shreffler's biography: that he'd been a CIA secret operative. If years of Bruce Willis movies taught me anything, it's that the CIA knows everything about everyone. So, as much as I was hoping there was something slightly mysterious about Shreffler's past, the fact that he hadn't even read my online resumé correctly was a bit of a letdown.

There were other signs that things weren't entirely right. He was as nervous as he was polite. Every few minutes, Shreffler's voice would go from a soft-spoken hush to a crowded-room bark, without warning. At other moments, as his volume rose, his right hand would reach over to tug his left shirt-sleeve, or he'd clear his throat for a few seconds. I tried to ignore it, but he volunteered that he had stuttering problems as a kid.

"I'd talk and get excited and pick up speed and volume," he told me. "I learned to catch it, but it looks to others like I'm losing my train of thought. I have these mannerisms that help me come back to where I was."

Born in 1959 in Ann Arbor, Michigan, Shreffler recalled being a quiet kid. His father, Donald Shreffler, was a University of Michigan human genetics research scientist. When Doug was a boy, his father became a rock star in the genetics world, courtesy of his pioneering work studying mouse genomes as a gateway to human genome research. Doug had little passion to follow in Dad's footsteps, as he dreamed of becoming an actual rock star. The Shrefflers bonded over a love of fishing. One of Doug's earliest childhood memories is getting fishing poles for Christmas and using them most weekends to catch bluegill and bass with his father and younger brother. They were much less in sync when it came to Doug's chances of making it in music.

Things didn't get easier when the elder Shreffler moved the family to St. Louis in the mid-1970s to start his own genetics department at Washington University. Teenage Doug enrolled in the Wentworth Military Academy, not exactly a breeding ground for the next John Lennon or Keith Richards. His music dream was put on hold, replaced for the time being by an interest in flying. One of Donald's friends was James McDonnell, half of the brain trust behind aircraft manufacturing behemoth, McDonnell Douglas. That connection, Doug explained, allowed him to learn how to fly Cessna planes "before I learned to drive a car."

When he got to this part of the story, Shreffler's volume began rising. He stopped, tugged at his sleeve and cleared his throat a couple of times. His right leg started to nervously vibrate, independent from the rest of his body. These were clear tells that his story was about to take an uncomfortable turn. The saga had been relatively plausible up to this point, except for that part about enjoying fishing. (I still don't believe people actually enjoy tossing a string with a hook on it into a body of water for hours on end.)

"One night Dad dropped me off at the NASA training facility at McDonnell Douglas. They had an underground training center, and I can't go into all the black budget stuff going on there, but I got my G4 (general staff level) clearance. I got to do a lot of prototype simulated work that impressed people so much that, not only did I get to see the rest of the other levels there, I earned a ride to the edge of the Earth in one of their planes. I chucked so bad! I still remember saying to myself, 'Doug, I know you're sick, but take a look out of that window because you may never see anything like this again.'"

It wasn't so much that detour into secret facilities and government clearances that seemed suspicious. The real strangeness came next, when Shreffler described how he spent his time when not flying in airplanes to the edge of the world. The way he remembered it, he delivered pizzas for the CIA and played rock 'n roll with Chuck Berry's sidemen.

"When I was 18, I was playing guitar in blues clubs on the east side of St. Louis, where white boys weren't allowed." He stopped to add a laugh, then quickly corrected himself. Like a true candidate. "I don't mean that prejudicially. I was just one of the privileged few that everybody knew. I worked at a place with Johnny Johnson, Chuck Berry's keyboard player. I'm not trying to name names here, but I'd get off work and sometimes Johnny would be playing a private gig somewhere and I'd play bass with him."

In his late teens and early 20s, Shreffler told me, he managed a local pizza joint. Having grown up around secretive government agencies, due to his father's work ("My dad was on the staff of advisors to various presidents"), he wasn't bothered at all one night, while making pepperoni pies, when a man approached him with what should have been a frightening request. Shreffler was unfazed, because for the last couple of weeks, suspicious "business type" customers inexplicably gave him $100 tips.

"Then this man came in one night and said, 'We'd like you to deliver something,'" Shreffler recalled, getting louder again. "I said 'no,' that I had a staff of drivers, and the guy said, 'No! We need you!' Then he explained why they wanted me. I already had classification from NASA. So I ended up going with two guys, along with a couple of pizzas and something in a sealed envelope. I didn't know what I was delivering or who I was delivering it to."

He remembered being taken into a room and frisked by two men, all the while noticing that nearly all the others in the room carried guns. Further in the back, sitting in front of a wall of weaponry, Shreffler spied a man he believed to be G. Gordon Liddy. And the secret envelope he was carrying inside the pizza box? That appeared to contain Liddy's clemency papers from President Gerald Ford. From that point on, Shreffler considered himself a CIA courier, delivering state secrets to military officials around the country.

"I'd stop by the courier's office, they'd give me something and say, 'Take this here or see this gentleman there. These are your passwords.' I was always going to highly secure bases. I'd have a solid red sticker on my car. Not the typical base sticker...this was military intelligence. It was White House clearance that allowed me on any base in the country."

Shreffler still believed he could live out his real dream of playing rock concerts for thousands of screaming fans. He was only doing the occasional errand for the government, while jamming in his own bands or sitting in on bass for groups he declined to name. One in particular ("a very, very popular '80s band" is all he'll say) approached him about joining them, because their bassist got into "a little trouble" in Florida. A Drug Enforcement Agency connection tipped Shreffler off to this little incident, which led to him sitting in for a show in front of 80,000 people. There was just one catch: the feds insisted he not use his own name onstage. If he did, such public visibility would mean his days as an operative were over. So, he used a fake name to keep the CIA happy.

"For me, music was a jump from being so isolated [with the CIA] to letting me see the world and find my place in it," he explained. "But I realized I had a choice to make: play music or not. The government guaranteed me something, and that tipped the scales. It's just that it isn't here yet. I'm still waiting on my pension."

For a moment, Shreffler stared off into the distance, no doubt looking back at that road not taken. Quickly, though, more pleasant memories drifted back and brought a beatific smile to his face.

"You might like this story. There was a general at a base in Oklahoma, a guy with patches on both sides, six months from retirement. He looks up from his desk, smoking a Cuban cigar. Here I was, a very young kid, and this guy refuses to give me the password I need. His boots were on the desk. I picked up those boots and put them on the ground, looked him in the face, and he got on the phone to call the White House war room. He spoke to a particular advisor there and his jaw dropped. I told that man, if he didn't give me that password, I was going to have two teams inside of 10 minutes sitting in his seat, close the base and he'd lose his rank.

"So what happened? He gets up and salutes me. I dismiss his men and he gave me the password. Then he said, 'Doug'—this is the most respect someone can give you—'Doug, in my 40 years of experience, I've never had anyone handle things the way you just did.' I figured that was the CIA's way of testing whether or not I was going to fold under pressure."

As it turned out, though, there was one significant problem with running covert courier missions for the government: Shreffler couldn't tell anyone about the work he was doing, and apparently there was a lot of it. He figures that from the mid-'80s to the late-'90s, he put in so many hours for the CIA that he was no longer allowed to work for the government. (If this really is the CIA's policy, I assume Jason Bourne must be long gone to his timeshare in the Bahamas at this point.) Shreffler was sent packing and told that a nice pension would soon be his. Until then, he needed to keep his federal missions private, which made it pretty tough to have any sort of social life.

"It's frustrating," Shreffler sighed. "I could never tell anybody what I was doing. My mom and family didn't even know. They tell me I can talk about things now, but I don't have papers or documents to prove anything. It's frustrating, because how am I going to tell a woman's family what I have done with my life and them not slam the door on me, laughing hysterically? I can't get past friendship, because I can't prove to anybody who I am. People get up and walk out on me when I'm talking."

I could relate. The deeper we got into discussing his life, the more I questioned the entire premise of my presidential project. Shreffler sounded exactly like the sort of political punch line most people expect citizen candidates to be (and that I was hoping to avoid).

After the interview, I reached out to the CIA and Liddy to see if there was any truth to Shreffler's tall tales. The CIA took forever to neither confirm nor deny Shreffler's employment, but Liddy actually left me a voicemail. Gasping like he was calling from an oxygen tent, he explained that he'd never heard of any Doug Shreffler, and had certainly never been served any clemency papers, in a pizza box or otherwise.

It was clear to me that Shreffler was slip-sliding perilously close to the edge of self-parody, which was precisely what I didn't want to hear; especially because he was such a sweet guy. I tried to justify keeping the interview going by reminding myself that he wasn't the only presidential candidate who had cornered the market on outlandish statements. Donald Trump referred to Mexicans in America as "rapists." Mike Huckabee wished he'd pretended to be transgender as a teen so he could get into the girls' locker room. Rick Santorum figured gay marriage was an evil on par with 9/11.

I wished Shreffler would show signs of being a bit more self-aware about all he was saying. That would help assuage any of my guilt about sharing his unbelievable words with the world. Mocking a nice guy who was only trying to help people was not quite the example I wanted to show my son. What if everyone else on my list was equally as...*expansive*, let's say, about their backgrounds? My admiration for people doing something seemingly impossible, like run for president, might seem as unhinged as the life story Shreffler was weaving for me. Desperate to yank our conversation back to Earth, I asked what I thought was a fairly practical question: Looking back on his courier/pizza/rock 'n roll days, did he have any regrets about the direction his life has taken? And that's when I found myself becoming sympathetic, if not supportive, of his plans.

"There's a long story there, and I'll go there for a little bit," he said, sighing yet again. "Like anyone else who served in government, I've wondered whether I should have had a family of my own. I've never been married. At age 56, I'm still hopeful. But I can see that it's better to have somebody who worries about you than to have a legacy and nobody to pass it on to. I just hope I can pass that advice on to others who will hear and heed it."

Before I could feel sorry for him, Shreffler asked me to

39

join him in the backyard of his apartment complex, where he had something important to show me. I thought he was going to point out specks in the sky that were actually spy drones chronicling his every move. Instead, he revealed something else with wings. One side of the yard was filled with sunflowers and birdfeeders; the other was lined with dozens of potted plants stacked on tables, and monarch butterflies zipping around everywhere. Shreffler showed me some of the clear plastic cups that had been attached to some of the plant branches. He beamed as he pointed out the little globs of fuzz inside several of the cups, not unlike the way I might grin about my son's curveball.

Every day, for at least an hour or two, he comes back here to tend to the multitude of plants and make sure the caterpillars he's protecting inside the cups are doing well. "I'm also raising new plants. You start with two or three, because every caterpillar that hatches needs two plants. I have a system going. Some caterpillars completely eat off all the leaves, so I move them to new growth."

As if on cue, a trio of monarchs fluttered over his head in a circle, a tactic that Shreffler is convinced signifies good luck in the Buddhist and/or Hindu world. His flock is apparently so popular that neighborhood moms and grandmas bring their kids and grandkids to see them. When he can, he'll even give the children a plastic cup with a chrysalis of their own to take care of. The caretaking, he explained, is "soothing and gives me something to do...keeps me out of trouble. It reminds me of when my mom used to take me to the Butterfly House in St. Louis. Nature keeps me grounded, keeps me peaceful."

Finding peace, it turns out, has been a pretty tall order for most of Shreffler's life. As we stood in the afternoon sun, surrounded by hummingbirds and butterflies, Shreffler dropped the self-importance of his fancifully spun spy stories. "I spent 30 years of my life being the likeness of Agent K, the Tommy Lee Jones character in those *Men in Black* movies. Nobody ever saw me laugh or cry or anything. That was the only way I could maintain control. My dad died and I never shed a tear. I was too proud. I wanted to be the perfect profile of an agent."

Shreffler got quiet for a long minute, until the roar of an airplane overhead snapped him back into reality—or, more accurately, surreality.

"Hear that? That's pretty routine for me. Those guys are keeping their eyes on me. Anywhere I go, they follow me. They get paid a set salary, plus time-and-a-half when I'm out away from home. I get such huge joy out of knowing that."

Shreffler possessed the same "Big Brother is watching" belief shared by media-saturated candidates like Rand Paul. At the same time, he's the only candidate who welcomes the privacy invasion, because he figures it's being done for a good cause. To prove how well-intentioned the entire Port Hueneme community is about ensuring his comfort and safety, Shreffler suggested we take a drive around the town to see what happens when he goes out.

We climbed into my car. As I cruised along streets lined with motels, fast food joints and strip malls, he continually pointed out pedestrians—like the mom pushing a baby stroller, the Sears-suited businessmen having a late lunch and the random skateboarding teens.

"You may notice a subtle nod of the head. Some kids may even salute you because you're with me. I want to tell them all thank you. I want to make sure all these people watching me know how important they are. Everybody says that, but I really mean it."

Leaving aside the fact that *nobody* says they want to thank the government for spying on them, there is something endearing about Shreffler's appreciation for the notion that nearly everyone he encounters every day is secretly checking up on his welfare. When I parked the car so we could walk around a local mall, he seemed to enjoy muttering "Thank you for your service!" and nodding ever so slightly whenever we wandered past anyone. For a guy who talks about how isolated and lonely he feels, he looked right at home sharing smiles with surfer dudes sucking down smoothies or young kids playing on a carousel. This is a guy who will never be voted in as president, though you might choose him as your favorite uncle. I figured we should probably talk some politics, seeing as how that was the reason for our meeting. I was trying to find out who was worthy of my support. Truth be told, deep down Shreffler was a decent fellow who would probably run the country with the same benevolence he showed his caterpillars.

As we drove back to his apartment, I asked what the first 100 days of the Shreffler administration would look like. He quickly answered with a litany of activities: completely eliminating federal taxes ("They're so high, we're starting to look more and more like what we left England for"); heading directly to Syria to personally negotiate an end to the violence ("I won't send anyone anywhere I wouldn't go myself"); and expanding the Department of Defense ("You need to give them the means to do what they want quickly and easily"). While he'd love to leave all this as his presidential legacy, there's one even more important thing for which he'd like to be remembered.

"How great would it be if the rest of the country would get behind a single man as president and, within his first term, see him have a wedding on the front lawn?" Shreffler asked me. "Do you think the country would get behind that? I'm still hoping for a wife, something that goes beyond even my desire to run for president and all those things. I deserve a chance for a life, even though it's so late." Shreffler's voice trailed off without a single throat clearing or sleeve-grab. "I almost want to cry just saying that."

The uncomfortable silence that followed lasted the rest of the car ride. As a distraction, I finally asked Shreffler to give me his plan for getting elected. Write-in candidate? Get on state ballots? Fundraisers? It's all part of the game he wants to start playing. He brightened up and explained that once his long-awaited CIA pension came in, he'd have more than enough cash to kick off a solid campaign. He'll "hit hard in the battleground states: Michigan, Ohio, Florida. You think the other guys hit hard? They haven't seen me yet. I want to sell out stadiums. I want to be a visible candidate."

This brief burst of self-confidence seemed to snap him out of his funk. The reality of his unfortunate situation hit him hard as he talked about wanting a family, so the fantasy of playing rock guitar at sold-out stadium campaign events offered the perfect safety net. I dropped him off at his apartment, shook hands and promised to keep him updated on my progress—even though, to be honest, in that moment I wasn't sure I meant it. As I started to drive away, Shreffler ran back toward me. Gasping for breath, he had one more question. Did he want a campaign contribution? Was he going to retract anything he'd told me? Was he offering me a future cabinet post?

"I forgot to ask—with all your experience, do you know Paul Shaffer? I really like him and it'd be great to jam with him sometime, if he is ever able to. Just keep it in mind, okay?"

Rather than crush any more of his dreams, I assured him I'd do what I could, should I ever run into Paul Shaffer. By the time I got home an hour later, Shreffler called and emailed me to say thanks for giving his long-neglected campaign some attention. He also shared the name and number of one of his neighbors, Teresa Balogh, who would be more than happy to talk with me about him, if I called. Which I did. Reluctantly.

It would have been so easy at that point to dismiss

Shreffler as just a nice guy with some credibility issues to deal with. True or not, the story he spun about his life was one that can now only lead to jokes and derision. Still, he was such a sweet man that I didn't want to give him the Politico.com treatment. They had previously done a piece on fringe presidential candidates and included a few sarcastic paragraphs about Shreffler and his CIA claims. I guess I was still a believer in the "If you can't say something nice…" philosophy.

It wasn't just that I'd spent four hours getting to know him that left me feeling like I owed Shreffler something. I was also keenly aware that he and I were almost exactly the same age. We both grew up loners. We were both looking for ways to leave a personal legacy before it was too late. So I felt obliged to call Teresa and at least get some independent insight into the man and his presidential ambitions.

She admitted right away that he is "very shy…the sort of guy who lets you go up to him, not the other way around. And if you're going to get out in public for politics, you have to get over that." His closed-off nature, along with his mysterious government past, "hasn't been the easiest" to deal with during the first decade-and-a-half of knowing Shreffler. "It gets frustrating for everybody," she added, although since he decided to run for president two years ago "to help people," she's noticed a major change in his personality.

"His attitude about life has gotten much better," she explained. "He's getting out more to meet people. He told me that his family thinks what he's doing is crazy and is giving him a hard time. But running for president is bringing out the best in him. It's given his life meaning."

And there it was. I thanked her and hung up, taking a minute to absorb the fact that she just crystalized my motives for taking on this challenge. Throughout my day with Doug Shreffler,

I'd started to do what most of us do, though I'd vowed to avoid it. Maybe it was his casualty of an apartment. Maybe it was the whole pizza delivery boy-turned-CIA agent thing. Maybe it was his conviction that everyone in his hometown was a government agent there to protect him. There were plenty of reasons to: a) turn his story into the standard stereotype we all have of the citizen candidate; or b) feel so discouraged by this less-than-spectacular start to my grand presidential experiment that I abandon it before really giving it a chance.

To do that would have proven me to be a...what's that term? ..."superficial dick," according to my high school graduate son. I needed to keep going. I needed to keep asking "why?" I kept coming back to what Shreffler's friend said: running for president made him a happier guy. In his mind anyway, it gave his life a purpose. Between the scotch, the therapy and the Prozac (more on that later, I'm sure), the total bill for *me* trying to get comfortable in my own skin was probably approaching six figures. Shreffler was doing the same thing for the cost of a few hundred bumper stickers and red, white, and blue business cards.

So who's the crazy one in that scenario? Instead of representing the foolishness of my presidential candidates quest, Shreffler became the symbol for it—do what you want to do and mockers be damned. If something (legal) makes you feel more alive, why not do it?

One week later, I was on the road.

Ronald Satish Emrit

I've never been a big fan of road trips. Pop culture chroniclers, from Jack Kerouac to Pee Wee Herman to Thelma and Louise, have romanticized the notion of piloting a car (or bicycle) across the country to the point where it's become a key piece of the American Dream. I'm sure there are good things to be said about the freedom that comes from hitting the never-ending highways and byways. You can eat all the biscuits and gravy and burgers you'd never dream of consuming at home. You get to stay in places that don't require you to make your own bed. All of which is great.

My problem with the whole idea most likely stems from a childhood spent traveling from upstate Washington to Kansas, Georgia, New York and back nearly every summer. The stated goal was to visit family, but I have a feeling the real reason we traveled was just so we could "make good time" on the open road. Thanks to my dad's pipe smoke, my mom making bologna sandwiches in the back of our speeding Ford Ranch Wagon and the used coffee can available for emergencies between designated rest stops, *National Lampoon's Vacation* seemed more like a documentary to me.

Nonetheless, to meet the Can't-idates, I *had* to hit the road. There was no way I could afford to fly to everyone. And if I really wanted to get a glimpse of the actual America that big name candidates yammer on about representing, I had to do it from ground level. I can't imagine a guy like Donald Trump jumping into a rented Nissan Sentra by himself to see the country—which is ultimately why I decided to do just that.

The downside was this meant missing the precious remaining weeks before my son's high school graduation, though that impending event was also the push I needed to get myself out there. I wanted to find some kind of graduation gift that might have an actual impact on his future, something with meaning. Writing a book about people willing to risk their reputations to attempt the impossible, teaching him to forget about fear and do what he felt was right...now *that* was a graduation gift. (Plus, I couldn't afford to get him a car.)

So I packed up a handful of T-shirts, my jeans and Chuck Taylors before heading to my first stop: Las Vegas. This was home to one Ronald Satish Emrit. I justified putting him on the list for a few reasons. To start with, he was *insistent* on talking to me about his campaign, to the point where he offered to come meet me in Los Angeles if I couldn't travel to him. I admired that passion, and I have to admit, I was also intrigued by the driving force behind his candidacy: he'd studied to be a lawyer, but after failing the bar four times, he decided running for president might be a more viable career option.

The other rationale for making the trip to meet Emrit? Vegas, baby! Don't get me wrong. I'm not one of those typical Vegas types. I don't gamble. I'm happy being in bed by 10 p.m., and perfectly content to be in that bed alone. Still, Vegas has always fascinated me. What other city in the entire world sells itself as the place where it's your right to be a drunken a-hole, and then have your misdeeds all buried and forgotten? This is heaven for people who would love a weekend pass in hell.

More critical to my journey, though, Las Vegas is America in one tidy little urban area. The city has become a symbol for our ever-expanding appetite for leisure and lust—one-stop shopping for anyone in search of discount lap dances or all-you-can-eat $7.95 seafood dinners. Or both. The legend of Las Vegas is enormous. That's probably why, as I drove along the stretch of U.S. Route 95 that passes by the Vegas Strip, I was surprised at how tiny the whole place looked. From the freeway these famous landmarks—from the Luxor pyramid to New York, New York's fake Statue of Liberty—have about as much significance and splendor as a McDonald's playhouse. They're just another rest stop for cheap hamburgers and a distraction for the kids.

Emrit lived a few miles north of Las Vegas, so driving into his neighborhood was like expecting to meet Brad Pitt and getting his computer business-owning brother, Doug, instead. Outside the gates that separated his complex from the rest of the neighborhood, men and women pushed shopping carts full of children and belongings. (Emrit had described it "like that show *Naked and Afraid*, where they drop you off in the middle of nowhere.") A supersized Wal-Mart sat across the street. Inside the apartment complex, despite the illusion of exclusivity indicated by the security guard at the gated entrance, the buildings were pretty much the standard issue you'd see in any American suburb.

It was virtually impossible to tell any of them apart, so Emrit met me at his garage door to guide me in. He apologized for his beach bum ensemble: baseball cap, scruffy beard, oversized T-shirt, and baggy shorts. "I figured this was just a casual interview, so I didn't dress up," he sheepishly explained as we walked up the stairs to his living room.

He wasn't kidding when he turned to me and said, "My thing is that I'm messy." Not only were the walls empty, the living room furniture consisted entirely of a couple of well-worn arm-chairs and a big-screen TV tuned to Fox News. I peeked in a few of the other rooms as we sat down in the aforementioned chairs, and noticed most of the floors were covered with piles of clothes and books. Before we started our interview, Emrit introduced me to a tiny, curly-haired woman who he said was his former girlfriend/current roommate, Nicole. She shyly apologized for the disarray, then moved on to the kitchen.

Before I could dig into his reasons for wanting to be president, Emrit blurted out, "I'm doing this for the experience. I'm 39 years old. There's really not another black candidate out there. (*This was months before Ben Carson emerged as a contender.*) I used to think that you had to be from a rich family to do this, but seeing how Obama just seemed to come out of nowhere and won, it kind of gave me hope. Plus, this will look good on a resume. People will see it and say, 'What? You were a presidential candidate? You must be making that up!' But I'm not!"

Don't get him wrong. He has an entire plan for his administration mapped out. It's just that politics was never at the top of his list of ambitions, despite growing up in Maryland, near Washington, D.C. His father, a native of Trinidad and Tobago, emigrated to the United States and became a nuclear engineer, while his mom ran a successful temp agency. Young Ronald was a self-described "dork."

"But when I turned 14 and hit puberty, I became more popular. I played sports and got respect for that—soccer and basketball. I was going to be a sports manager. I wanted to be a guy who'd draft for professional sports teams."

His dream of a sports career died—and Emrit nearly did

too—not long after enrolling at Brown University. He joined one of the school's fraternities, but instead of endless parties and secret handshakes, he walked away from the experience with depression and post-traumatic stress disorder.

"The guys had all of the fraternity brothers gathered, and the guy who was pledging me told me to tilt my head to the right," Emrit recalled. "And this 300-pound guy took his hand and slapped me on the side of my neck." He paused for a breath and glanced at Nicole, whom he met and dated while they were both at Brown. "She points to that day as changing my life. If you're looking for a traumatic event in my life, everybody talks about that one, because I was hospitalized for a while afterward."

The injury to the nerves in his neck and the subsequent recovery was physically and emotionally devastating. It took Emrit weeks to return to his classes, after weeks of recovery and worry about the repercussions. The reception he received from his fellow frat brothers was less than pleasant, which I gleaned from his cryptic description of those years: "I don't know if you know about Masonry, but a lot of [fraternities] are a part of the secret society. Which is a culture where you don't complain, because if you do you'll be viewed as a 'snitch,' and that is unfortunate."

After leaving Brown, Emrit bounced from career to career for nearly two decades. There was the time he toyed with being a doctor. (He worked as a lab technician at the National Institutes of Health, learning how to separate DNA.) That was followed by what he said was four years in Miami, getting a degree at the Saint Thomas University School of Law. (Which was followed by those four failed attempts to pass the bar.) Mixed in along the way have been weeks as a first grade teacher, car salesman, paralegal and assorted gigs at Target, Office Depot and Verizon.

He blamed at least some of this drifting from gig to gig on the fact that "I can work for a certain amount of time, but after a while the depression gets to me to a certain extent. You can acknowledge that I'm disabled. I have worked over 30 or 40 jobs in my life, but I am on disability now. I would say that actually gives me more opportunity to do something like this, because if I had a job as an attorney, I wouldn't have time to run for president."

Now *this* was more like it. Imagine someone like Hillary Clinton or Marco Rubio explaining that the most fortunate part of their campaigns is that they have a disorder that keeps them from working a regular job. Sure they can act like they're mentally unstable—something Donald Trump and Ben Carson seemed to have cornered the market on—but admitting any emotional problems is a campaign killer. Emrit is the perfect *anti*-candidate: what might be political Kryptonite for a mainstream nominee is, in his eyes, more like Popeye's spinach. His flaws are what make him more sympathetic and more real, precisely the opposite of how we tend to view our better-known politicians.

I have to admit that at this point, I was starting to feel like I had with Doug Shreffler. Clearly Emrit had some...let's go with *delusions of grandeur*...going on. Was this a trend? Did every candidate, famous or not, have to be a little nuts to run for president? Part of me was ready to bag the interview and ease on down the road. But the truth is, Emrit reminded me of a lot of guys I knew in high school. Their ambitions far outstripped their abilities, but there's no denying they were kind of charming in their eccentricities. So I stuck with it.

Finally, we got around to talking about what brought me here in the first place: that whole thing about running for president because he failed the bar...repeatedly. Each attempt had cost him $1,000 just for the test, and there was more than a financial cost to his repeated failures. Emrit had been married. But he says when it became clear that practicing law was most likely not in his cards, that marriage ended. His wife remained in Florida with their daughter (now 12), and the newly single Emrit eventually found his way to Las Vegas a couple of years ago.

"It'd be nice if I was president, because then I could go to my ex and say, 'Hey, I'm the president now. Can I get custody of my daughter?' She could come to the White House," he said. "I haven't seen my daughter in a couple of years. It's a sensitive issue."

Which is probably why he took a breath and shifted our conversation to the positive side of his bar issues. Failing the exam freed up time to fully explore the dreams of hip-hop success he'd briefly mentioned on the phone. Emrit loved music when he was a kid, to the point where he and a friend formed a rap duo called Mr. Hyde and Da Beast. He's recorded on and off for the past decade as Satish Dat Beast, turning out what he proudly referred to as three "commercially announced albums" as well as winning "a *Billboard* award contest."

It's not that I doubted this. It's just that after Shreffler's CIA stories, I was somewhat more circumspect about what these people told me. But sure enough, before I left LA I found a handful of music videos online featuring a somewhat slimmer Emrit swaggering around sexy women, sporty cars and swanky locales, in songs with titles like "Searching for my Dimepiece" and "There She Goes Again." Seeing these videos felt like watching Dr. Dre or Snoop Dogg's eager distant cousin trying too hard to get into the family business—with 10% of the budget.

(It's too bad Emrit only gives himself a .1% chance of making it to the White House. How cool would it be to see an inauguration where the nominee arrives in a jacked-up Chevy, wearing a baseball cap and baggy jeans and sipping Hennessey from the bottle to meet Ruth Bader Ginsberg in her skintight black hoochie mama robe?)

To be fair, Emrit's music and videos are a perfect reflection of his presidential campaign: both feature a regular dude just trying to survive in a world unkind to regular dudes. He's awkward, but sincere, tossing out blue-collar rhymes like, "I'm losing my home / You know that just sucks / I called every hotline, but I ain't got no luck."

It seemed natural that he'd create his own presidential rap to perform at campaign stops. But he shook his head and explained why that probably won't happen.

"I was really excited when I first started making music," he said. "But when you've been doing it for 10 years like I have, it just gets kind of boring after a while and politics seems a lot more fascinating. They say to shoot for the moon, and if you miss, you'll still be among the stars. That's what I'm going for here. I am trying to be president. And I'm trying to be a record label exec and make it in Hollywood."

I had to give Emrit credit for an honesty you seldom see from the bigger names in the presidential race. Most of these people will never admit that they're really just running for reasons that would do Sarah Palin proud. They know they can never win the election, but the name recognition they get will lead to increased fame and less gray hair than being president. At least there was one guy in the race who freely acknowledged that rebuilding this nation is about building a personal brand.

I am guessing at least some of Emrit's outlook comes from Nicole, who has been there to support him no matter what project he's moved onto. Even though it's been awhile since they had a romantic relationship, they do still enjoy watching the news and having philosophical debates together. They can spend hours kicking around such topics as ancient Egypt.

"I can talk about the Battle of Actium, where Cleopatra took on Octavian." He paused, laughing at whatever joke he was hearing in his head. "She doesn't just like me because I'm good looking!"

They can agree on politics in the year 31 B.C. The year 2016, however, is more problematic. "I remember him saying, 'I qualify! I could try to run for president,'" Nicole said from across the room. "I thought it was a crazy idea. I thought that to become president, you had to have some kind of political background. There are people more qualified than he is, like Marco Rubio and Hillary Clinton. If he goes up against Hillary, he's going to lose."

Not exactly the sort of homefront support that inspires confidence in a candidate. But Emrit was unfazed by Nicole's comments. He's used to it.

"I just told my mom yesterday. She kind of chuckled a little bit, then said that it was good. I am kind of hoping that she will tell my dad that. My dad is a no-nonsense kind of guy."

Undeterred by this lack of interest, and taking advantage of his vast amount of spare time, Emrit has taken the campaign seriously enough to contact 40 states about getting on their ballots. He's had at least one success to show for his efforts. He bounced out of his chair and disappeared for a few moments, returning with a piece of paper.

"I was able to get on the ballot in Florida," he explained, waving the document around. "I wrote their Secretary of State and gave them my Federal Election Commission ID number. And that is that. They put me on the ballot."

While he explained, I glanced down at the note. It was indeed from the Florida Department of State and said that his name will appear on its Division of Elections webpage. Unfortunately, Emrit neglected to mention the rest of the sentence: "… this does not automatically mean that your name will appear on the ballot for either the presidential preference primary or general election." For that to happen, there were plenty of other political party hoops through which he'd have to jump.

I saw no reason to ruin Emrit's jovial mood with this little detail, so when he suggested taking a ride to show me where Dat Beast hung out, I immediately accepted. As he left to get his car

ready, Nicole came over to make sure I realized one very important thing about her friend's campaign.

"Running for president has had a positive impact on him,"
she said, looking quite serious. "It's made him happier. He seems
more motivated. Even this interview with you was something he
was looking forward to. When he feels like he has a goal, he can
be a real go-getter. That's why he got into this argument the other
day with his best friend. The friend told him, 'You know you have
to come from some political background if you're gonna do this.'
And he said right back, 'Don't tell me what I can and can't do!' So
if this experience just makes him happy, then I support him."

She then walked me downstairs to the garage, where
Emrit waited with another apology. He hadn't thought to clean
out his dusty old black Mercedes, so he was hoping I could drive
instead. With no other options, we hopped into my Nissan and hit
the road. As we drove the fast food and payday lender-lined
suburban streets that led into the heart of downtown Las
Vegas, the conversation drifted to what he liked to do when *not*
running for president.

Emrit's a big sports fan ("you can't really politicize sports");
he doesn't mind the occasional gambling trip to a local casino
(though he's not a regular on the Strip); and despite not being a
lawyer, he spends much of his time in courthouses filing litigation.

"I've been able to litigate over 100 cases," he explained.
"About 60 cases and about 40 appeals. So, to say that I am not
experienced in law, that just doesn't make sense. Because I have
been involved in all of these lawsuits. Ten of them are still open,
according to the court. This just shows you that the average citizen
can walk into court and file lawsuits by themselves."

He's an equal opportunity non-lawyer, with a wide variety
of lawsuit targets. For instance, Emrit claimed to have a 2001
case in Providence, Rhode Island just going into the discovery

phase now. In that case, he alleged police harassment "for false imprisonment, negligence, intentional affliction of emotional stress and malicious prosecution." He's also suing the Social Security Administration and Medicare for denying benefits to Nicole. And of the 100 cases he's got percolating, his guess is 50% of them are taking on the recording industry in one way or another.

It's no wonder he guided me to the Federal Courthouse in downtown Vegas. "I was just here this morning," he told me, as we parked. Sure enough, when we walked in the security guards gave him one of those "Yeah, I see you" nods of recognition you give a co-worker you see in the lunchroom for the fifth time that day. Emrit led the way to the clerk's office, demonstrating his litigiousness with the same loving pride Shreffler displayed with his caterpillar collection.

Using one of the court's computers, Emrit called up a list of cases that was so long, I couldn't get through it until I got back to Los Angeles. That's when I noticed the roll call included suits against everyone from Bank of America, to the Archdiocese of Miami, to Universal Music Group. One suit we did look at, though, involved his battle with the Federal Election Commission He was accusing the agency of not accommodating his depression. The only problem was, he wasn't quite sure of what he wanted them to do.

"The burden is on them," he said, smiling.

As much as I would have loved to delve deeper into his desire to spend time in court, I was feeling a little freaked out by how the quiet, nearly-deserted courthouse felt as spooky as life after the apocalypse. I told Emrit that I really needed to get back on the road—there was a biker in Boise waiting for me—and he seemed sort of sad, asking if we could at least make one more stop before I left.

That stop, as it turned out, was a casino a few blocks from his apartment. Emrit led me through a maze of slot machines, blackjack tables and sad grandparents, suggesting we grab a drink before I hit the road. I knew this was Las Vegas, where it's as normal as tea time in England to enjoy booze at three in the afternoon. Still, I settled for a ginger ale as Emrit returned with something that appeared to have vodka in it. Then we sat for a few minutes to shout about politics over the sound of bells and alarms that meant somebody was going home with a nice plastic tub of change.

I asked what an Emrit administration would look like, and he eagerly ticked off various policy positions: Relations with Cuba would go way beyond what President Obama has already done; anyone who needed marijuana for medical purposes would be allowed access to it; and, at the same time, his presidency would be seen as the one "that went after the drug cartels...if the Americans wanted to end the drug trade, they'd send in the Navy SEALs to Colombia to dismantle those cartels."

Despite constantly minimizing his chances, Emrit did lay out a social media plan of action that he would use to get some attention. Just start using all the Facebook/Twitter/Instagram tools out there and "you'll get 10 followers, then 100, then 10,000 and then 1 million. That happens if you keep working at it. So, to a certain extent, things don't happen overnight. But as long as you are trying and making an effort, they could. I have always learned luck is where opportunity meets preparedness."

Luck is also finding what I was after with this first travel stop. Even amidst the swirling and silent desperation of a Vegas strip mall casino in the middle of a Monday afternoon, where the conflicting smells of cigarettes and cheap air freshener battled to the death, I'd gotten to the reason why Ronald Satish Emrit was worth including in my Can't-idates collection: If Doug Shreffler was the guy running for president to get himself out in the world to become a better person, Emrit was the guy doing it to prove anyone can (and maybe should) try it. Running for president was no bigger a deal to him than, say, starring in a rap video. Don't worry. Be happy.

I am far more a Shreffler than an Emrit when it comes to my life. Yet, for some reason, as I dropped Emrit off and drove away, I started thinking about an incident in Boston decades ago. A neighbor I barely knew invited me to her friend's party. I subsequently spent two hours walking all around the neighborhood where her friend lived, sweating like a drunk in a sauna about the idea of going into a party where I knew nobody. Finally, I knocked on the door and when the hosts invited me in, I said I was just there to find Ann because I needed to get a message to her. They told me she hadn't arrived yet—which was perfect, since I had no message anyway. I said thanks and practically ran the three miles back to my apartment.

In many ways, I'm still that insecure guy. Which is why I envied Emrit. Okay, so I have no interest in failing the bar four times, or being in rap videos, or living in public housing across the street from Wal-Mart. But the one thing he had was a complete lack of fear when it came to trying pretty much anything. Emrit was Tom Cruise in *Risky Business*—"Sometimes you gotta say, 'What the fuck!'" I was Tom Cruise in the tabloids—nervous, misunderstood and awkward.

His was a world where running for president was no riskier than trying the free cheese-and-meat sample a stranger hands you at Costco. I had planned to immediately hit the road to Boise. In the moment, though, it felt like I needed to do something out of character. Something appropriate to Sin City, the place where people go to do everything their parents warned them about—but only after they did it themselves. Which explains why I decided to stop at a place called the Adult Mega Outlet.

Sitting in a strip mall on the edge of the freeway entrance, it featured signs promising such accouterments as a "fresh lingerie and toy section" and "peek-a-boo booths." The place had all the anonymous, yet enticing, charms of the Sears-adjacent strip club in the neighborhood where I grew up. A giant banner promised a sale inside and I'm all about saving a buck. So I opted to enter the forbidden zone.

For those who've never dared enter a porn store, picture a 7-11 in the shady part of town. Replace all the day-old hot dogs, Slurpees and "energy" aids with comically large dildos, erectile enhancing devices and DVD boxes featuring cover girls who vaguely resemble the cheerleaders that ignored you in high school. I needed proof that I had dared to enter this place, so I figured I should buy a souvenir. I was going to go with a copy of *The Texas Vibrator Massacre*, but they were all out. Likewise for my second choice, *Forrest Hump*. So I settled for the penis and heart-shaped cookie cutters, in case I'm someday overtaken by a sudden urge to serve pornographic baked goods at a holiday party.

I was officially a rebel now, courtesy of Emrit. So it was on with the trek…

Harley Brown

Ronald Emrit had gotten me feeling rebellious, but this was the most anarchistic act I ever performed. As a kid, instead of going to sleep at bedtime, I'd pull out the little white transistor radio I'd stashed beneath my pillow, crawl under the covers and listen to AM stations for hours. Because fewer stations were broadcasting in the middle of the night, the signals of the country's biggest AM outlets would reach all the way out west to the mountains of Washington.

KSFO in San Francisco. KOA in Denver. WLS in Chicago. WJR in Detroit. On an exceptionally clear night, I might even make it as far as KDKA in Pittsburgh. Traveling the country just by listening to late-night news and weather from other cities was more enjoyable than those pipe smoke-reeking, warm bologna sandwich-eating vacations with my family. I'd lay there for hours, imagining what it'd be like to get out and discover new things.

Forty years of playing it safe later, that wish was finally coming true. So for my trip from Las Vegas to Boise, I decided to spend the 10-hour drive listening to nothing but AM radio. Except for the lack of Carpenters and Seals & Croft songs, not much had changed since those 1970s nights under the covers. Eager evangelists and self-absorbed talk show hosts still ruled the airwaves, just as God intended. Here's the thing about AM radio: How many people listen to it for anything more than weather and traffic? Exactly. So the AM radio audience is primarily people in very old cars and/or assisted living centers. Hence, the relentlessly conservative tone of every conversation. It may not represent a peek into what the majority of voters are thinking, but there is probably no better way to monitor the mood of the *motivated* electorate than listening to AM radio. It's easy to get lost in the big media mania of Los Angeles, a land where we can all arrogantly indulge in whatever and whomever we like simply because we want to. Not that there's anything necessarily wrong with that. But even the most committed Angeleno has to admit ours is a pretty self-absorbed city. That's why hearing what people really thought, hundreds of miles from the nearest BMW dealership or air-conditioned juice bar/health club, was refreshing. Scary, but refreshing.

For most of the morning and early afternoon, religious shows dominated the dial with predictions of social Armageddon if and when "those people" were allowed to marry. I got sucked into one pastor's hour-long treatise on resurrection, especially when he used the caterpillar-into-butterfly metaphor to explain what glorious fate awaits the faithful. I thought of Doug Shreffler's backyard and smiled.

I edged closer to Boise, closer to a state known for its potatoes and white supremacist encampments. The radio mood shifted from spiritual to something much more earthbound. Namely, the death and destruction liberals were planning to rain down upon us. This was the first time on the road that the notion of *liberals versus conservatives* even occurred to me. The Can't-idates were all people, not politics, as far as I was concerned. But when in

61

Rome—or Idaho—it's easy to see how people can become po-
larized listening to AM talk show hosts rant about the evils of
Hillary Clinton or the imminent federal government takeover of
Texas, courtesy of a military training exercise known as Jade Helm.

I had vowed to be as apolitical as possible on this trip,
trying to listen to and learn from, rather than ignore and yell at,
everyone. (So much for promoting this book on cable news...)
I even tried to remain neutral while the host on a Utah station
groused about how his oppressive, nanny state just made not
wearing a seatbelt while driving an expensive ticketable offense.
(For the record, roughly two-thirds of the states already had that
same law.)

About an hour outside Boise, I found a host named
Alex Jones, someone fond of using the word "liberal" the way a
personal trainer would use the words "Big Mac." I'm sure he'd
consider himself a "None of the Above" kind of talk show host.
To a first-time listener such as myself, it seemed like outside of
his dog and his mother, there aren't many creatures Jones trusts in
this world. And the dog had been acting a bit sketchy when fetch-
ing lately. On this particular evening, he was talking to Chuck
Norris' son Mike about a "patriot movie" called *AmeriGeddon*
that Norris had just directed. The film (which not coincidentally
featured a Jones cameo as an evil politician) tells the story of a rebel Army officer who must fight a sinister American government
attack on its own people not unlike the aforementioned Jade Helm.

At one point in this discussion, Jones took a break from
the doom and gloom to talk up his sponsor: Patriot Blend 100%
Organic Coffee, from the mountains of, yes, southern Mexico.
I'm sure the coffee is great. And perhaps Jones has no personal
qualms about hiring Mexican immigrants. Still, I could easily
imagine his hardcore, blank slate conservative listeners getting
hyped up on all-American coffee grown by people they didn't

particularly want moving into their neighborhood. I wanted to measure exactly how many gallons of irony went into this, but I pulled up to The Busted Shovel in the Boise suburb of Meridian instead.

The place was precisely what Harley Brown had promised. There were a few motorcycles parked out front, indicating the heavily tattooed types who liked to frequent the joint. Inside, at least from what I could tell given how dim the lights were, the left half of the club was all pool tables and video games. The right side was all tables, chairs and cigar smoke. Lots and lots of cigar smoke. Most of which, I noticed, came from a table occupied by a hefty man who looked like a leather-clad, tooth-challenged Santa Claus, replete with leather vest, cap and gloves. He sat across from a much younger guy in a red flannel shirt and leather vest with "The Bombers Motorcycle Club" stitched on the back.

I recognized Harley right away. Of all the people I was visiting on this trip, he was one of the few who had actually gotten some national exposure for his political ambitions. In 2014, he ran for governor of Idaho and, through some Machiavellian machinations courtesy of incumbent Gov. Butch Otter, ended up as one of four candidates in a televised Republican debate. All his talk of being chosen by God to become president quickly made him a viral sensation, with everyone from Stephen Colbert to Chris Matthews plugging him on their shows.

"Welcome to The Busted Shovel," boomed the 61-year-old Brown. He introduced me to the younger guy, Mayhem, whom I deliberately choose not to question about his name. Brown informed me that his young friend was sergeant-at-arms of their biker club, then handed me a cigar.

"Step into our formal meeting area!" said Mayhem, whose goateed, pop idol good looks made him seem barely old enough to be in any bar, let alone this one. Brown quickly jumped in.

"Don't worry! They wiped up all the blood. We thought about going to the other biker bar in town, but that place is a little rowdier and more violent. You can do an interview here."

He already had a pint of beer waiting for me as he pulled out a match to fire up my stogie. "I warn you," he bellowed. "Sir, that's an exploding cigar! I keep them for the fuckin' liberals. Hey! You're not a liberal, I hope."

For the briefest of seconds, he glared at me. As self-preservation prompted me to insist I was completely non-partisan, Brown erupted into the kind of rumbling, self-satisfied laugh usually reserved for Bond villains and assured me he was just screwing with me. He likes screwing with people. He does it very well.

"People think I'm a certified lunatic," he roared. Perhaps it comes from a lifetime of hanging out in biker bars, but volume control is not one of Brown's virtues. "I'm used to people telling me that I'm crazy. It's like water on the duck's back to me."

Mayhem eagerly joined in. "A lot of people right off the bat don't understand Harley, but I've had him over for my family dinners and stuff. They are kind of iffy about him at first. But then they get to know him and start hearing his stories and his dream of being president, and they start thinking, 'Yeah, you're the guy to fix all this.'"

By day, Mayhem operates cranes and other heavy equipment. By night, he's doing whatever it takes to get Brown running this nation. First and foremost, he does it because bikers have to stick together. And second?

"This country's lost touch with the regular guy, who's out there busting his balls just to eat! We need someone who's real in office. And Harley is a go-getter. He sees something he believes, he goes for it. Even the younger crowd wants that. Look at our committee for his campaign. We're mostly 20- to 30-year-olds."

In fact, a lot of his supporting cast grew up watching him regularly run—and lose—races for public office. Over the past 20 years, he's not only tried to become Idaho's next governor, he's failed to win so many contests that "my entire political career has been like one of those 1950s rocket launches…it gets about 10 feet off the ground and goes out with a spectacular explosion. I've run for senator, congressman, mayor…it all started when I ran for county highway commissioner around the year 2000."

I was worried that his presidential bid would crash and burn before I'd even made it to The Busted Shovel on that rainy Tuesday night. Right before I left Los Angeles, Brown called to give me some bad news. Due to a lack of funds, he was folding his 2016 campaign. Unlike Emrit or Shreffler, he was bringing all his friends into the fold and trying to pay them for their help. This was admirable, but also a bit misguided, since it was sucking away several thousand dollars. Most of that money paid salaries to the dozen or so friends working for him who, like Mayhem, had specific campaign duties.

"I used to have a pretty good credit rating," growled Brown, a jack-of-all-trades who has lately done everything from construction jobs to driving long-haul trucks. "I financed a beautiful Softail Deluxe motorcycle in 2009 and was making payments on that, but things were tough. We weren't getting the campaign funding and I had to pay the guys on my staff. For this particular campaign, I've spent about $35,000 in cash—and lost that motorcycle. Then I thought I could get a Rat Shovelhead (another bike), [but] then I found that I had to pay these guys again. So I told the guy with that bike just to keep the $2,000 and that I'm sorry, I couldn't fulfill my obligations. And that was just this year!"

He slowly shook his head, blew out a long stream of cigar smoke and watched it drift away. "Two bikes, man, two bikes…" His voice trailed off like the smoke. If you totaled the amount of money he's spent on all his campaigns, things look even worse. Brown estimates he's spent around $150,000 on his political career, with nothing to show for it. Inheriting money from his father, another Navy vet, helped offset the cost. Unfortunately, it hasn't done anything to get him closer to the presidency.

This failure is at least partially God's fault. Make no mistake. Harley Brown is a God-fearing Christian and has been ever since his Waterbury, Connecticut Catholic school days in the '60s. He still remembers how to say his Hail Marys in Latin (which he demonstrated for everyone at The Busted Shovel). Even when he couldn't find a job after becoming the first man in his family to graduate from college—the University of Connecticut—he had faith that God would show him the way. Which God did, escorting him into the Navy's construction battalion (a.k.a. "the Seabees"), and a career as a professional engineer.

I confess that I get a little jealous whenever people start talking about their relationship with God. My mom's side of the family was Methodist, though nobody ever fully explained what "the method" was. (I knew about the rhythm method, but the Catholics had already claimed that one). When I was younger, we were regular churchgoers. I spent many hours in Sunday school, but mostly because the teachers were cute college girls. I never did think that plan through thoroughly, as church was probably not the best place to lust after older women.

When I meet people like Brown, whose faith is steadfast, I feel as out of place as the guy with a seafood allergy whose surprise birthday party is at a sushi joint. I've tried to understand religion. My kids both went to a Presbyterian pre-school. I wanted them to have at least some understanding of what God may or may not be up to, but I ultimately used the "I don't want to force religion on them" excuse as the lazy way out of taking them to actual church.

So I wasn't sure whether to laugh at or envy Brown as he

told me about the time God "pulled my balls out of the fire." It was decades ago, after he alienated his military superiors by asking for a leave to propose to the Scottish woman he'd just met in a bar. The Navy was set to ship the newlywed to a post in the Aleutian Islands, but a paperwork mix-up sent him to a munitions storage base in Indiana instead. Rather than freezing his butt off in Alaska, Brown got to watch over 450 civilian employees and 750,000 tons of explosives in Indiana.

He also had a duty that, in looking at this husky, bearded, 6-foot-4 wall of a man, was hard to imagine ever being assigned to him. His gruff demeanor makes him seem like the last guy you'd want knocking on your door to tell you your loved one had just been killed in the line of duty. And yet, he did just that for nearly two years.

"It loosened a few screws in me," Brown admitted. "How could it not? If you don't have a heart, you could do that job. But I was supposed to say this blurb: *'The Secretary of the Navy said...'* Fuck that shit! I wasn't gonna say that. I'd walk up to the door and they'd see my uniform and start thinking about their son. Then they look into your eyes and see the expression on your face and say, 'Oh, Jesus!' You have to confirm their worst fear. I had a lady who had a heart attack on the stoop of her home. I didn't know what the fuck to do."

For one of the very few moments in the evening, Brown sat silent. "That fucked me up in the head. It just changed my whole attitude. It completely stripped me of a façade of political correctness. After doing that shit, you don't care."

I would love to hear that sort of gut-wrenching honesty from any of the cable news-ready, gung-ho, pro-military presidential candidates. Sure, I've never served, and I'm too much of a chicken to even join my son at his annual paintball party. Then again, I don't want to be the boss of the armed services.

That's why it was fascinating to learn about this part of Brown's background. If *he* were the president sending our boys into combat, at least he'd know, more than any other candidate, what the cost of that move would be.

Not surprisingly, things unraveled for Brown after that experience. He traveled the country, working military construction jobs in Missouri, California, New York and Alaska. He went to Reno to start his own engineering firm. When that didn't work out, he moved north to Idaho with his second wife, her two kids and the two children they had together. Brown started driving a cab, enjoying the company of the "crazy bastards" he'd shuttle around town, because, he said, it gave him "close exposure to mankind and the stark reality" of what this American life was all about.

But living his life was rapidly becoming like riding one of his beloved motorcycles along 100 miles of pothole-filled country road—far too many bumps, with no end in sight. There were moments when it seemed like the suicidal alcoholics Brown was picking up in his cab might have had the right idea. He and his wife were having problems, and the run-in he'd had with the local authorities didn't help.

"I came home after working the day shift and my ex-old lady was crying. I said, 'What the hell's the matter? Where are the kids?' She said, 'They took 'em!' I said, 'Who took 'em?' Turns out Health and Welfare and the cops had been there and took our kids. I'm an Irishman, right? And that kindled my wrath. I had a big fuckin' Hell's Angels red beard, about 18 inches long. I fire up my old Shovelhead and go right down to the Health and Welfare Department, madder than hell."

Brown was as diplomatic as you'd expect. He barged into the department director's office, leaned over the man's desk and explained that he'd had a dream where bikers took over Boise and "we marched all you motherfuckers who steal our kids away without due process of the law down Main Street with bayonets into a concrete truck. Then we threw in a couple hundred pounds of medical waste and dumped you all into an open grave."

The situation was eventually straightened out—a clerical error had sent the authorities to the wrong Brown family—but not before the outburst landed Brown in prison, where one of his jobs was to serve meals to the guys on death row. A judge eventually determined he was "obnoxious, but not a menace to society," so Brown went home, only to end up alone again when wife number two dumped him. By the fall of 1994, he was broke and alone, living in his buddy Fat Jack's cellar.

After all of that, you'd think that God would finally ease up on him. So did Brown, who continued to have faith, even though nothing was going right. To keep himself occupied, he became fond of confronting his down-on-their-luck cab customers by asking, "If you were to die right now, would you go to heaven or hell?"

"Here I am, this big biker, saying, 'How would you like to be guaranteed to go to heaven and party with all us bikers forever?' The guy would answer, "Yeah, I'd like that.' So I'd say, 'Hold my hand!'" Brown would extend a biker glove-covered hand while barking at his passenger: "Repeat after me! Dear Jesus, save my ass from hell! Alright, that'll work on Judgment Day. Now get the hell outta here. I gotta go back to work."

And then, on a cold, dark autumn night in Boise, everything changed.

"Business was lousy and I was depressed. [So I] cried out to God, 'What the hell am I doing driving a taxi? You didn't make me the youngest fleet commander in the Navy for nothing. How about putting me back on active duty and [making] me a battalion commander of 1,000 men to fulfill my wildest ambitions?' I think I was 40 years old at the time.

"And then God talked to me. Not audibly, but to my heart. He said, 'Harley, I have a much higher rank in mind for you.' Being an Irishman, I said, 'What? Secretary of War? Being in charge of all the troops and planes and tanks?' He said, 'No, son, I'm gonna make you Commander in Chief!' I said, 'Wow!' Then it hit me and I thought, 'That's the President of the United States. What the hell do I know about politics and protocols?'"

Not much, clearly. "I said, 'Besides that, Heavenly Father, you give someone like me that kinda power and I'm gonna have to take over the whole goddamn world! Because that's all those assholes can understand.' I was thinking about Iran. And then the answer comes back. 'I know what I'm doing, son.' I was like, 'Holy shit!' The next day I went out and got the presidential seal tattoo on my arm!"

Lest you think the body ink was a bit premature, or that God might have made a wrong turn at Spokane and ended up in the wrong cab with a citizen politician fond of the phrase "nuke their ass and take their gas," consider this: After God nominated Brown, he met "this guy out of Africa." The Rev. Bishop Thomas P. Ngira Abungu, to be exact. He was a man of the cloth who just happened to visit Boise about the same time Brown received his divine message. To prove his spiritual support, Brown produced a campaign brochure, which featured the entire notarized affidavit from Rev. Abungu. In that letter, the Reverend confirmed "by the Holy Spirit that in November, 1994, God did indeed tell Harley D. Brown that He would make him the Commander in Chief... the general time frame for the promise to come to pass is 20 years, during which time Harley is to prepare for the presidency by accomplishing a number of specific tasks, among which is to serve at least one term as a state governor."

Not everyone was as excited to hear about Brown's new career move. Friends and family thought he was nuts. Fat Jack's old lady wanted him out. His response to the doubters? "Screw you! I got a promise from God!"

"I developed the nickname Psycho Biker From Hell," recalled Brown

Some might view this as a reason to *not* vote for him. Still, as I puffed my way through a second cigar and a fourth glass of beer, it became easier to identify with the well-intentioned, yet crass, ramblings of Harley Brown. Sure, he's a Hell's Angel who promises America's enemies that if he's elected president, "they'll be wetting their pants about this redhead getting a nuclear bomb." But how is that different than, say, Ted Cruz stating that ISIS should be bombed "back to the Stone Age"?

I've always hated when candidates accustomed to ordering from the top shelf suddenly become bottom-shelf guys (and gals) when in Iowa, New Hampshire or Ohio. If we really do want to elect more people who have experienced the blue-collar world most Americans inhabit, you don't get more bottom-shelf than a biker who's been married four times, has no filter and makes sure he takes care of his pals when he runs for office— even if he can't afford it.

I wanted to ask Brown if he'd be my surrogate fun uncle, the guy who lets you get away with all the stuff your parents never would. I was just saving the request for when we got back to his place. In the weeks leading up to my visit, Brown had offered to let me spend the night at his nearby house, appropriately located on a road called Happy Lane. Once there, I could meet his fourth wife, Joni, and their two kids. (He'd also volunteered to use the pimping skills he honed while driving a cab to find me some company for the evening, but all I had so far were four beers and two cigars.)

Brown met Joni through an online dating site and married her back in 2001. It's hard to imagine this man in leather as peaceful, but apparently Mrs. Brown has mellowed him immensely.

"She's got his back through thick or thin," offered Mayhem. "And she knows he's got this dream to be president, and she'll do anything to help him."

Brown would do anything for her too, including become a parent again—even though he was in his 50s at the time. Joni's son from a previous relationship had passed away at age 22, and Brown told me how "she took it so bad that she was on medication." She wanted to have more kids, so for about $70,000 ("the price of a new Suburban"), they recruited "a 29-year-old volunteer chick" as a surrogate caretaker of Brown's sperm. Eventually, along came Baron Tiberius (now 7) and Bronson Augustus (now 6).

This meant Brown was my first interviewee so far who could relate to my difficulty of trying to be a decent role model for my boy. I mentioned my fear of fatherly failure and how I wanted this presidential project to teach my son to never let anyone trample his hopes and dreams. Brown stopped me with a wave of his hand and stepped over to the vaguely better-lit section of the bar. He had me follow him, with my iPhone camera ready. We stopped alongside a pool table, where Brown suggested I record him delivering the following video message to my teenager:

"I wanna quote you something! 'The only thing to do when a son of a bitch looks cross-eyed at you is to beat the hell out of him right then and there.' Who said that? Gen. George S. Patton. Study hard, go to college and get good grades so your old man doesn't have to bust his balls putting your ass through college. Thank you for your support."

Definitely a different direction than I tend to take when offering advice, but maybe this was a good thing. After all, if I was going to continue what Emrit had inspired me to do—expand the boundaries of my personal comfort zone—sending my son a video of an ex-sailor swearing at him like, well, a sailor was probably an appropriate move. I hit "send" and headed outside to say goodbye to Mayhem and ride home with Brown.

Sadly, Joni had called to tell him it would be much better if he didn't bring home any guests this evening. So I would not be meeting Harley's family. Instead, Brown suggested meeting for breakfast, when he would produce a few more surprise guests.

Which is how I met Ken Henderson. The next morning, he and Brown were waiting for me at Sunrise Café, a couple blocks down the street from The Busted Shovel. It was the kind of folksy, biscuits-and-gravy diner that had me feeling two Duke boys short of being on a back road in the South. I found the guys in what I assumed was their customary booth, where Brown introduced this Taylor Swift-thin, 50s-ish man as the brains behind (and sole member of) the Harley Brown 2016 IT department.

They'd connected a couple of years ago, during Brown's gubernatorial campaign. Brown may be comfortably in the "Kids, Get Off My Lawn" demo, but he was well aware of the importance of the Internet if he wanted to attract the young guys who Mayhem predicted would love him. So he found and hired Henderson, who had been through some tough times of his own.

A recovering drug addict, Henderson choked back tears when I asked about his background. Rather than fill me in on all of his 65 years, he skipped ahead to the night a couple decades ago when he realized he was "a fucking monster." The desire for drugs had consumed him and he sat in front of a space heater in his freezing dump of a home in Colorado, "begging God to help me. I am crying, and I don't cry pretty—snot coming out of my nose, my face all swollen. I had never in my life had total despair until that moment. I was utterly hopeless. And then the great thought came in: 'Why do you think you need God?' Within a second, I'm laughing at the absurdity of my conclusions of what life was all about, that I couldn't do it. All I needed was to be willing to try. I don't need to accomplish anything. I just need to be willing to try."

Henderson cleaned himself up starting that night, and eventually found his way to Idaho and gigs as a website developer. He told me he'd worked on sites like GunnersGuru.com and Spiritual-Insight.com, a thematic contrast that perfectly captured Henderson's far-ranging views on the world. Even though he and Brown just met in 2013, they had the playful chemistry of a couple who've been married for 40 years. They can't talk about the bacon and eggs we had for breakfast without arguing, but you know their quibbling will probably end with a bro hug.

"Being around Harley, I started to understand him more and learned sometimes I just have to put my hand in his face and say, 'Shut up and listen,'" Henderson said softly. "At first, that was kind of scary, because Harley is a pretty big dude. But that's how hard we pushed one another. He lets me shout and scream for a while—and I let him shout and scream. Because if we don't do that, we're gonna go a little crazier. He thinks I'm trying to help get him elected, but I'm really trying to get him to think."

He looked over at Brown, who was grinning back at him. So Henderson continued: "He thinks about what needs to be done and then takes action. And I appreciate it. When he first talked to me about working with him, I was almost afraid to be associated with the guy because it would ruin my reputation. He's nuts. [But] should a crazy man have the opportunity to say what he thinks? I came up with, 'Absolutely!'"

There's a genuine compliment buried somewhere in all that, but Brown still growled back, "How can you say I'm nuts? You're not a psychiatrist!"

"It depends on if your thought chain is rational or not, and frequently your thought chain is not rational," Henderson shot back. "You can go ahead and be fuckin' nuts. I like it that way."

"I just propose an idea and a course of action," Brown answered. "I realize I could nuke North Korea, but that might not be the best thing to do."

"It's not crazy to want to be president, but from where we're starting..."

Brown's original playful attitude seemed to be fading. "It's my God-given destiny!"

Henderson was undeterred. "That remains to be seen. Harley, from a rational viewpoint, you thinking that you might be elected the President of the United States, starting where you're at right now, is fuckin' nuts!"

Brown moved his gloved fists onto the table. "The Bible said that the carnal mind is the enmity of God."

"Harley, you can spout all the bullshit you want to!"

"It's in the fuckin' Bible!"

I tried not to laugh hearing the phrase "fuckin' Bible."

"Harley, I'll just say this. I don't need the Bible to figure it out. If God takes a hand in this, you'll be president. And if he doesn't, you won't. It's very simple. You believe it. I don't. So what the fuck difference does it make?"

"He told me and He can't lie, so the deduction is that He's gonna make it come true!"

The more worked up Brown got, the more laidback Henderson became.

"You could be the Commander in Chief of the Boy Scouts, I don't fuckin' know! Go convince somebody else—you're not gonna convince me! God is going to direct me as He sees fit, and for whatever reason, He has me here helping you. Whether it's to get you elected or not, I don't know and I don't really care."

Brown smiled, leaned back and pulled a piece of paper from his pocket. Then he grabbed a pen and started to scribble something. He was out of the discussion now, so Henderson turned to me.

"It was not a leap of faith that connected me to Harley. It was very thoughtful consideration. I sat down and asked myself,

'What are the fuckin' Democrats and Republicans doing to my world?' They're fucking it up. Will Harley fuck up my world? I don't think so. I think he'd make it better."

It was clear to me that when it came to the campaign, Harley Brown was definitely the id and Ken Henderson was ego and super-ego. Brown's charm was his brash impulsiveness. He was a human Kalishnikov who may fire a shot in any direction at any moment. Henderson was the practical thinker, someone who liked to reason things out before jumping into any debate.

"He brings out the best of me," Brown said, looking up for a moment from whatever he was drawing. "I would never have given a damn about those enemy combatants that we got locked up in Gitmo. He was ramming it up my ass, saying, 'Hey, what does the Declaration of Independence say? All men are created equal, thank you very much.' He says the guys at Gitmo are being held without a trial for 15 years and are entitled to due process of law. It's political suicide to say we should give them all trials, and if we can't convict them, set them free. But I realized Ken's right. Righteousness and truth should prevail over political expediency."

It's talk like this that makes Brown so captivating. He can be downright liberal, despite his earlier threat to wipe the floor with such freethinkers. Then he'll talk about abortion being a sin "that's worse than a million gays marrying each other." After that, it's back to the left to discuss gay marriage.

"I've picked them up in my taxi and they are just like everybody else. And they love each other. The Bible says that love covers a multitude of sins. Yet here are all these religiously-correct motherfuckers trying to make your conscience be your guide, coming down on these people that can't be married and shit!"

As long as we were talking issues, he mentioned that he and Henderson agreed that the national debt is a problem that needs fixing, no matter what one's political leanings might be. Brown grabbed the drawing he'd been working on and slapped it down in front of me. On the reverse side of a computer printout chronicling the rise of said debt from zero in 1915 to $18 trillion now, he'd sketched out a pie chart to illustrate the federal budget. Two-thirds of the pie had been labeled "Social Programs (unconstitutional)" while the other third was called "Gov Ops."

Looking at the paper the way a five-year-old looks at a plate of Brussels sprouts, Brown snarled, "Two-thirds of our $4 trillion budget goes to social programs and the rest is for the government itself. And I'd say that a good 75% is unconstitutional bullshit! The national debt is running out of control. Big government is hemorrhaging our money and our grandchildren's money!"

Henderson smiled back at his friend, happy to see how worked up Brown is about this particular topic. Before they could get into another debate, however, Brown realized he and I had somewhere else to be. He wanted me to meet his attorney on the other side of town, so we had to hit the road right away. I gave an unexpectedly rushed farewell to Henderson, with a promise that I'd follow up with more questions once I got home.

Minutes later, I followed Brown as he weaved through Boise with the speed and reckless skill of a former taxi driver. We ended up at a tree-shaded office park alongside the Boise River, and as we walked over to his attorney's office, he briefed me on what to expect.

"This guy, T.J., is my Hell's Angels-approved defense attorney," he boomed. "There was this lawyer in town, Gar Hackney, and he and T.J. had started a practice. I went to see them for some other law issues and eventually got [them] involved in the campaign."

The way he just left the phrase "some other law issues" hanging there like a piñata prompted a few new questions. Before I could ask any of them, though, Tony Shallat, one of the rising star attorneys at the Angstman Johnson law firm, met us at the door. He had the gung-ho attitude of a high school quarterback, with the conservative look of a student body president. Because he grew up in Boise, Shallat has known about Brown for most of his life.

"After I told my friends Harley was my firm's client, they got really excited," he explained as he led us into a conference room. "He's a local legend. When I first realized that Harley Brown was a client here, I went out and snuck a peek to see what he looked like, because I'd heard a lot about him over the years."

As a student of history and politics, Shallat was pleased when asked to counsel Brown about fundraising. The more they talked, the more of a believer he became.

"Harley takes the whole playbook on how to run for office and stands it on its head."

Brown leaned back in his chair, soaking up the joy that came with an outsider getting what his campaign is all about. Then Shallat's boss, T.J. Angstman, walked in.

"I disagree with Tony a little bit," explained the man who has been working with Brown for nearly 20 years. "I don't know all of Harley's campaign platforms, but I do know him well and I think the money thing is a big point. His stand on the issues might make him more appealing to people, but just to get on the ballot in one state costs a tremendous amount of money. We're going to need a fortune."

In many ways, Angstman is a more outgoing version of Henderson—a reality check Brown keeps in his circle so his mouth doesn't race faster than any of his bikes. He's been with Brown since before the burly biker was known as Harley. ("I changed my name for political purposes...Harley Brown, now that's a name for a man...But after I become president, I will change it back to Robert, on account of my poor Irish mother, God rest her soul.")

That was back in the late '90s, Angstman recalled, when Brown would pull wads of cash from his pockets and slap the bills down to "make a show of it." That cavalier attitude about money didn't impress the attorney. It took time, but once he got past Brown's leatherwear and tendency to smell like a cigar bar, Angstman was struck "not by the outrageous parts of his character, but that he is really smart. And it makes life more interesting to be around people that are clever, smart and self-aware." He paused for a moment, glancing at Brown to make sure he hadn't riled the man up.

"Has he heard the story about the M1 Garand at the airport? Mind if I tell it?"

Angstman brought us to precisely where I wanted to be: those aforementioned "other law issues."

"Go right ahead," Brown shot back with a laugh. "You're my mouthpiece."

While Angstman was not Brown's attorney for this case, he was around for all the pertinent details. Apparently, not long before 9/11, Brown had gone to the Boise Airport to pick up a female friend. Brown leaned forward, eager to take over his own story.

"It was a Marine Corps World War II issue rifle with a 16-inch bayonet. I was running for Congress and I was concerned about any liberal villains out there. I had that thing fully loaded, with a round in the chamber and wires strapped around the trigger, so it wouldn't go off without me pulling it. The guard looked at me like a raccoon looking at truck headlights. They came out and tackled me and put me in handcuffs. They walk by with my rifle and I started singing, 'Take good care of my baby.' So they busted my ass for a misdemeanor."

He went to jail and bail was set at $300. He had exactly $299 in his pocket and none of the local cops would loan him the extra dollar. That meant he had to spend the night in a cell while his female guest went back to his house. Upon getting home, he did what came naturally to a recently incarcerated psychotic biker from hell—he threw a party.

"It was a total Level 3. Level 1 is your church party with kids. Level 2 is all-you-can-drink beer and rock 'n roll. Level 3 is a full-blown Level 2, but you put a spin on it with strippers. So it's six in the morning, the sun is coming up and I got sick of this kid not leaving my house when I asked him. So I grab him by the throat and throw his ass out the front door. And he won't leave my front lawn. So I got a 30-ought-6 hunting rifle and fired a round in the air, then pointed it at him and said, 'The next round is going into you.' That should have been incentive for his departure. But all of a sudden I hear a knock on the door, and I see a light across the street. [I] hear a chick's voice saying, 'Harley, this is Officer Shane. Come out with your hands up.' I said to my friend, 'See! This is Idaho! Come on vacation and leave on probation.' Everybody laughed their asses off. And in the end, the cops didn't bust me, so it was one helluva party!"

He laughed again, spinning the story in the same boastful way I tell people about the night I spent stranded on a mountaintop with nothing but a case of Corona, a bottle of tequila and Jon Bon Jovi. Stories like these at least start with facts and drift along from there, creating the perfect macho, badass mystique. Brown works very hard to come across as a pit bull. However, while I'm sure he wouldn't want to hear it, he actually seems like a big, cuddly St. Bernard.

He poses as the kind of dad who grounds any son who doesn't fight the school bully. But so many of his stories end with him trying to entertain everyone around him, I suspect his darkest secret is that he's actually the kind of dad who would read his kids bedtime stories until the day they left for college. He genuinely cares for everyone around him, as he demonstrated by making that video for my son. Which is why he not only feels the need to keep the world laughing with his antics, he also wants to protect it by becoming president.

"This will make him mad, but not mad enough to injure me," Angstman interrupted. "Inside of him is a very kind and caring man. I've seen him tear up having heard that his words had a negative effect on another person. That's more recent, in the last five years or so. And the value of having someone like Harley to our country is enormous. And his message about political correctness—I really understand that. He's not trying to discriminate. What he really wants to say is, 'Let's get over ourselves and stop getting so bent out of shape with just words.'"

I was shocked at how quiet the room got. Compliments are apparently not something Brown is used to absorbing. His world is so full of blunt talk and bluster that when his campaign actually does get taken seriously, it's tough for him to know how to react. Luckily, Angstman and Shallat were needed elsewhere, so our meeting broke up quickly. As Brown headed out the door, he stopped at the receptionist's desk, bringing things back to true Harley-ness by asking if she knew the difference between men and bonds. She smiled politely and shrugged, and he barked, "Bonds mature!"

He let out one more self-satisfied roar before we headed to the parking lot. We stopped at my car and, to be honest, it felt a little weird. Brown has this unique ability to make sure everyone around him feels attended to. But now he seemed distracted and upset.

He looked off in the distance and said, with a hint of melancholy, "God does some bizarre shit. Who the hell does He think He is, anyway? Whenever He gets involved, all bets are off. This [presidency] has to happen or God is a fucking liar, which would destroy the whole fabric of the universe."

Whereas Emrit and Shreffler were ultimately running for president as a lark or to feel useful, Brown was doing it for a more divine reason. He was doing it for God. I realize how ridiculous that sounds, but standing there in a Boise office parking lot after meeting people devoted to the guy, I got it. This man is all about passion—for women, for motorcycles, for parties. Twenty years ago he poured all his passion into fulfilling what he was certain was God's plan. Now he was growing frustrated because that passion had yet to pay off.

Brown turned to me as I got into my car and laid this on me: "What I'm doing is keeping the campaign nominally official until you get this book squared away. That's the thread we're hanging on by right now."

Great! I was already doing this to prove something to myself and to my son. Now I apparently had to do it to prove the existence of God. No pressure there…

Josh Usera

Back in the '80s, I worked as a rock critic because I figured it would: a) get me into lots of shows for free and b) make me seem cooler than I actually was. "B" never really had a shot at becoming fact. However, not only did I get into all kinds of concerts without having to pay, I received plenty of after-party access as well. One of the most memorable moments of my rock critic life happened backstage following a show by one of the least remembered groups, Spandau Ballet. If ever there was a song made for proms and first dances at weddings, it's their classic tune "True."

Spandau Ballet was big thanks not only to their soon-to-be-dentist office-worthy smooth grooves. They were also a momentary phenomenon courtesy of handsome band members, sharp suits and screaming fangirls. I went back to meet the group after one of their Seattle shows, but they were so mobbed I ended up chatting with a guy standing by himself alongside the food table. He wore wire-framed glasses, a baggy jacket with rolled up sleeves and a frown, so I naturally assumed he was a geeky rock critic just like me. We chatted about the show while watching the band pose for pictures and gulp champagne. Finally, I asked my new friend where he worked.

"I'm with the band," he casually explained. "I play keyboards. But you probably didn't notice me, because they have me stand behind the partition." When I asked why, he happily told me it was "because, well, look at them and now look at me. I totally get it. I mean, they still pay me, so it's all cool. And who wants to have people staring at you every time you go out?"

With that, he became my new favorite role model—someone content to do his job adjacent to the spotlight, but not actually *in* the spotlight. He went back to eating stale potato chips and carrots, while I felt reassured knowing I wasn't the only one who was totally happy to exist as far in the background as possible. It wasn't due to shyness or a lack of self-confidence. It was simply less stressful. Which is the one thing I didn't understand about the people I was interviewing. We've all seen those before and after pictures of presidents, where they go from looking like a grinning groom on his wedding day to the hollow, haggard guy who just lost big on his divorce settlement. Who needs that?

In particular, I couldn't understand Josh Usera. It would be hard to find someone with a personality more diametrically opposed to my own. Talking to him on the phone had been like talking to a combo platter of high school homecoming king/star athlete/student body leader. Usera bubbled over with a positive, can-do energy, almost to the point of parody. Some might call it crazy. He calls it enthusiasm.

Even after we finished our initial chat, he continued to text me motivational thoughts about not just his campaign, but life in general. *Not* including him in my list of interviewees would leave me feeling as guilty as telling a girl scout her cookies caused diabetes. So my next stop was Rapid City, South Dakota to see the man who wants to start the "Us Era" in America.

The 36-year-old Usera wanted to meet at nearby Mount Rushmore, where he hoped to hold his first official campaign rally in my honor. However, a steady, chilly downpour and smothering cloud cover changed the plan. Instead, we connected at Usera's house to figure things out.

I pulled up across the street from the split-level rental house he moved into when his martial arts teaching business went under. Usera came bounding out with the same sort of energy that had burst through during our original talk. He was, as he put it, "dressed for success" in dark slacks, blue dress shirt and dark tie. That bid for mainstream respectability stopped shortly above his receding hairline, where what was left of his hair had been shaved into a tightly cropped Mohawk.

"This is for you," he said, laughing. "It's partially a joke because there's not much hair up there anyway. So I've been buzzing it most of my adult life. But it's also symbolic of warrior shit, Native American tradition."

Usera has the compact, buff look of that guy at the gym who's always asking if he can "work in." The tattoos on his arms and hands complete the picture. Despite their threatening appearance, he insisted that the Japanese symbols on his right hand represented "Truth" while the ones on his left hand spoke of "Love."

Rolling up a pant leg to show off more body art, he told me, "I also have tattoos on my shins. The martial arts thing that I grew up doing is on this leg...this is the five elements: Earth, water, fire, wind and nothingness."

When he spoke, he buzzed with the unbridled eagerness of a TV weatherman ("call it ADHD or whatever"). We walked into his sparsely furnished living room and he excused himself to make a peanut butter and jelly sandwich before we started our day. He left me in the company of his friend, Jonathan Old Horse, also dressed up for this occasion in a dark tie, argyle sweater and lips pursed into a smile that seemed constantly in danger of slipping into a scowl.

As he told me about himself, I could understand why he was an important piece of Usera's life. A native of Colorado, he ended up in the Army for several years until he was wounded in an IAD explosion. His ancestry is Lakota Indian, so he eventually ended up in South Dakota, where the total population is nearly 9% Native American. The state has the third highest percentage of Native Americans, with seven separate reservations, which you'd think would make Rapid City a good place for Old Horse to settle.

However, South Dakota is home to Wounded Knee, the tiny town where U.S. troops massacred 300 Native Americans in 1890. It's also where activists with the American Indian Movement confronted corrupt tribal officials, leading to a 71-day siege and standoff against the U.S. government in 1973. Old Horse's teenage son lives there now, but it tears him up to visit his boy "because it looks like a Third World country. It's one of those secrets that nobody wants to talk about, because it's 2015 and it shouldn't be that way."

While Old Horse had adjusted to all the "bad racial labels" that got tossed at him on a daily basis, he worried about his son growing up hearing those taunts. So to toughen the boy up a couple of years ago, he sought out a martial arts teacher. Everyone he spoke to in Rapid City told him he had to check out Josh Usera. The two men have been friends ever since.

Glancing over at the Bible on Usera's mantelpiece, Old Horse calmly elaborated. "If Josh wasn't in my life, I would have probably tried to kill myself. He met me during the early years after I left the military. It was difficult to adjust. He's a good friend. Someone I could talk to and not look down upon me for some of the things that happen when you're f-ed up. I address him as a

Khola, which, in the Lakota language, is someone that you would give your life for. He really does a lot for the Indian community. And when you're in his dojo, the only color that matters is the one on the belt of your uniform."

Upon hearing this, Usera charged back in with a PB&J sandwich in his hand and a fire in his eyes.

"The Native Americans are the people, at least in this community, who the Caucasians can point their finger at and say, 'Our lives are not happy because you guys keep messing it up,' you know what I mean? That's ignorance. That's fear. That's not open-minded thinking."

Old Horse turned to me in earnest and asked, "So in your journey so far, have you found more people who think like Josh, than there are people out of touch with the reality of being a human being?"

It was a good question, one I hadn't ever anticipated being asked when I left Los Angeles. We all read the stories about white cops shooting unarmed young African-American men. But like most decently well-off suburban Caucasians, I sleep easier at night by convincing myself the problem exists exclusively in big city ghettos and sweaty Southern towns I'll never visit. To be confronted right off the bat by someone who lives in the heartland and deals with prejudice left me without an immediate response.

Usera jumped in to describe his own racial struggles. His dad's dad was originally from Spain, his grandma from Puerto Rico. His father was born in Brooklyn, but moved to Rapid City to be with Usera's mom. Julio (a.k.a. "Mutch") and Deb Usera became one of the only non-Native American minority families in town, a vantage point that allowed young Josh to "sneakily look through the window and see reality from both sides," according to Old Horse.

His ethnic background didn't seem to be much of a

drawback in school. He was voted homecoming king and was a martial arts star, thanks to all the training he did at his dad's dojo. At 13, he was teaching adult classes there. At 15, he got his black belt. After graduating high school, Usera went off to Radford University in Virginia. He'd never strayed far from South Dakota, but Radford had a martial arts program that he wanted to join...until he got there.

Six months in, Usera realized he didn't need a college professor to teach him what he'd been studying his whole life. So he moved back home to open his own dojo, while working his way up as a mixed martial arts fighter. He was also back to the party that was his life in Rapid City. Featuring hot women. Fast cars. Plenty of booze. It was, as he recalled, "good to be me."

As he talked about this homecoming, I couldn't help but put it in the context of a presidential campaign. We're always going after candidates because they are too isolationist. They haven't fully experienced everything the world has to offer, so they couldn't possibly understand what's best for us. In Usera, we had a contender who attempted to expand his personal horizons, but then felt it was better to return to the comfort of the world he already knew.

He was ready to show me that world, but there was just one catch: Usera let me know that I'd have to drive today. He didn't elaborate, just noting that he "had a criminal background... which will definitely add to your story." So he climbed in the front seat, Old Horse piled in the back. And we were off.

The first stop was a 10-minute drive through the foggy morning mist—to the elementary school where Usera's son Nate attended third grade. Usera is very open about *his* parents' divorce ("I was 13 or 14 when my parents split and it shook my world up in a way that I'm probably still dealing with"), but he spoke very little about what happened between him and Nate's mom.

Instead, he marched Old Horse and me into the school, insisting that talking to me was going to blow his son's mind.

We approached Nate's classroom and peeked in to see most of the kids sipping milk and eating pizza. Usera got the teacher's attention and she was soon stepping out into the hallway so he could explain that he wanted to introduce his son to a very important visitor. The teacher walked over to a kid wearing an *Adventure Time* T-shirt, whispered something in his ear and then led him out into the hallway.

"Meet Nate the Great," Usera boomed. Turning to Nate, he said, "I wanted you to meet somebody. He's a writer doing a story on me and he wants to know what you think of your dad running for president."

Clearly, Nate was his father's son. Rustling with the same energy, he told me, "It's pretty cool. At first, I thought it was a little nuts and a little cool. But now it's totally cool."

I asked if he'd learned anything from seeing his dad become a candidate. "If he accomplishes it," Nate the Great happily explained, "I'm thinking I can accomplish anything, too, when I'm a grown-up."

To be honest, this all sounded more than a bit scripted, although maybe that was simply because it was almost word-for-word what I'd been saying about what writing this book meant for me and my son. Whether this was a setup or not, though, I have to admit father and son seemed so in sync with each other that it was kind of sweet.

Usera asked Nate if he wanted to spend the day with us instead of at school. The boy didn't hesitate.

"Yeah, it's pizza day and I hate it!"

Within two minutes, we were now a foursome as we headed back to my car. While we drove to our next mystery stop, Nate's dad started reminiscing about his own school days.

When he was his son's age, Usera always saw the world "as my playground, which is what I thought everyone would think. Why wouldn't you?" By the sixth grade, he was already fascinated with the idea of being Commander in Chief. "There was this thing we did from elementary school into middle school called the Presidential Forum of Famous Faces. Each student had to pick a president and perform and act like that president. I was George Washington one year and Ulysses S. Grant in middle school. That particular one got me the furthest to the state competition."

I pulled into a strip mall parking lot, in front of a red awning with the words "Sound Pro" across the front.

"This is where I work," announced Usera, as our quartet got out of the car. "I told you I used to do the dojo deal, but I retired from that. And I still need money, right? So this is how I stay active. This is a business owned by the same two guys for four decades now, and when I campaign, I'm going to use this as an example of your classic American dream."

We walked into the small store, a mini-me version of your local Best Buy. Striding in as confidently as he did at Nate's elementary school, Usera led me over to three men in red polo shirts standing behind the counter: J.T., Tony and Russ, Usera's co-workers. Also, just like at the school, Josh wanted to do some of my work for me.

"This is Craig. He is writing about me running for president and he wants to find out what you guys think of it."

As it turned out, the first time any of these guys found out about his presidential ambitions was when he showed them the interview request I'd sent three months earlier.

"My first thought was, 'This is crazy,'" admitted J.T.

"First of all, what a crazy job to want, right?" Tony added.

That didn't mean Usera wouldn't get their votes.

"This guy is such a free spirit and has such a great

attitude about what is going on in the world, why not vote for him?" Russ explained. "It's America. Anything should be possible, but it's not."

He didn't say this in a discouraging way. Rather, he actually seemed hopeful. They all did.

"Every time you meet someone like Josh, it makes you think that getting out of your comfort zone is probably not a bad idea," Tony said. "When we hired him, he didn't have the skill set we needed, to be honest. He's not a techie. But he had a willingness to learn and just a great attitude. And honestly, that means more than anything."

I followed Usera down a hall to the office of owner Barry Shaw, who couldn't wait to throw his support behind Sound Pro's future most famous employee.

"I'm jealous of Josh because I've had this fantasy for years about what I'd do if I was president," Shaw said. "I look around at all the groups of friends I have and, no offense to Josh, but many of them would make a better president than what we have right now. I think he'd be very good at it, even if he doesn't have the skill set of a career politician. Look at these other candidates. 'What did you do? You were a first-term senator, you ran HP into the ground.' I'm just looking for someone with a good core set of values and common sense."

No wonder I'd been so impressed by Usera's self-confidence when we first spoke. Whereas the majority of candidates I talked to had been branded nutballs by family and friends, the people in Usera's world were simply taking his campaign at face value. If this was what he wanted to do, they'd be there to support him. At least, that was the case until we made it to our next stop: his dad's morning martial arts class.

As we traveled across town to the mall where Julio Usera taught, Josh explained he and his father haven't always been on the same page about many things—including Josh's various life goals.

While he loved studying and practicing martial arts, I detected a hint of resentment as he explained that he "was never able to choose to start this, because I grew up living with it. My parents were sensei. I was the only person in any dojo I'd go into that didn't know what it was like to not go to a dojo. I eventually became imbalanced...you know what I mean?"

Usera tried to emulate his dad, opening a dojo when he was just 19. However, Julio was "the only person telling me back then *not* to open a business. I thought it was because he didn't have faith in me. But what he knew and I didn't was how hard this was going to be."

Josh set up shop in three different locations over the course of 15 years, before eventually declaring bankruptcy and moving the business "into my dad's hands, because he is my sensei." He admitted that he'd gotten lazy, so the failure was, at least partially, on him. Before he could offer more details, though, we walked into the dojo where the senior Usera was putting a dozen students through their paces.

"My dad's the top instructor here, but we have other instructors who help legitimize our system," Josh explained. Yet again, he proudly announced my presence. "This is Craig. He's doing a book on presidential candidates and is interviewing me."

Julio stepped away from the students, looking like a shorter, post-*CHiPs* Erik Estrada. I sensed my visit was completely unexpected, particularly when I asked him what he thought of his son campaigning for the presidency.

He paused for a long moment before recalling reading the news on Facebook and thinking, "it's a good exercise if he wants to go through that exercise. Josh thinks big and *this* is thinking big, for sure. Anytime he sets his mind to do something, he does it. He learns from his mistakes and he has made mistakes. I just want him to have a good career and a good family and, basically, be able to take good care of himself."

According to Josh, his dad also had an interest in politics for a while, to the point where the South Dakota Democratic Party asked him to be their chairman. Julio apparently said no, his son added, "because of his corporate job. (He manages public affairs for Black Hills Power, one of Rapid City's most prominent businesses.) He's more of a Republican. When he told me about it, I said, 'If you're not going to take it, I'll take it.' But I think in his mind, he'll retire and probably pursue politics."

Meanwhile, according to Julio, Josh's interest in politics only surfaced relatively recently. The awakening came in 2008, when another unknown seemed to come from nowhere to run for president.

Barack Obama's election changed Josh and "his desire for politics has come up...he's been very inspired by Obama." The elder Usera smiled, admitting that he didn't know "if [Josh's] ideology is more Democratic or independent." Then, with a slight laugh, he added, "I don't know if he has my vote. I haven't heard about his stand on the issues yet. So I don't know yet."

Maybe it was just my hypersensitivity to father-son relations that kept me from making eye contact with Josh after hearing his dad hold back support for his son right there in front of him. Neither side of the father-son paradigm had ever been my strong suit. I guess it was my destiny. After all, my biological dad was burned severely, along with my very pregnant mom, a few weeks before I was born. An explosion tore through their home in a tiny Kansas town. Several days later, he died and she gave birth to me. A few years later, when I was still too young to process any of this, my mom remarried and her new husband adopted me. For the next three decades, I didn't realize any of this—and nobody bothered to tell me any of the news.

There were a few odd moments growing up. Like when I once found a set of encyclopedias with the name Craig Lee Donley in them. I wondered why I had books that used to belong to a kid with my first and middle names, but figured it was just coincidence. Ours was a family raised more to abide situations than question them. So I let it go.

It wasn't until I turned 33 and had to find my birth certificate in order to get my first passport that I finally figured it all out. After noticing a check in the box marked "Expired" and a name I'd never heard of—Buddy Donley—listed as father, I called my mom to find out what the deal was. Beyond explaining that my biological father had passed away not long before I was born, she offered no details.

As odd as it sounds, upon sensing how uncomfortable the topic made her, I decided not to press the issue. I didn't blame her for keeping this secret. She had her reasons for insulating herself from what happened. At least now I knew about my past—which is ultimately all that mattered. Besides, after 33 years, blame seemed like a moot point.

That doesn't mean I wasn't curious, though. I traveled to Kansas, looked up all the local newspaper stories about the incident and even found an aunt I never knew. She, in turn, took me to see my dad's grave, shared a box-load of his pictures and memorabilia, and even had me meet up with a bunch of my dad's friends at the local bar (which, just FYI, was a trailer). None of this was easy. But it did help explain why, other than the fact that we both require oxygen to live, my adopted dad and I had so little in common.

I have to admit, I've always worried about discussing any of this. It feels kind of dishonest, as if I'm handing out family secrets like they were Halloween candy. I never wanted to dredge up bad old feelings, only to hurt people who I know cared about me. Ultimately, I've come to understand what really counts is how you grow up *after* a tragedy—do you use it as a damn fine excuse to hate the world or do you lie awake at night vowing you'll do better when you have kids of your own?

I like to think I've gone the latter route, trying desperately to be the best dad ever to *my* son right from birth. Time will tell how successful I've been, probably when I ask to borrow money from *him*. Meanwhile, as we headed with Nate and Old Horse back to the car, I asked Josh how he felt about his dad's reluctance to endorse him.

"The deal is going to come down to if my name is on a [ballot]," he said. "As long as my dad doesn't have that piece of paper with my name on it, he will always be able to be the devil's advocate."

Despite Usera's chipper attitude, something felt different as we drove to meet up with his mom. Everything seemed a bit more serious. He pointed out the high school where he gets occasional gigs as a motivational speaker.

"I want to motivate people to see themselves more clearly." He had wanted to take his inspiration one step further and become a teacher. He even got a teaching certificate. But... well...he can't get the gig because of "the criminal background I mentioned earlier."

He'd skated past this bit of information before, but after his dad's dose of reality, he seemed more willing to have that conversation.

"I have three DUIs," Usera explained. I peeked in my rearview mirror to catch Nate's reaction to this confession, but he seemed far more distracted with the view zipping by outside. "2004 and 2005 were the first two. I was 24 and 25. And then in 2013. There's a 10-year period that clears your deal and, well, nine years in, I got another one..." He stopped for several seconds as the windshield wipers *thwapped* away to help break the silence.

"I hate to say this, but I have a lot of fun. I feel very comfortable in my community, but that's not an excuse…I'm currently on probation from the third one. I've never been accused of something where it's, 'Josh beat so and so up.'"

Except when it was legally sanctioned. Usera got seriously into mixed martial arts fighting in his 20s, traveling to fights in nearby states whenever he could. He fought dozens of bouts as an amateur. In the late 2000s, he competed in the World Combat League, a team-based martial arts league that didn't have traditional boxing rings—but *did* have Chuck Norris as its founder.

"I have video of me going all the way back to when I was seven, winning fights. Every night I was fighting people. I didn't lose very much. There weren't a lot of people that were more experienced than me. I'm not saying I was unbeatable…"

This was a time when, according to Old Horse, Usera was like the "rock star" of Rapid City. He ran a successful business. He was a champion fighter.

Still, "everywhere I went, it was, 'Oh, you're Julio's son,' holding me up to some upper echelon when I'm just normal."

Usera enjoyed being the center of attention, but "I think people would be put off by him, because of his honesty," Old Horse explained. "People like that are very few and far between, so you don't know how to act around them."

Eventually, Usera realized his life had gone from "too much fun" to "too much loneliness." There were the DUIs. His business headed toward bankruptcy. He grew more insecure, losing fights and blowing relationships. Before we could dive any further into all this, we drove across railroad tracks and into the gravel parking lot of the grim, gray liquid fertilizer plant where Usera's mother worked. Our traveling party headed into an enormous room filled with cabana-sized plastic tanks, where we were greeted by Deb, a tiny woman with grey hair and a round, red face that never seemed to stop smiling. ("Your classic cowgirl," Josh had told me earlier.)

As Deb talked, it became clear from which parent Josh inherited his spirited style. She was somebody who had no qualms about going from being a marketing director, to a regional vice president for a local mall, to operating her own insurance company, to running the office for a liquid fertilizer plant, just because she was curious to try new things.

Josh stood by her side, beaming brightly as she explained how years ago she "opted to drop out of corporate America and just do something bizarre. And I've been doing bizarre for a while. Bizarre is where you learn. I hope that idea has rubbed off on Josh. I think it's a good thing to have the willingness to be comfortable going against the grain and being outside your comfort zone."

As uncomfortable as I felt watching Josh and Julio interact, it was the exact opposite seeing him standing there with one arm around his mom and the other around Nate. There was something comforting about a mother and son who could connect on both an adult and parent-child level at the same time.

"After high school, he started having the passion to be an entrepreneur. Everybody looked at him and said, 'You're only 18. How do you expect to run a dojo in Rapid City, South Dakota? You're crazy! The whole idea is bizarre.' But he did it. He's always been one that is comfortable being outside of the box."

Running for president when nobody knows your name is certainly an activity located roughly *120 miles* from any box, so I wasn't shocked Deb seemed as pleased with her son's plans as if he was 12 years old and just brought home a report card with straight A's.

"Whether he becomes the President of the United States or not is beside the point. And the reason it doesn't matter to me is that he's going after his idea, he's taking steps, he's bringing people along with him. Some of them are going, 'What the hell? The idea is crazy.' Others think it is pretty cool. But regardless about what side of the fence it is, they are talking about it."

Sure there were the DUI arrests and the whole bankruptcy thing. But this was Josh's mom talking, and to her, he's still the little kid who once came home to tell her he had to help a homeless man he'd just met.

"He felt compelled to get the man a care package and take it to him. The unfortunate part is, though Josh had the compassion and willingness to put himself out there, the homeless person told him, 'If you had just given me some money or drugs I would have been better off.' I think that day might have crushed his spirit for a period of time."

Josh smiled, hugging Deb and Nate slightly tighter as he took up the story from there.

"I assumed that I knew how he was feeling. It looked like this person needed help. And I was always out there trying to help people, making sure that everyone was alright. It was one of the first times that I saw that maybe there was a different side. Maybe there is actually more than what I see. It started the process of me developing perspective intelligence, just trying to make sense of reality."

I suppose this comes with the territory when you've studied the martial arts practically from birth. Thus, we have the arc of Usera's life: sensitive kid becomes popular grown-up, thanks to his ability to beat people up ("it was fun to do what most people weren't allowed to do"); he takes things too far, and now seeks to make up for it by serving humanity. That's where running for president comes in. If you're going to seek redemption, might as well shoot for the moon.

"I've gone through a lot of metacognition—thinking about thinking," he explained as we said goodbye to Mom and headed back toward town. And that thought process helped him realize that his days as a wild child were really "a lot about attention."

I have to admit that, at first, as intriguing as it was, his relentless positivity had all the sincerity of a life insurance salesman a few thousand dollars short of the free trip to Bermuda. Having now met both his parents, though, I was starting to believe how much he believed in his campaign.

I thought a lot about his "attention" comment as we continued our road trip, which started to feel more like *show and tell*. He was brandishing me like a weapon in front of everyone he knew, or wanted to know. It was his way of telling these people he wasn't crazy. He wasn't joking. He was *somebody*. He was serious about bringing America into the *Us Era*, and this outsider proved it.

At a local trophy shop, Usera introduced me to the owner, to whom he still owed money. At the local high school, he had me meet the teacher and students to whom he'd given a motivational speech earlier that morning. At the *Rapid City Journal* newspaper office, he had the receptionist call the city editor to see if he'd come out and interview us both. (All we got was a bored intern who pretended to take notes while we talked, then beat a hasty retreat back to the newsroom with an empty promise to push his editors to do a story on both me and Usera.)

Our next-to-last stop was the county courthouse to meet his probation officer. Once again, not exactly typical candidate behavior. Here was a convicted felon (which, by the way, meant he couldn't even vote for himself, should he end up on a ballot) wanting me to sit down with the person who knew the details of his past indiscretions.

Nate sat outside the door getting jacked up on candy and soda from the courthouse vending machine, while Usera and I went into an office. Clearly I wasn't the only one surprised by this meeting. So was the probation officer, who seemed shocked that: a) he had a writer following him around for the day to document his presidential campaign; and b) that he even *had* a presidential campaign.

Upon hearing this news, she feverishly typed something into her computer, then announced, "Josh, you *do* realize that there's a warrant out for your arrest, right?" As it turned out, he did not. She explained that he'd neglected to pay a speeding ticket and was headed for jail again unless he took care of it ASAP. We rushed downstairs and across the parking lot to the sheriff's station, making it inside just before they closed for the day. Old Horse had gone home, so Nate entertained me with a failed magic trick involving a disappearing quarter. After a couple minutes, Josh motioned for me to come over. I reached into my wallet for my credit card, certain it was going to be up to me to bail him out of this. Instead, he had already taken care of the payment and just wanted to introduce the clerk behind the counter to the writer who was covering his presidential campaign.

By this point it was getting late and the rain was coming down even harder. I knew I had to hit the road soon, but Usera insisted we make one more stop. The local Fox TV affiliate had apparently once done a story on his DUIs, so he thought it was only fair to convince the station to do a news story on his campaign. With an author in tow, how could they refuse? I could have said no, especially given our lack of success with the local paper. However, the notion of generating some free press for the book was not lost on me, so we drove through the soupy fog to a building at the top of a hill on the edge of town. This was KEVN, whose slogan—*"Real People. Real News."*—was plastered on the sign in front. If that's indeed what they cared about, Usera was certainly going to put it to the test.

We spoke to the receptionist, who seemed to recognize him. She said she'd get someone to talk to us. Although I'd kept warn ing Usera not to expect much from this visit, a man who looked like an older, wearier Stephen Colbert emerged. It was the news director, Jack Caudill, who also seemed to know Usera, but instead engaged me in conversation about my project. When I explained I was traveling cross-country to meet real people with real stories who just wanted to take advantage of their constitutional right to run for president, he gave me that "yeah, the crazy people" look that I had grown used to. Then, out of nowhere, he asked me to hold on for a minute and came back with a camera crew.

Caudill assured Usera that he'd talk to *him* another day, then did a quickie interview with me. As we left, he told me this would air on their local newscast Sunday. On the way back to his home, Usera looked incredibly satisfied. And it wasn't just because this day hadn't ended with him back in jail.

"Today is for me," he said, confirming what I'd assumed from the start. "Especially that trip to my work. Your being with me legitimizes what I've been doing. I've tried to be humble. I'm not running into Sound Pro going, 'Yay! The president's in the house!' But I haven't been able to convince people this is real until today."

I was the tool to help him rebuild his life. Redemption was his motivation to be president. Today, he'd been able to show those he wanted to impress that he was getting his act together. Somebody in the outside world was taking him seriously. I suppose being used like this should have pissed me off. Still, as I dropped him and Nate off and headed out of Rapid City, I knew I was a willing accomplice. I was using Usera pretty much the same way he was using me. He was running for president to get attention for himself—and I was talking to him about running for president to get attention for *myself*. With every stop I'd made, I got to be the most powerful person in the room, because I was The Validator. My superpower? Improving the self-esteem of strangers with a single visit.

I felt a little guilty about all this...assuming, in a totally dick-ish way, that I was somebody whose very presence could launch anyone's candidacy from obscurity to viability. Or at least impress their friends and family. Then again, what is American politics without ego and a fair amount of dick-ishness? I would fit right in if I kept this up. All I had to do now was find a way to boost my bank account by approximately $99,999,990.23, and powerbrokers like the Koch Brothers had better watch their backs.

Doris Walker

Ever since Harley Brown had essentially anointed me the third Blues Brother—I was, after all, on a mission from God now—I'd been looking for signs this trip was indeed the right thing to do with my life, rather than a way to run up a credit card bill I had no idea how I'd pay off. I like to think that sign came to me the morning after Josh Usera.

I'd spent the night in Mitchell, South Dakota, planning on enjoying a "me" day stopping by the small Minnesota town, Mankato, where I lived as a child. I tried to get up extra early to have enough time for the side trip, which meant swinging by the County Fair Food Store to load up on snacks, iced teas and anything else with too much sugar.

Even at 9 a.m. on a Saturday, though, the place was jammed. I went to get some snacks from their bakery and ended up waiting 20 minutes, watching dozens of people in front of me pick up boxes with cakes, cupcakes, deli platters and more cakes. When I finally got to the register, the cashier apologized for my wait in that polite, guilty manner common to pretty much all Midwesterners—

and I say that as a guy who spent his first decade-and-a-half as one.

"Sooooooo soooooorry! It's just been crazy here because it's a big day," explained the frazzled, grey-haired woman, drawing out the vowels to emphasize her regret. "It's high school graduation day and everybody is here picking up what they need for their parties."

Okay, so maybe this divine intervention wasn't exactly John the Apostle emailing to say, "Keep up the good work!" Still, seeing all the anxious parents transporting cookies and balloons to celebrate their kids' major milestone reminded me of my ultimate mission: be a better example for my own soon-to-be-high school graduate. There wasn't anything positive or forward-looking to be gained from wasting an afternoon in Mankato visiting sentimental childhood haunts. So, I chose to head straight for Chicago and Doris Walker.

She had plenty of reasons *not* to run for president. As an African-American female, the odds against her were stacked even higher than they were for a broke biker with a prison record. I had to find out what made this a viable career option for her. I'd just have to do it at a bit of a distance. Unlike everyone else I'd met with so far, Walker was insistent that we not meet at her home, or a bar, or a casino. I wouldn't be getting time with her friends and family. Instead, she would hold a campaign rally I could attend at the Oak Park Public Library.

I'd been to Oak Park before, almost exactly 30 years ago to the day. It was my last quarter at Northwestern University and I had one final project standing between me and my master's degree in magazine journalism: a 5,000-word piece with a business theme. So I did what any graduate student trying to keep from being bored by business journalism would do—I interviewed a Yuppie. As in, Young Urban Pornographer. Through some connections back in Seattle, I'd found a guy in his early 20s who had started a successful S&M magazine called *Collars and Cuffs*. (Historical footnote: there was a time when people could only get their porn by going to X-rated movie theaters and patronizing liquor stores that sold magazines full of naked pictures.) I met the young porno prince at a Burger King, where I was surprised to find a guy with the physique of a Macy's Thanksgiving Day Parade balloon, and facial hair that would make a 13-year-old boy feel macho. He talked loud and proud about the time he lost his cherry to a guy, much to the dismay of the nearby moms watching their little kids in paper king crowns celebrate a birthday.

From there, we walked to the two-bedroom apartment he shared with his mother. As we sat at the kitchen table, where he showed me photo albums of the recent orgies he'd been to, Mom occasionally wandered by in her housecoat, slippers and curlers to ask when he was going to clean up his room.

Meanwhile, the buxom young woman who was intro-duced as his personal slave sat silently, occasionally pointing at a piece of fruit to see if he'd nod his head and allow her to eat it. At one point, she decided to lift up her top to reveal her pierced nipples. When I winced and said, "That must hurt!" she simply gave me a glare that said, "Yeah, what's your point?"

Our day ended when he asked for a ride to the train station, because he had to go meet some "investors." (I would later learn that Oak Park is home to many a mobster with ties to the porn industry—allegedly.) I agreed to give him a lift, then watched as this man—who'd been showing me far too many naked photos of himself—moved behind the couch to change his pants. I was impressed by the sudden and unexplained modesty.

As I headed toward the Oak Park Public Library to meet Doris Walker, I was tempted to seek out my Yuppie friend to see if his moustache had ever grown in. I had to assume that the lifespan of a guy going to meet mystery financiers in mob country so he could sell more sadomasochistic pornography was somewhat less than 30 years, so I simply headed for the second floor of the library instead. I asked the woman sitting at the information desk which of the meeting rooms had been reserved for the Doris Walker campaign event. She looked bewildered and told me none of them had been reserved.

Enter an out-of-breath Walker, who rushed up the stairs apologizing for being late. Just as Usera had done, she'd dressed up for our meeting. The short, curvy African American woman in her early 40s was clad in a sleeveless pink and black dress. Along with a pair of white running shoes. She clung tightly to a thick packet of papers and folders. Trailing a dozen feet behind her was a boy who couldn't have been older than 12. This was the youngest of her four children, and he would keep that distance from her for the rest of our interview.

"I live less than a mile from here, so it's a good walk for me," she explained, catching her breath. "I've lost about 60 or 70 pounds just in the last year. I've been changing the way I eat and getting tons of walking in. It's been getting easier and easier."

I broke the bad news to her. The library had no conference room reserved and none were available until much later in the day. Working hard to show confidence rather than embarrassment, Walker launched into a negotiation with the woman at the front desk. She insisted she'd called earlier in the week to reserve a room, but there had been some mix-up regarding a credit card deposit.

"You want cooperation and you want things to flow seamlessly when you're running for president. And it is not," Walker said, more to herself than to me or the librarian. "I'm sort of disappointed. I put it out there on Facebook for church people to show up. What can I tell them now?"

After a few minutes of negotiation, we reached a compromise. Although there were no big conference rooms available, there was one small meeting room open for the next hour-and-a-half. It could hold about a half-dozen people, so at least we'd have somewhere to start. When more voters arrived, we'd figure out where to go from there. Walker went to say something to her son, who then wandered off into the depths of the library. We went to the nearby meeting room, which was like a giant fishbowl with a table and some chairs. Walker set her stack of documents in front of her, and for most of the next 90 minutes she stared over my shoulder and past the glass door to see if anyone was showing up for her rally.

During my preliminary interview with her, she made many valid points about how hard it is for women to achieve success in this world. But it wasn't like she believed *she* hadn't achieved plenty already. Walker told me all about running a production company, as well as a few clothing lines geared toward curvier women. ("They are calling this 'the new beauty,' and not the traditional Anglo-Saxon porcelain Barbie doll beauty.") Still, she seemed like the sort who was never satisfied with whatever success she might find. This was a highly confident woman, who spoke in paragraphs, not sentences. I doubted she could ever be president, but I had to at least admire her aggressive confidence—a trait I've been unable to master.

Growing up primarily on Chicago's west side with her mother and grandmother, Walker was a lonely child who felt "awkward, sort of strange in the sense that I didn't have a unique look. We all know it is a given that beautiful people get more attention. The more attractive you are, the more attention you garner. It's a scientific fact."

Every summer, she and her family would trek to her grandma's hometown in rural Mississippi. Her grandparents, aunts and uncles would buy her sodas and jewelry, letting her play around in the cotton fields, where they started their work day at four every morning. My eyes must have given away the white guilt I was experiencing, something that reflexively happens every time I hear stories involving race. Sensing my discomfort, Walker tried to put a positive spin on her past.

"I think that had a profound impact on me, because I was able to see people who did not have a lot. Nonetheless, they existed and thrived and were happy. They had this common sense about them that is unmatched, compared with people from other areas. So I'm happy I had that exposure."

Her mom and grandma took great care not to limit Walker's creativity, something her classmates interpreted the wrong way.

"If it comes across that I am overconfident, the reason is, I was never given any limitations or boundaries on what I could, or could not, do."

She was a quiet kid back in those days, biding her time alone and reading as many books as she could get her hands on. I could totally relate, having spent the bulk of my elementary school days poring over every Encyclopedia Brown and Hardy Boys mystery in library carrels and on bookstore floors. That sort of intellectual, but isolated, childhood can take you one of two ways: you withdraw and keep that intellect to yourself until it all pours out (fingers crossed) in a hit book / song / film; or you realize you're smarter than 95% of the people in any room you walk into and gain confidence from this. Walker seemed to have gone the second route.

Most of the presidential candidates I'd met up to this point didn't come across, at least at first, like natural politicians. From Shreffler to Usera, they were regular folks whose path led them all over the place before they wound up on a campaign trail. Walker was different. Listening to her dynamic and constant speech, it's as if she was destined to run for office. Either that, or host infomercials.

"Growing up, there are other children who will make you feel like you're the teacher's pet, and that's followed me since kindergarten," Walker mused, her eyes focused over my shoulder and to the right, where nobody continued to walk up the stairs or exit the elevator. "I feel compatible with people in leadership positions. I feel I was born with natural leadership prowess. If my teacher gave me instructions, I followed them meticulously. If she said something, I could finish her sentences. But teachers are perceived as the enemy by kids, because they're trying to teach you something. But not by me. Others interpreted what I was trying to do as winning points with the teacher. I was just a little bit ahead of my time."

Walker is the epitome of that older student who has gone back to college and annoys all the underclassmen by asking questions long after the bell has rung. However, what probably sounds in print like arrogance comes across in person more as naiveté. Like when she explained that for most of her childhood, "I never knew that I was black." It sounded like something a "guest expert" on Fox News might say to prove some misguided point about the end of racism in America. Walker, though, clearly meant it.

Because of the sense of fairness and justice that she learned from her grandma and mom, Walker just thought that "I was the flower child of love, peace, sprinkles and sunflowers. I'm telling you that when I went to school, if I looked at you, I didn't say, 'Hey there's a white guy.' I would have just thought that there's another kid, you know? Someone had to slap me and say this is the way that it is."

That first blow was struck when she was in her mid-teens, and another (white) teenager came up and told her, "I know you probably don't know who your father is." Despite her relatively sheltered life, she understood the implications of the remark.

"He was saying that, simply because I was black, I didn't know who my dad is. It was a blanket, random statement. Until that moment, I never knew that I had to categorize myself. So that pinched a little."

When Walker told her family about the insult, her mom's first question was: "What color was the kid?" That's when she began to notice that she was surrounded by white faces every time she traveled to school on Chicago's North Side. She'd already felt isolated because other students resented her eagerness to please the teachers. Once race entered her consciousness, "more incidents occurred." Walker tried to mask her sensitivity and insecurities with an attitude that came across as brash and off-putting. As a result, she felt like "the world was closing in on me" and her studies suffered. Looking back now, she wishes she'd just "blanked everyone else out [and] kept quiet at all costs."

Instead, she spoke her mind without considering consequences. Like the time when she spotted the boyfriend of one of her few female friends hitting on somebody else. She told her friend about this apparent transgression, even though most teenagers would see the danger in this. The result?

"It was bad. It was really bad," she said softly. "I felt terrible. I felt like I betrayed him and I didn't even know him. I went to my friend and was, like, 'Girl, why'd you do that? I was just telling you something for your own good.' I learned a lesson early. It was the first time I realized that people can put a spin on a situation, interpreting your actions as demonic, even though what you're doing is pure-hearted and simplistic and naïve even."

I asked her if things got any better after high school. She smiled and told me how great it felt when she enrolled at Texas College in Tyler. A counselor had visited her high school, touting the many virtues of the tiny institution. For Walker, the conversation was a religious experience.

"He was so *Christian-ly*, so upright. I said, 'Wherever you're going, I'm going.'"

College didn't disappoint, at least at first. She developed a personal motto: "Every day you're going to learn something. What you choose to learn is up to you." One of her teachers explained that students are supposed to "take everything out of [an instructor's] brain." That's why Walker decided that with each person she met, she'd do "something like a *Star Trek*-Klingon thing... 'I'm touching your brain and I want to know what you know.' And now I have more compiled intelligence than most people."

I thought *I* was somebody who preferred to let intellect outweigh emotion—the former is something in my control, the latter is most definitely not—but Walker was a gold medalist at this technique for keeping the world at a manageable distance. There had to be some way to catch her in a natural, real moment, so I asked about the word "Collier" that was tattooed on her right shoulder. She looked at her arm and, probably without even realizing it, reached with her other hand to touch the name.

"That was my first husband's name," she said slowly. "He is deceased. A friend of mine wanted me to get a tattoo of his name on my shoulder."

I have to make a confession here. I've been a journalist most of my adult life, and part of the job description involves possessing a somewhat Grinch-like heart. We don't wish people ill, of course. But if something bad has happened to them, we zero in on it. Maybe we're just depressives by nature and looking for ways to share the misery, but when the person you're interviewing hints at a sad moment in his or her life, you rip into it like a five-year-old with a wrapped birthday present. Tragedy equals reality, and we always want reality. So in I went...

Walker met the 21-year-old Charles Collier, who came from a military family, when she was still in college. He saw her walking down a Tyler street and said, "You look lonely." It may have been just a standard pick-up line, but it struck a real chord with Walker.

"There are some peoples' lives that I want to be a part of because they are so special, and he was one of those people—kind, gentle, very soft-spoken. When my little evil person would come out, he'd calm me down, make me quiet. And I was like, 'Wow! Look at him!'"

The couple married and moved to Wyoming, where Collier joined the Air Force and they had a son. They may have been young, but they were in love, and Charles "thought enough to say, 'My wife needs this. She needs that. My son needs money when he's born.' The Air Force recruiter had been calling him for three years. So when I told him I was pregnant, he called back and enlisted."

Eight months after their son arrived, however, a service-related accident took Charles' life. Walker wouldn't tell me exactly what happened, saying only that "it was friendly fire…it was a debacle, I'll just put it to you like that. It's confidential, a sealed case, and I can't talk about it. But it was something that could have been prevented."

Not surprisingly, it's also something that even 22 years later is too traumatic for her to revisit—which, naturally, is what I tried to make her do.

"It's one of those things," she explained in a halting way that made it clear this was far more than just *one of those things*. "You have to be able to move on. You have to stay sharp. You have to stay focused. Nothing can prepare you for something like that. Ever…ever. And when you are not the person that is dead, it hurts you so bad that you want to die. Death happens to people on a daily basis, but I wasn't ready for it…for that. My heart is still tender."

She eventually remarried and had three more kids—including the boy wandering somewhere out there in the library—

but it's clear from her tattoo and her expression when speaking his name that Charles is still her inspiration. If he could see her running for president, she's certain "he'd tell me to go for it. He was always one of my biggest cheerleaders, always backing me up in whatever I wanted to do."

With everyone I interviewed, I hoped to dig until I found *The Reason* for their impossible dream. Whether it was redemption or religion, it became clear that everyone on my list had something unfortunate happen to them, and running for president was a way to fill that hole. Losing her husband seemed to be exactly that for Walker. Not surprisingly, she didn't see it that way.

"It's not just about one person's death," she sternly explained. "It will never be about just my husband's death, or my trying to get vindication for him. It has nothing to do with that. I would honor him and honor his memory, if I could, in any type of way. Other than that, that's not what this is about."

What it is about, she insisted, is her plan to whip America into immediate shape once she takes office. She'd get more engineers and mathematicians in the Treasury Department. She'd track how money flows into federal agencies to see where waste is happening. She'd reform the education system so we can compete with China and Russia. On the other hand, she'd never tell anyone whom they should marry and who will get their benefits in the event of a tragedy. And she'd never ever let developing nations that are "suckling from America's breast" get away with putting us down. When it comes to Americans stuck in neighborhoods that are "unsavory and unlivable," she'd make sure that families did whatever it took to make their kids' lives better, rather than just accepting government handouts.

"If and when I do pass, I have safeguards in place so that my kids will not be left destitute or wandering around in America, becoming someone's social problem." She kept talking, but I was stuck on the phrase "if and when I pass." Since when is "if" an option? Meanwhile, smiling and laughing, she added, "I am going to live forever! I am going to walk up into heaven like Elijah!"

She was joking. Probably. But that's the kind of statement that would instantly turn a mainstream candidate into late night comedian fodder and prompt relatives to see if maybe you need to rest for a while. Walker didn't seem to care how outlandish she might sound. Probably.

"If there was a familial situation where people were saying that their family members were not competent, if they don't have any concrete proof to prove that this person is, for some reason, mentally unstable or imbalanced, that means somebody is hating," she explained, moving forward in her chair. "They should be gathering around their family member. It is not like you are making a proclamation that you are Jesus Christ or anything. Right?"

She paused for an uncomfortable laugh, then continued.

"It's not as if you are proclaiming to be Miss America or anything. You are saying you are competent, you can read, you can write, you have some legal background experience. You know how to read and write legalese. You know how to write a law, and if you don't, they can show you how to do it. You know how to put laws into effect. That's what the president does."

I had to give her credit. She was getting into some pretty touchy, as well as potentially heart-breaking, stuff. Yet Walker almost never stopped smiling. Sometimes her smiling looked more like wincing. Still, she seemed quite adept at one important presidential skill: Never let them see you sweat.

Certainly a candidate also needs some experience in government, and Walker has that. One of her early jobs after losing her husband was working for the Cook County Board of Review in Chicago, helping people find and file the proper paperwork to make sure they were paying the appropriate property taxes. ("I was behind the scenes, a very intricate player in the legal process.") Later she moved on to be a liaison for a "high-ranking government official" whose identity she has to keep confidential. Part of being a lifelong journalist is being devoutly skeptical, and anytime somebody keeps something confidential, I assume said information doesn't actually exist. However, Walker seemed so supremely satisfied with her story that it was more interesting to listen to her than contradict her.

The most influential job she's held, though, had to be her time working for the Cook County clerk's office. She helped citizens with summons find the correct courtroom. As a result, Walker "met every lawyer and law clerk that was in personal injury and tort." She loved the idea of helping people find their way through bureaucracy and might still be there had it not been for a dust-up with her co-workers.

Walker had moved her family out of Cook County and believes other employees mentioned this to her boss. That felt like a betrayal—"Why would you do that? I have to earn a living just like you!"—and she ultimately "fell out with the whole process and quit." The job was done, but her outrage about how it went down continued to burn.

"I was literally harassed out," she told me, slipping back into her grimace-smile. "It sparked my sense of indignation toward persons that abuse power, and I decided I needed to be part of the solution, not part of the problem. I said to myself, 'I must stand up. I must make my voice heard.' So I started looking through some books just to see what it takes to be qualified to run for president."

Up to that point, the thought of a woman, let alone an African-American woman, running the country had never occurred to her. After watching fellow Chicagoan Barack Obama succeed,

Walker began to feel like a run for the presidency was not only possible, but probable. In fact, ever since she filed her paperwork in early 2015, she started to see the job as her "birthright." Her personal research even revealed that her ancestry goes all the way back to past Commanders in Chief like Washington, Jefferson and Lincoln.

(If, say, Donald Trump or Ted Cruz made statements like this, I'd be tempted to challenge the questionable genealogy. But the advantage of being a Can't-idate is that details aren't nearly as important as attitude. Walker definitely had attitude. And I saw no reason to interrupt that.)

I realize how crazy that sounds to anyone who wasn't sitting with Walker in the Oak Park Library on this spring afternoon. And I don't mean a cute, "my puppy did the wildest thing" kind of crazy. I'm talking a real, "somebody with a medical degree should be called" kind of crazy. And when she started speaking with all the modesty of Donald Trump about "The Doris Effect" that was changing American politics, I began to get that same sinking feeling I had walking around town with Doug Shreffler.

But then Walker explained what she meant.

She was running for president "to say that I joined the ranks of the other females that ran, to put my name with that long list of warriors who have been throwing pebbles into the pond and causing ripple effects."

In so doing, the plan is that "someone would be encouraged, someone would be inspired, someone would get up and get a job, someone who has been oppressed or fired for no reason would feel the courage to get up, go out there and know that they still have something to offer this world. Don't let people get you down. I know, because I've been a recipient of that. But because of my overconfidence, my overzealousness, I'm able to bounce back under the harshest of circumstances."

The Can't-idates may not be cursed with the same force field of self-awareness that blankets most of us throughout our adult lives, but that's not insanity. It's simply ignoring logic in favor of the notion that *they* know more about making their lives better than outsiders do. Before Walker could explain her campaign any further, a slight, balding man holding a stack of papers even larger than hers pushed the door open. It was his turn to use the room and we had to get out...without ever getting to meet any of her supporters. Although I didn't remind her of this, Walker seemed compelled to explain their absence with a happy smile that contradicted every bit of bad news she was delivering—another valuable political skill she's mastered.

"I may not get one person here, but I may get hundreds of people in six months, depending on the condition of the economy, depending on what happens. What seems so strange to me is that people will take your ideals, your inspirations, but they won't give you a vote. That's very strange to me. My son and I discussed this. He said, 'Mama, do you think there are going to be a lot of people here?' I said, 'Nope. Not unless we were serving fried chicken dinners.'"

As we parted, I didn't know whether I should feel sorry for the low turnout or happy because nobody had come to enable her. I went with admiring her for happily ignoring any evidence that might make her doubt her master plan for saving America. Confidence and logic don't necessarily have to travel together *all* the time.

The rest of the world will look at Doris Walker and see somebody living in a land much different than ours. I'd rather look at her and see somebody following her passion...even if that passion will ultimately be unrequited. We'd probably all be a bit better off occasionally stepping outside ordinary expectations, despite the inevitable mocking we're destined to endure. Or at least that's the excuse I planned on using when I got home and friends realized I'd spent a month chasing down citizen candidates, rather than chasing an actual job.

Bartholomew James Lower

I wish I could say that when I woke up two days after my time with Josh Usera, I'd totally forgotten that we'd been interviewed for a local TV news piece. But the truth is, our piece was to have aired the previous night. So, like every guy who has ever done a man on the street interview for their local newscast, I was thinking of nothing but how I would look on TV. Which explains why the first thing I did that Monday morning was to Google "Rapid City + KEVN + Usera + president." Right there at the top of the list was "Local Man Makes Big Decision to Run for President." (Go ahead and check for yourself. I'll wait. Just tell me that my hair looks decent.) I clicked on the link, which led to a three-minute piece about Usera and his campaign, including a minute or so of me discussing *The Can't-idates* as if it was already a bestseller revolutionizing the American political process.

I've been on TV before, back during my days writing for *People* and *TV Guide*. But that was always to relay such newsworthy information as whom Jennifer Aniston was breaking up with or which new TV shows weren't worth your time. This experience was different. This was about me, about something I did on my own. Without any celebrity gossip.

I realize that the total viewership for a Rapid City TV station after 10 p.m. on a Sunday night is maybe 100 people more than for my TV station. And I don't have one. Still, there was something about seeing myself on the KEVN clip that lent a sense of credibility I hadn't felt just two days earlier. It's the same reason drunk guys jump up and down in the background when local news anchors report on a triple homicide. If you're on a screen, it means somebody, somewhere has to pay attention to you.

So now I was for real. I must have watched the piece half a dozen times, and then emailed the link to everyone who knew I was working on this project. Seeing myself talking about my work was seriously addicting, which I realized, when I snapped out of my fixation, was a micro version of the macro reason why money has corrupted politics. The cycle works like this: You have to possess a fair amount of vanity if you even want to run for public office. Running for public office costs a lot of money. That money is used to get you on TV as much as possible. Being on TV as much as possible can't help but pump up your vanity. Vanity requires ego—and where there's ego, there's most likely going to be money.

Eventually, I was able to pull away from watching myself. It was time to head out to the day's destination: Ionia, Michigan. I was in the heart of the heartland by design. Being someone who spent a lot of his youth as a Midwesterner, I've always been fascinated by how the country views these so-called "flyover states." I admit that my memories of the Midwest are a bit dated and jaded. I was just a kid for most of the time that I lived in Kansas, Illinois and Minnesota—a skinny guy with braces, Coke bottle glasses and clothes his mom picked out for him. Which is why most of the Midwestern memories I have feature bullies smacking me around in the hallways. Whenever I think of the *real* Midwest—not the idyllic, black-and-white part of *The Wizard of Oz* Midwest—I see Steve's face. Steve was my third grade best friend, a handsome, freckle-faced kid who was all "Yes, ma'am" and "No, ma'am" to the teachers at school. One day, he invited me to the park to play, so I ran over to find him there with a group of other guys from our class. Without warning, he called me "four eyes" and smacked me in the nose. I fell. They laughed. And he walked away, never to speak with me again.

So, when Bartholomew James Lower bounced out of his beat-up Ford Expedition and into the roadside coffee shop where he'd requested we meet, I had a flash of Steve. Lower had the same blonde hair, the same can-do energy, the same kindly air my former friend had—until the moment he clocked me. At the same time, with his buttoned-up white dress shirt with blue stripes, dad jeans and habit of pointing a finger at you and saying "Bingo!" whenever you say something agreeable, Lower reminded me of a kindly high school principal.

His wife Nicole helped make arrangements for this visit, but she had to go to Detroit on a business trip, so Lower was in charge of the couple's children that morning. The oldest (Nicole's son from a previous relationship) was 18 and off at college, but the three younger kids (10, 5 and 2) had just been dropped at school and would need to be picked up in a few hours. Lower promised that would be just enough time to give me a grand tour of the Ionia streets and parks "I used to go to when I was little, and where my parents, and *their* parents, and their parents went." For five generations his family has lived in this "one McDonald's town," a rural community of 11,000 that has supported itself with a mix of farming and manufacturing. Since it's about a two-hour drive to Detroit, the auto parts industry used to dominate the local economy—emphasis on "used to."

"What you have to remember is that they just put the cars

together in Detroit," the 38-year-old Lower said as his truck clanked its way onto the country highway in front of the coffee shop. "They don't make the parts. You've got thousands and thousands of suppliers that make everything from the little rubber thing that goes on your tire, to the brackets that hold your bumper on. So when you hear about the automotive industry slowing down, I don't think people fully understand the massive impact that has and the depth that it reaches."

Lower knows, though, because he's a factory town lifer. His grandfather sold tractors here. His dad started out with dreams of playing drums in a rock band, but ended up marrying at 19 and having kids. So he went to work making auto parts in town before starting his own metal stamping business. During high school, Lower spent many an evening cleaning up that factory by pouring buckets of water and chemical cleaner on the floor, then mopping up the grime. After getting his degree at Eastern Michigan University, instead of going out to see the world, Lower pulled a George Bailey and returned home to stick with the family business.

Upon returning home his dad said, "Now we're gonna teach you what you *need* to know." Within a year, Lower was operating machinery. Then it was unloading steel trucks before he eventually became director of quality. In my comfy West Coast world, the idea of operating any machinery other than a laptop and maybe a microwave is unthinkable. However, in the Norman Rockwell world of a rural Michigan boy, this kind of hands-dirty work creates a "passion for trying to make things reach their potential." For instance, when he noticed the mood of the factory workers was dragging, Lower suggested to his dad that they paint everything in the shop white, because it would brighten things up.

As he reminisced, we drove along a country road that wound past a couple of cattle farms. We approached a clearing with a large sign that read: "Bart's Golf Center." This couldn't be a coincidence.

"That was my first business, which I started when I was 24," he told me as we passed a tiny (and empty) driving range. "When I was a kid in school, I was going to be a professional golfer. That is what drove me to do everything. I was a mediocre student. Looking back, I was probably a little bit ADD."

Lower was always small for his age. As a high school freshman, he was 4' 11" and barely 90 pounds. I could relate to that feeling. He discovered, just like I did, that being physically unimposing inevitably leads to "coming into contact with your fair share of bullies." And he realized, as I eventually did, that when it came to getting picked on, using your brain offered a longer-lasting solution than your fists. (I just didn't learn the lesson until a kid in 10th grade called me "Beak" because I had a big nose, and I decided to cry in front of him to make him feel bad. He never bothered me again.)

"You've got two ways to handle a bully: you either take matters into your own hands, so to speak, and smack a bully back," he explained with a confident smile. "Or you figure out how to be friends with the bullies. I learned the latter skill very early on in life, so when I got to school I ran with everybody. I hung out with athletes, with kids who were in garage bands."

The plan clearly worked. Long before he decided to run for President of the United States, Lower befriended enough popular kids to be elected junior class president, then student council president. From that moment on, he's "gravitated to the leadership positions in any groups I was in. It was almost like they were a natural fit."

He did end up coaching and playing golf in college, but opted to open Bart's Golf Center right after 9/11, only to discover that "the golf industry [was] declining, and has been ever since." Getting soaked by a bad business venture in an already ailing economy would leave a lot of us drunk and weeping on the kitchen floor. Not Bart Lower. He's so self-assured that he discusses this failure with the same casualness most of us would use to describe watching a dropped coin roll away. No big deal. If he had any regrets, he stayed true to the legendary stoic Midwestern nature by never letting on.

Lower cruised past a long razor wire fence protecting a large, square, drab compound that, at first, seemed like either the worst elementary school or the fanciest Army barracks ever. It was the maximum security Ionia Correctional Facility, one of five area prisons. The auto industry had long since jilted this place, but the inmate industry was apparently booming.

"Two of the five have popped up in my lifetime here, and for the town in general [the prisons] have just always been there," Lower said as we slowed down to look at the town's oldest prison, the Riverside Correctional Facility, a former insane asylum that looked like a less inviting version of the hotel from *The Shining*.

He's got plenty of friends employed by the prisons who report that going to work is a lot like going to jail.

"Those guys will talk about going into those facilities and just the aura itself, just the feeling of the anger and the frustration, you just can't help having the feeling dribble into their souls... Politicians all say they know what normal Americans are going through, but they don't know. They can't know. It's not their fault. They just don't live in it. They've never lived in it. And I do."

He's more generous than I would be. I do think it's their fault. I'm a big proponent for a constitutional amendment banning all politicians from using the phrase "what the American people want." If it's not the most disingenuous phrase ever used by someone in public office, it's at least a close second to "I did not have sexual relations with that woman."

Unless there was an Evite to an American people

convention that went straight to my spam folder, I don't know how these people have determined what all of us want. We're a pretty large group with different points of view. The reality is, the pols who claim to know what Americans want only know what people they've paid tell them Americans want. It's not quite the same thing. When it comes to finding a candidate who will work harder to create jobs, for example, doesn't it make more sense to listen to someone who has repeatedly been laid off? Someone like Lower, perhaps.

"I've gone through layoffs on both sides...I've been the one losing my job and the one telling people they were losing theirs. I'm not sure if there are any politicians currently running that had to go through what I've been through."

After working for his dad and opening his golf course, Lower got a job in sales for a school supply distributor. From there, it was on to sales and marketing for one of the nation's largest homebuilders. Later, after a stint as an assistant golf coach at nearby Michigan State University, he became a sales and marketing consultant for an international company that made accessories for four-wheelers and all-terrain vehicles. That was followed by time as a sales advisor for an IT company. And, most recently, he worked at an agency that helps train military veterans re-entering the work force. ("We've got 22 veterans a day that are killing themselves—*22 a day!* Another thing that the Commander in Chief isn't even talking about!") Then...the job offers stopped coming.

It was nice to find a fellow unemployment statistic. I was going on six months of unemployment at that point, and the experience had become far more isolating than I ever expected. Dealing with being out of work felt a lot like being diagnosed with chronic depression. Both are clearly traumatic experiences that leave you feeling powerless. There's a certain amount of shame with both, because you feel consumed with your own failure. And at first, when word gets out about your situation, people will console you—but it doesn't take long for them to want to move on. Even though you can't. The difference was, at least I could take pills to ease my depression. Getting a new job? I was doing what I could, but the end result felt like it was left up to a very fickle outside world.

Lower slowed his truck down as we swapped unemployment stories, pulling into a long driveway just outside of Ionia. A sign in front advertised his latest business venture: Danny Boy's Drive-In Theater. The placard offered $1 popcorn and a double bill of *Avengers 2* and *Cinderella*. A little more than two years ago, he and some family members decided to buy an abandoned motocross track near the municipal airport. The goal was to bring back "a thing people don't even realize they miss—the drive-in. They've been gone so long, people don't remember what real family fun is like."

The plan worked and business boomed at Danny Boy's. Cars lined up along the road waiting to get in. Then, in April 2014, Lower was preparing to open for the summer by pressure-washing the large, inflatable movie screen. (The city wouldn't allow him to build a permanent screen, a lesson in bureaucracy that still gnaws at him.) A gust of wind came and flipped the screen over on top of Lower. He fell 25 feet to the ground and ended up with broken bones in his foot, femur, hip and back. Lower nearly died. He spent the next three months in bed, unable to move.

"For 12 weeks, I was supposed to just lie in bed. And they said, 'If you do something stupid, then we will have to do surgery, and that will be another 12 weeks.' I was a good patient, but it was kind of funny. After the first week in the hospital, someone came to visit and said, 'So, are you solving the world's problems?' I just kind of laughed, 'Well...'"

Because that's precisely what he was doing. Lying in bed,

with his laptop and cable news to keep him company, Lower started following current events with a new intensity. Whether it was education, or the economy, or the Middle East, he studied the issues of the day and formulated what he felt were reasonable solutions to each and every challenge. Gradually, he began to feel like running America wouldn't be that much different from running the production line for his dad.

If you make car parts that aren't coming out right, you try to figure out what's going wrong. Ask the question as many times as it takes to get an answer. Has something in the line outlived its usefulness? Is something misaligned? Take a moment and really look at the final product, and that will tell you all you need to know. So, when he started following the issues dominating the news, "you see we've been complaining about the same things for decades. But no one has come up with any solutions, because they didn't ask 'why?' enough times."

During his recovery, Lower had nothing but time to ask that question. The more he looked for answers, the more he realized that in his own personal life he'd already processed every crisis that America faced. He was in a hospital, which told him how the health care system failed people. He'd seen family adjust to life after the auto industry crumbled. He worked with veterans at New Horizons, so he knew how they were getting screwed over. Whenever he had to lay somebody off, he put in extra time trying to find those people new jobs. So he learned how tough the job market was.

Lower would see problems with America's education system firsthand, too. His five-year-old, who couldn't wait for his first day of school, saw "his fun turned into a nightmare" because he suffered from ADHD and the teachers weren't trained to handle it.

Gay marriage? Like his friends and neighbors, Lower was apprehensive when a lesbian couple moved into his subdivision and adopted a child. But realizing that the little boy was the off-spring of a drug addict and "these two gals put everything on the line to help him," Lower became convinced that true Christians shouldn't judge other people. "These women should have the same rights my family and I do."

Before his Danny Boy's accident, Lower was thinking about running for some kind of local office. Afterward, though, he knew that we all get just one shot at this life, so you might as well go big if you're going to go at all.

"I talked with people about some of the solutions that I was starting to develop, and more and more people went, 'That would work. That would really work, and that would absolutely work.' Then part of me began to say, 'Well, if our country keeps heading the direction it is heading for another decade, what is it going to look like?' So part of deciding to run for president was me saying, 'If my ideas could work here on a micro level, they'd work on a macro level.'"

I realize that as you're reading that quote, Lower could come off as pretty delusional. He's like Harley Brown without the leather and Josh Usera without the probation problems—a nice guy with impossible ambitions. Still, either I had already been at this too long, or he was the sort of sensible guy I was hoping to find on my road trip. That became even more apparent with our last stop of the day: downtown Ionia.

Lower pulled up in front of the local courthouse and we hopped out of his truck. I took a long look down Main Street, where the construction workers fixing the road outnumbered the pedestrians using it. I'd never been in Ionia before, but as we walked along the red brick streets past three blocks of buildings, none of which were more than two stories tall, I felt like I knew this place by heart.

You want to talk Main Street, USA? This was it, a reminder of all the small towns in which I'd also grown up. Or at least this used to be it. You know something isn't right when the sound of the wind whipping down the street is louder than the sound of people talking on it. When I grew up in one-street towns, those roads still had businesses like the dime store (yes, that's what we called it) that sold my favorite *Mad Magazine* books, and the corner grocery (a one-room store owned and operated by my grand-parents). Ionia's Main Street, however, was primarily filled with storefronts that had *For Rent* signs hanging in the windows—including a realtor's office.

"Look around," Lower instructed as we walked, constantly pointing at one empty structure after another with the same sighing recognition one uses when seeing high school yearbook pictures of friends who've died since graduation. "See the signs—*For Rent, Available*. That building's empty. That one's for sale. That one just switched hands again. See that green building? That used to be my in-laws', and it was a bar they ended up closing because of the economy. This whole corner building has been vacant for a decade. That one on the corner that kind of looks like a bank? That's been vacant for a decade, too. That one there? Empty. That one? Empty." He stopped on a corner for a moment to take it all in. "Truck through downtown Ionia and this *is* the rest of the country. The big cities are the big cities, but what you see *here* is the rest of the country."

I admit you can't judge a book by its cover. (Unless that cover has a teenage vampire on it.) Still, sometimes you really *can* judge a town by its storefronts. And according to Lower, the fact that there were so many pregnancy clinics and drug counseling centers downtown showed exactly what was going on in Ionia.

"That's Straight Street," he pointed out as we walked by a storefront that used to be an optometrist's office. "Everybody knows that's a drop-in center for anyone hooked on drugs. The number one cause of accidental death right now in the United States is drug overdose. I hear all of the politicians talk about all these issues that we have in the country, but they are not talking about that. There are over a million Americans hooked on heroin. *Over a million!* It's never been more prevalent in our country than it is today, and it's hit this town hard. We've got kids overdosing on heroin almost on a weekly basis."

He has a very personal relationship with one of those drug abusers. When Nicole's son was 16, she and Lower learned he wasn't just using drugs—he was dealing them as well. A line had been crossed, and Lower truly believed that "if you can't hold people accountable in your own family, how can you expect to do it on a national or global level?" So, they turned their own child over to police custody.

I had no idea how to respond. We're so conditioned as parents to protect our children, no matter what, that the idea of handing them over to someone else for punishment seems unnatural. We preach tough love because it sounds good, especially when it pertains to someone else's children. I like to think that everything I've ever done for my son, this current journey of mine in particular, has been done to inspire him to do the right things—rather than scare him into avoiding the wrong things. Here was a man who felt the same way, yet still handed his oldest child over to the authorities. He had his reasons.

The way Lower saw it, "when kids are under 17, you have a window where you're trying to make a change that doesn't end up hurting them the rest of their lives. He couldn't follow the probation, so I finally looked at the judge and said, 'He needs real consequences.'"

Candidates talk all the time about their willingness to make a tough decision. Well, they don't come any tougher than this one, and Lower made it. He let his son go to a detention center for 90 days in order to start weaning himself off drugs. The decision definitely strained his relationship with the now 18-year-old.

But I didn't sense a second of regret as Lower told me about it.

"For all the battles we've had over the years, he knows my running for president is good for our future," Lower finally said. "It's hard to swallow that when you're 18, but I know what will happen, because I was an 18-year-old once. When you're 45, you eventually thank your dad."

Mental note: remind my son of this and put it on my calendar.

Lower and I kept walking down Main Street, passing the family planning centers. Much like drug abuse, teen pregnancy is nearing epidemic proportions in the Ionia area. According to Lower, Ionia County has roughly twice as many teenage girls giving birth than the national average—a phenomena that, perhaps not coincidentally, began when Ionia's Planned Parenthood clinic shut its doors a year earlier.

"And look over there," he said pointing to a small, beige storefront with the words 'Pregnancy Services' painted on the front window. "The county's Pregnancy Services office is only open two days a week, Tuesdays and Thursdays. They don't even know there is funding out there that can help them." That's why he joined the agency's board of directors: to help them navigate the bureaucracy to find more money to help troubled Ionia girls.

It was nice to see someone not spit fire when the conversation turned to abortion. More than anything else, it's an issue that can ruin a family dinner or outing with friends, should it creep into the conversation. As far as Lower is concerned, both sides are missing the point. Most people leap to discussing the back end of a problem, instead of dealing with it from its start. It's not about babies or control of one's own body. It's about sex and the ultimate outcome.

"[Anti-abortion advocates] are missing the boat on this," he explained. "They keep talking about the babies, but the babies aren't the issue. The babies are fine. The babies are not the problem. They are with God. If you are a Christian, that is what you believe. The people that are hurt most, physically and emotionally, are the mothers. An abortion follows a mother her entire life."

He also knew this too well. Drawing in and then exhaling a long breath, he told me that's because "my wife is one of those women." Though he was spare on the details, he did explain that Nicole had had an abortion before they met. Instead of letting this be a deal breaker in their relationship, Lower listened to his wife's story and gained a perspective that a lot of men will never have.

During their 12 years of marriage, Nicole has told him several times that since her abortion, "one of the things she was most angry about was that nobody ever told her how she was going to feel when it was over. Everyone just said, 'We will support you in anything you want to do.'" As the weeks and months went by, though, she fell into a deep depression. And when she and Lower decided to have kids, the mental scars were so deep that "she said there wasn't a day that went by where she didn't have an overwhelming feeling of anxiety that something was going to happen to one of our kids, because it was karmic justice."

She overcame her feelings of shame and fear left by the abortion and had three children with her husband. Even more remarkable to me was that Nicole was willing to let Lower share her experience with total strangers in the hopes that they may feel less shame and fear. Once more, I tried to imagine any major candidate openly discussing something this personal. And yet again, I couldn't.

Lower continued defying any attempt to nail down where his political heart called home. One minute he'll explain his plans to limit federal regulations and the power of unions in a way that would make even my slightly-to-the-right-of-Ted Cruz uncle happy. "Our ancestors didn't hop on boats and leave everything behind because they heard there were good schools in America. They didn't do it because they heard there was a factory hiring over there. They did it because they heard that they could make their own way."

Minutes later, Lower will sound more like all my Bernie Sanders-supporting California friends by complaining the federal income tax is unfair to the have-nots, and special interest money is destroying faith in our political system. And gender pay discrimination?

"Here's another thing I'll throw at you," he explained. "My wife works in the IT industry and the position she held prior to this one paid $40,000 less than the male counterparts on her team. And she was the number one sales person on the team. So you want to talk about another personal experience that drives me? Is there a war on women? Absolutely there is one! We know because we've lived it firsthand."

When we climbed back into Lower's truck, I asked if I could get some video of him for my Facebook page. He quickly declined, since he wanted to hold off on making any announcement of his campaign "because it's very important that we launch this the right way." Midwestern modesty in action. Or maybe it was Midwestern distrust of us city folk. I wasn't sure. Either way, I was surprised at how quickly he shut me down, seeing as how everyone else on the trip had leapt at the chance to get a little free publicity.

As downtown Ionia faded into the background while we headed toward the coffee shop where the day began, there was one thing I had to find out from Lower. We expect our politicians to have lived perfectly spotless lives, where everything constantly goes right. At the same time, we want them to be real people who know the tough stuff the rest of us suffer through on a daily basis. These are conflicting desires, making it pretty much impossible to please all the people all the time. So I asked Lower what a nice guy like him was doing in a strange world like politics.

"You can't live in a small town like this and just kind of go about your life and not pay attention to things," he told me. "But when you are paying attention, [Ionia] is a microcosm of the rest of the country. And I've learned here that the only difference between hope and sadness is somebody with a vision that makes sense. If you've got someone that has a vision that everyone can see, sadness turns into hope really fast."

With that as my send-off, Lower dropped me at my car, while promising to keep me posted when he was ready to make his campaign official. By now, I'd become used to these awkward Can't-idate goodbyes. They felt like most of the first dates I'd been on—we spent time checking each other out, trying to decide if there was enough of a reason to get together again. Up until now, they'd been the ones wanting to stay in touch and I was the "wait and see" guy. This time, though, I felt like I'd come across the ideal citizen candidate—and the best I could get was a promise that he'd call me sometime.

Talking to Lower wasn't like talking to everyone else. The political discussion was fascinating and important, rather than just a way to let the interviewees vent. He really was the stereotypical Midwesterner: open, honest and innocent. I realize I can display a certain smugness that, for better or worse, comes with a writing project like this. After all, I'm in charge and everyone had to dance for *me*. Lower brought me down a few pegs. Even though I could imagine voting for the guy, I still needed to get my ego back on top.

So there was just one thing to do. When I stopped for the night in Cleveland, on my way to meet an inner city minister, I spent 20 minutes repeatedly watching a local news story about a writer traveling across the country to meet real people with no chance of becoming president.

As George Bush might say—mission accomplished.

Rev. Pamela Pinkney Butts

There are a few things that seem contradictory about the phrase "comfort zone." First and foremost, we're always being told to get out of it. Why? It's a *comfort* zone. If we feel good inside it, what's the point in leaving? Secondly, we're always urged to leave these zones because they are too confining. If that's the case, shouldn't it be easy to get out? It's much quicker to sneak out of a tiny space than a large one. My comfort zone has roughly the dimensions of one of those boxes magicians use to trap their assistants. I still listen to Huey Lewis and the News. Even worse, I sing along. I don't trust self-checkout lanes at the grocery store. I refuse to believe that coconut water is water. It's not that I mind trying new things. It's more that I'm afraid if I like them, I'll have to move into a new zone. Which could lead to another, and another…and at my age, I can't even summon the willpower to try a vegan cupcake.

Still, I'd committed to expanding my horizons by taking this presidential trek across the country. So if I was truly going to commit to it, I had to meet the Rev. Pamela Pinkney Butts. Nobody on the list lived further outside of my comfort zone, which is why I chose her. (Well, that and the fact that at the end of our phone chat, she led us in a prayer for the success of the book.) She's female. I'm not. She's African-American. I'm so white I make milk hip. She's extremely religious. I haven't even done the Christmas-Easter church thing in decades.

Nothing, however, represented our differences more than my drive into the east side of Cleveland to meet her. I'm a born and bred suburbanite who can't imagine life in an area without at least three apartment complexes named after trees. Meanwhile, the apartments I was driving past had all the charm of those prisons I'd seen back in Ionia, with fences and barred windows everywhere. It's seldom a good sign for a neighborhood when there seems to be a church on every other corner—an indicator of how much praying the residents must do to get through a day?—and discount stores and pawn shops squeezed between the houses of worship. I had to assume this was not the part of town that would be hosting the Republican Convention when it rolled into Cleveland in a year.

Rev. Pinkney Butts wanted to meet at a diner in one of Cleveland's oldest and best-known suburbs, Shaker Heights. When I arrived, the reverend was nowhere to be found. Which gave me time to sort out whether the drive here left me feeling: a) guilty b) depressed c) fortunate or d) all that and then some. I was leaning towards "D" when an out-of-breath Rev. Pamela Pinkney Butts burst into the diner and immediately grabbed me.

"I'm a hugger! Hope you don't mind," said the 54-year-old as she threw her arms around my shoulders. "You drove through the Valley of Death! But you made it!"

She was late because she'd spent the morning 30 miles away in Akron, at a protest against the local utility company, First Energy.

"I'm very upset," she explained. "First Energy is using coal

137

and making people spend money that they don't get any benefit from. They have investments in our stadiums, and in our events, and in our entities downtown—but the poor people are suffering as a result of that. I beg to differ on accepting something like that."

With a blue headband, blue kerchief around her neck, plaid jacket and dark slacks, she had the disheveled—yet still somehow elegant—look of somebody who may be living in a sub-basement, but vaguely remembers how things look from a penthouse view. Talking to her was a similar experience in contrast: she was incredibly open and chatty, yet practically never made eye contact. Without waiting for me, she turned around and headed back outside, eager to show me "how people really lived" around here. That included shops that gave her pleasant memories, like Dave's Supermarket. ("He's someone everyone knows," she said of the store's owner, presumably named Dave. "And he gives people jobs, a second chance in life.") She then pointed out places that had more of a bittersweet sting, like the local barbershop. "It's black-owned," she said, quickly noting with a sigh that such an establishment "is rare to see staying in business here."

As we walked over trolley tracks to the other side of the square, the reverend pointed out a storefront where she once witnessed "some white police officers surrounding a black guy. Somebody accused him of taking something out of a store without paying. The police really bothered this guy, and I stood there to make sure they didn't do anything to him. When they found out he hadn't stolen anything, they took his phone so he couldn't even call for help."

Other than LeBron James and a few guys on the team in *Major League,* I'm not particularly familiar with Cleveland. Most of what I did know came via the nightly news, and practically none it was good. Exhibit A would be the 2014 report from the Department of Justice that features commentary like:

1. *"Our investigation concluded that there is reasonable cause to believe that the Cleveland Police Department engages in a pattern or practice of using unreasonable force in violation of the Fourth Amendment."*

2. *"We found incidents of Cleveland Police Department officers firing their guns at people who do not pose an immediate threat of death or serious bodily injury to officers or others and using guns in a careless and dangerous manner, including hitting people on the head with their guns, in circumstances where deadly force is not justified."*

3. *"Deeply troubling to us was that some of the specially-trained investigators who are charged with conducting unbiased reviews of officers' use of deadly force admitted to us that they conduct their investigations with the goal of casting the accused officer in the most positive light possible. This admitted bias appears deeply rooted [and] cuts at the heart of the accountability system at the Cleveland Police Department..."*

Cleveland has a 53% African-American population and elected its first African-American mayor nearly 40 years ago. But whenever you hear about the city, it so often seems to be about incidents like the shooting of 12-year-old Tamir Rice by two white cops while he clutched a toy gun. Or the death of Tanisha Anderson in 2015 while she was in police custody. Or the report by 247WallStreet.com that found Cleveland to be the most segregated city in the country, with a black poverty rate of 33% and a white rate of 9%. Reading stats and stories about racism is one thing. Walking down the street with a black woman while you notice white cops in a nearby car carefully watching you is something else altogether.

Lest Fox News followers swear they now see my left knee

jerking and my heart bleeding rainbows, let me clarify something: I can't pretend I haven't had my own racist thoughts in the past. You'd be hard-pressed to find an adult of any ethnicity who hasn't, however briefly. When I was growing up in Kansas, we learned the childhood nursery rhyme as, "Eenie Meenie Miney Moe, Catch a N****r By the Toe." Even now, when I hear about a shooting at a concert or nightclub, my knee-jerk reaction is to wonder if it involved rap stars. I'm not proud. This is a response I'm consciously trying to change.

These kinds of reactions are the products of fear, control and conditioning. We humans work very hard to separate ourselves from each other, so there can always be somebody to blame over *anything* for which we don't take responsibility. I've thought this through enough to realize that if everyone in the world had the same skin color, we'd *still* find something to make us feel superior to one group or another. Right-handed cab drivers would boost their self-esteem by refusing to pick up left-handed passengers because, frankly, southpaws are just weird. Short people would make the world a safer place by having six-footers sit in the back of the bus so those freaks of nature wouldn't block their view.

Rev. Pinkney Butts and I made our way back to the diner, and the place was now buzzing with the conversations of a sizable lunchtime crowd that included a mix of white, black, Asian and Hispanic patrons. This was the middle-class neighborhood where she grew up, with a dad who worked as an artist and photojournalist, and a mom who was an elementary school teacher with two master's degrees and a PhD.

She recalls being a toddler when her parents moved to a new place that was next door to a white family. This was the first moment in her life that race became an issue. Pamela used to watch the neighbor kids through cracks in the backyard fence, eventually seeing that family pack up and leave "because of our skin color. That's when I felt different. That's when I knew I had something to do in my life."

While her classmates dreamed of being ball players, athletes or doctors, the reverend developed a far more ambitious plan.

"I wanted to be the world leader that would make peace in the world. I remember sitting at my desk at Randallwood Middle School and Eastwood Middle School, imagining that I was that person who made peace in the world."

A noble dream, but one she probably should have kept as an inner thought. She never believed friends or family rallied around her Gandhi-esque ambitions, leaving her feeling "very lonely growing up...very, very lonely. And that sticks with me even today."

In fact, there's really only one friend from her childhood that has apparently never let her down: Jesus Christ. Every Sunday her mother would put young Pamela in a nice dress and bonnet, then take her to church.

"One of the key moments ever for me was when I want to the Aldersgate United Methodist Church'" recalled the reverend. "I was singing in the choir when I was in elementary school. I remember singing, *'Give me a clean heart so that I may serve thee.'* That song took me to the next place. Music has always done something to bring me through. Whether it had been a good situation or great turmoil in my life, music has always done something to bring me through. Music has not only been the peacemaker but [also] a peace-giver."

Whitney Houston's "I Look to You," Barbra Streisand's version of "People," Elton John's "Bennie and the Jets." Feel-good anthems like "We Are the World" and "I'd Like to Teach the World to Sing." They were all on her hit parade.

Her favorite was "Just You Wait" from *My Fair Lady* because "I love what it portrays," she said, closing her eyes to envision a memory she wouldn't share with me. "I love that it shows it doesn't matter where a woman comes from or what she comes through. She can always be successful and victorious."

Music was such an important part of her life that she studied it at Bishop College in Texas. She remembers singing in *Carmen* and even got a chance to achieve her dream of playing Eliza Doolittle in a production of *My Fair Lady*. Not everyone figured this was a good thing. She says her dad, for instance, used to tell her when she was very young that "those love songs are going to get you in trouble!" Her grandmother was the one person she felt truly understood her. She was "the one who kept everyone from treating me like a misfit. She was a protector. I could always go to her and she would give me words of wisdom. Actually, my campaign is dedicated to her."

It's a sweet sentiment, but it also comes with a fair amount of sadness. When her grandma passed away, even music wasn't enough to console young Pamela's lonely heart any longer. That's the period when, as the reverend puts it, "the devil went crazy in my life."

From our initial hug, I'd started to like Rev. Pamela Pinkney Butts. She seemed to be one of those people who, for better or worse, *feels* the world more than most of us. This is a good thing for a public servant, because it means he or she will truly care about righting the wrongs of society. However, it's a bad thing for one's personal life, because it leaves a person raw and fragile. Which was to be the reverend's case. Perhaps that's why I began to feel protective of her in a way that I hadn't with the other Can't-idates.

That's also why it was depressing when she began to spin stories of abusive husbands and boyfriends. Of being forced to take drugs. Of living in homeless shelters. Of legal troubles that led to her losing custody of her children. Each tale seemed more incomprehensible than the last, and they all had a theme: the world couldn't understand or appreciate the talents she brought to it. I could tell she had a lovely heart. At the same time, I felt like it might be wise to move on to my next interview, rather than exploit someone who has some real issues to work through. And if I couldn't adequately delve into her life the way I had with all the other people on my list, what was the point? As I decided whether or not to continue or just hit the road, a younger African-American wearing a job interview dress and carrying a massive stack of files rushed to our table.

"Hi, I'm Charlena," she said, extending her hand toward me. "Sorry I'm late. I'm a presidential correspondent—President Obama precinct captain. In fact, Obama's campaign office is right across the street."

I'd totally forgotten that Rev. Pinkney Butts had mentioned earlier she'd invited friends to come talk about her campaign. Those "friends" turned out to be a lone friend, Charlena Wells Bradley, the reverend's biggest believer and the supporter who'd helped file her campaign paperwork. The pair met three years earlier, when Bradley saw the reverend on the subway and thought "she just looked like she needed someone to help her."

Bradley was inspired enough to assist Rev. Pinkney Butts in filing out all the proper paperwork for each of her presidential bids. (The reverend also ran in 2012.)

"A lot of times, if violence happens in the neighborhood, Rev. Pamela Pinkney will be out there picketing and speaking up to say that we will not stand for this violence. That's why I think people will see her as a voice not just in Ohio, but across America. I believe that people are beginning to respect Rev. Pinkney, even though she may not see the fruit of it. She will eventually."

That's also why, at least according to Bradley, the local news has started to interview the reverend whenever she shows up for local protests, like the recent demonstration to fight a recall of Cleveland's mayor.

"That's why they are filming her on TV," said Bradley. "It's not because they are trying to lock her up. It is because they are seeing the light."

As if on cue, a stocky African-American man in a flashy suit (dark jacket, white tie, blue and white pin-striped dress shirt) waved to the reverend from his table across the room. Smiling proudly, she led me over to meet him. This introduction process was starting to feel familiar.

"This is Pastor Aaron Phillips," Rev. Pinkney Butts explained. "And Pastor, this is Craig. He's interviewing me about my presidential campaign. Do you want to tell him anything about me?"

I soon learned she befriended the pastor years ago, and that they'd both been at the First Energy protest earlier in the day. Pastor Phillips smiled, put down a fork full of salad and happily told me his friend "is vital to making sure there's someone standing up for the voiceless. I appreciate how she advocates for African-American women. If we didn't have her voice, there'd be a huge void."

But would he vote for her? I asked.

Pastor Phillips and his lunch companion, Pastor Vincent Barry, looked at each other and laughed.

"Who wants that job?" he finally said. "I wouldn't want it! I don't think Obama wanted that job. Look at him now. So her aspiring to this very difficult task is admirable. She represents those folks that don't do it—but need to."

Not quite a ringing endorsement. Still, it was enough to keep the reverend beaming. We said goodbye to Bradley and the pastors, then walked to my car. Before I hit the road again, I decided to drive over for a quick visit with at least one of Rev. Pinkney Butts' children. "My oldest daughter lives around the corner," she told me as we headed east from the stately single-family streets of Shaker Heights. Before long we were navigating the ramshackle roads of a far less elegant neighborhood. "She's 20," the reverend told me. "As a matter of fact, she's going to be officially legal on Friday. She doesn't think that I need to be there for the party, because she knows what I disagree with."

She directed me down some blocks that made the neighborhoods from *The Wire* look like *Beverly Hills 90210*. Many of the dilapidated Craftsman-style houses were boarded up, probably 20 years removed from their better days. Meanwhile, despite it being mid-afternoon—when schools should be letting out—the streets were nearly deserted.

We pulled into the driveway of one of the few non-abandoned houses, a faded blue two-story that was the home of the reverend's eldest child, Kitt. While I waited in the car, she stepped onto the rickety porch and knocked on the front door. I couldn't see what was happening, but a minute or so later, Rev. Pinkney Butts strolled over to me with a pretty girl who didn't look a day over 16. She had the look of someone who wasn't expecting company, wearing black sweatpants and a grey T-shirt, tightly pinching a freshly lit cigarette.

Kitt seemed cautious. I couldn't tell if it was because a stranger with a tape recorder had just arrived at her home—or because the mother she rarely sees had just shown up. The reverend already warned me that her daughter had asked her, "Ma, why do you have to do this?" when she filed her campaign papers for 2016. So I was surprised when Kitt launched into a discussion of her mother's political ambitions.

"She really does have great ideas," Kitt said between heavy drags from her cigarette. "Like on women's rights. I'm a survivor of domestic violence, and she goes out there to march for people like that. She goes out there about police brutality. She hates violence. When we were little, we weren't allowed to be spanked. If we kids fought, we'd get in trouble—but never spanked. She was always saying, 'No fighting. Be nice. Be sweet.'"

At one point when her children were little, the reverend caught someone stealing from the family home. Instead of having the person arrested, according to Kitt, "my mom gave him her last five dollars. She did it just so he could get home, so he could get food. She's like that and I've learned from her."

Kitt was also a mom, with two babies napping inside the house. At the moment, she's trying to start school, find a job and launch a singing career—all while living on the $500 in public assistance she gets to attend classes every month and feed her kids. As she told me all this, her baby face began looking edgier and edgier.

"Welfare makes me check in with them every month with an attendance sheet. That is one more paper for me to carry. I took 16-credit courses and I failed two of my classes because of welfare and some stuff going on with my daughter and my son. My son is kind of delayed a little bit. I just wish I could get more help."

As she spoke, I felt like a guy who goes out searching for the Loch Ness Monster and finds it's just some guy in a kayak. Never believe a myth. I grew up on *The Legend of the Welfare Queen*, a fiction that Ronald Reagan used to terrify conservatives. The creature was like a reverse Babadook, scaring decent taxpayers by *having* kids rather than *snatching* them while accepting all the free government handouts that came with the process. The truth, for those willing to search for it, looked a lot more like Kitt.

"People think that we just sit around and don't do anything," Kitt explained. "I have heard of certain girls that do it, but I have motivation. I don't want to be here forever. I have dreams for my kids. My dream is to go to Puerto Rico. I want to own a house in Puerto Rico."

Her mom eased a couple steps closer to her daughter,

adding, "She loved Spanish when she was a little girl."

Kitt quickly agreed.

"I want to go to Spain. I want to go to Barcelona. And if I can go to France, I want to go *there*, too."

(Note to self: Never again complain about plane flights any-where, because there's always somebody who wishes they could be doing precisely what you're moaning about. One person's gripe about a middle seat is another person's dream come true of escaping to something and somewhere new.)

The closest Kitt says she ever came to getting out of Cleveland was three years earlier, when she claims to have made it a few rounds into the audition process for the Fox talent show, *The X Factor*. But then "my phone got turned off after I made it through the fourth round, so I never found out what happened... Maybe I'd made it all the way to actually meet Simon Cowell."

She stared down at the cigarette butt she was grinding into the ground with her toe, the long silence finally interrupted by the rumble of a white van bumping along the rough road in front of Kitt's home. She flinched and took a step toward her front door. As the van kept going, she let out a very audible sigh.

"I thought that was the utility people," she explained. "Every time they come around, I get scared. I always ask, 'Are they coming over here?'"

We all watched as the van headed away and a relieved Kitt eagerly changed the subject to something much happier—her 21st birthday party that would take place in three days. That's a special time for anybody, the official starting point for life as an adult. For her, it would be something more. When she was very young, Kitt was shuttled around in foster care, so she never had a birthday party. As she got older, something always seemed to keep her from celebrating. She told me she'd been in the hospital on her special day the past two years—last year because she was pregnant with her son, the year before because of what she'll only refer to as "domestic violence."

"I'm so excited!" she said, vibrating with the sort of eagerness my son had when he turned three and got to spend his birthday at a *Thomas the Tank Engine* party. "I get one day where I can just have fun for me. I never get a day for me. Everything I do, I do for everybody else. I need to learn about getting more time to myself."

Friday night was going to be epic, unlike anything she'd ever experienced. So epic, in fact, she was even letting her mom babysit the kids—something that almost never happens. Her friends were going to kick in with food and alcohol. If they don't show up with either, they'll be required to give Kitt $10 as their present. Best of all, at least according to the reverend, Kitt was finally going to spend an evening wearing something besides her trademark sweatpants and sneakers.

"Do you want to see my outfit?" she asked. Without waiting for an answer, she dashed into the house to retrieve a printout of a silky, billowing white harem-style jumpsuit. "I used to be a straight-up tomboy. My sophomore year in high school, I started wearing makeup and all that. I still hang around with guys all the time. But I want to look pretty on my birthday."

"Hallelujah!" her mom laughed as she raised her hands to the sky. "There is hope. She is going to be beautiful and not brassy for her birthday!"

There was just one problem, the same problem Kitt always seemed to have: money. She burned up all the excess cash she had on her outfit, which left nothing for shoes or accessories. As mother and daughter argued over which shoes would be most appropriate and least expensive for the party, my head went in another direction.

I thought of the picture my daughter texted me a day earlier. She was wearing the brand new superhero boots I'd ordered just before I left—new shoes she probably didn't need. She didn't even ask for them. But I knew she loved Marvel comics, and I'd seen this pair online that featured images of all her Marvel heroes. So I splurged and had them sent to her. Given my current lack of income, spending money on a pair of unnecessary boots was probably a dumb idea. Still, I did it without thinking twice. I was just operating on the same instinct all parents are supposed to have—we discover our bliss by pleasing the people who give our lives meaning—and logic just doesn't apply. It's rare to get into relationships where doing something for the other person benefits you just as much, if not more. But that's what being a dad felt like to me.

And since Kitt wasn't that much older than my son, I felt very paternal as she told me her story. In that moment, it just felt wrong to let a girl go without having a pair of shoes she loved for her big night. To the outside world, I imagine it looked as though I was playing the role of *The Charming Caucasian*. You know, that saintly white person in blockbuster movies about racial inequality who absolves all racial guilt by stepping in to save a helpless minority character's day. To me, it just felt like a way of being a dad when my kids were 2,000 miles away.

Okay, so maybe this didn't exactly move me into Gandhi territory. Still, I could see how just the thought of fancy footwear boosted the self-esteem of someone who had already survived more than I would ever have been able to withstand. I interrupted the reverend and Kitt, offering to get the birthday girl some nice shoes as a gift.

There was just one slight flaw in the plan. They were concerned it might look rather odd for a paunchy, haggard old white guy to walk into a shoe store with an attractive young black woman to buy her some fancy heels.

So we settled on a different solution. Instead of picking out the shoes with her, we'd go to the nearest ATM and I'd get $80 in cash for Kitt to buy them on her own. Leaving Rev. Pinkney Butts behind to keep an eye on the babies, Kitt and I drove to a cash machine a couple of miles away.

"You're going to see a lot of ghetto people on the street here," she explained the way somebody else might casually offer tips to avoid traffic. "I just want to let you know that. They don't really bother anybody. They are just hanging out."

I got money from the ATM, noticing that Kitt had subconsciously turned her back to me. She was now facing the door like she was my security force. At this point, I suppose my comfort zone should have been compressing upon me like that *Star Wars* garbage room Luke and his gang get stuck in. But Kitt's subconscious gesture was so thoughtful and reassuring that it didn't even occur to me that some might consider what I was doing dangerous or foolish.

I grabbed the $80, handed it to her and we bounced along the pockmarked streets back to her house. While we rattled along the still relatively deserted neighborhood, she said, more to herself than to me, "I just which they would fix the streets though, because they fixed the streets downtown for no reason, when we have all these messed up streets."

The reverend was waiting for us on the porch, reclining in a butterfly chair with a folded piece of notebook paper in her hand. As Kitt continued to thank me, I could tell there was still something her mom wanted to add to the conversation before we left. When Kitt was discussing her dreams of becoming a professional singer, the reverend had suggested mother and daughter sing a duet for me. When Kitt declined, her mom looked disappointed.

"She gets embarrassed when I sing."

Now, though, she reminisced about how she used to listen to her little girl sing a hymn called "His Eye is on the Sparrow."

"I wish she'd give me just a bar of that," the reverend said.

Kitt also turned to me, explaining that "she's the one who taught me that song." Caught up in the moment, Rev. Pinkney Butts softly started singing the tune. After a few seconds of hesitation, Kitt joined in. And for the next minute or so, the pair gently harmonized on this tune about keeping one's faith intact no matter what. The reverend kept her eyes on me, something she'd barely done all day. Kitt looked heavenward. This moment was very tender, but I felt uncomfortable. I worried my presence was trampling all over their private moment. They never looked at each other. Still, the way their voices coiled around each other was all the proof I needed that, no matter what had transpired between them in the past, they still had a future together.

There was clearly a lot that still needed to be said between these two, and maybe never would be. Although, who knows what would happen over the weekend when the reverend got to spend quality time with her grandbabies and Kitt got to finally enjoy her life? As the reverend and I said goodbye to Kitt, the young mom promised to email me pictures of her new shoes as soon as she got them. I'm not sure if she was saying this because she wanted to show off that future purchase or because she wanted to prove that's what the money would be used for. Frankly, it didn't matter one way or the other to me. She seemed happier when we left than she did when we arrived, and that was well worth $80.

The reverend and I got back into the car and she handed me the folded piece of paper I noticed her holding a few minutes earlier. I set it aside with a promise to read it later. Then she asked if we could make one more stop. Her mom, Betty, worked in a law office a few miles away and would be thrilled to speak with me— because "she's really been wrestling with how people have been treating me. She's been very displeased."

I wasn't exactly sure how I fit into that equation, which left me worried as we arrived at the law firm. We were taken to a conference room, where we sat alone for a couple minutes. When Betty finally came in, she took a seat several chairs away from her daughter. Neither smiled at the other, and I felt more uncomfortable than I had the entire day—which was saying something, considering some of the streets I'd driven down earlier. We chatted briefly about how chilly the weather was that day, but as soon as I brought up the fact that her daughter was running for president, small talk in the room died a quick death.

Betty looked at me and said, "I told her that she has the right to do what she wants. But I have a right to vote for who I want. She got furious. That is one thing that I still believe in, that I have the opportunity to do that. I told her, because it takes millions of dollars, millions of staff to run for president. That is reality."

Rev. Pinkney Butts steamed like a volcano three minutes short of an eruption. Eager to keep things moving, lest a major meltdown occur, I mentioned the difficult times in the reverend's past that she'd shared with me. Betty frowned, then told me her daughter was no different than "a lot of people who make bad choices, the wrong choices. I, for one, believe that she should stop telling people all that stuff, because it impacts her children. They don't want to read about it."

The eruption was getting closer.

"I don't have anything to hide," the reverend bristled. "I don't have anything that I'm afraid of."

"It's not always only your life," her mother shot back. "It's other people's too, and this is about whether they want [that information] out there or not."

Turning to me, the reverend tersely said, "A lot of family members don't speak to me. My cousins don't even speak to me."

With every sentence her daughter spoke, I could see more tension in Betty's face and her posture slumping. I wasn't sure how to tell her that, as a parent, I could not only see her pain—I could *feel* it. The relationship between parents and children feels, more often than not, only slightly less dysfunctional than the relationships in any *Real Housewives* episode. Think about it. It's naturally going to be a messed up situation.

Parents start out doing everything for our kids. Eventually, if we're lucky, those kids end up doing everything for us one day. Parents want nothing more than the success of our children. If they fail, we feel like we failed somehow. At the same time, if they succeed, they may not need us anymore. Either way, there's a lot of pain and resentment to work through on both sides.

Maybe I was just projecting my own insecurities with my kids, but it seemed like this same dynamic had been playing out in the reverend's life all day as well. First, there was the occasionally awkward connection between her and Kitt. And now, there was an equally strained feeling as she and her mom talked. Pamela and Betty clearly wanted the best for their daughters, even though it was sometimes hard for that message to get through. Kitt and the reverend clearly needed and wanted a solid connection with their mothers. It's just that, like Los Angeles smog, it's hard to see how to get where you're going when you're in the middle of it.

Oblivious to the tension in the room, Rev. Pinkney Butts asked her mother, "What do you see as unrealistic about this?"

Betty retained her composure. "It takes a lot of people. It takes a lot of support. It takes a whole lot of money!"

"To identify this as not realistic puts me into a negative light with my campaign. It puts me in the light like I'm doing something no one has ever done before, something weird."

"Who's putting you in that negative light?"

"A lot of people. When you've labeled me into a category of doing something unrealistic, that means I have goals that aren't reachable. So I'm trying to figure out what is unrealistic about me doing what other people are doing or have done already."

"The lack of reality I'm talking about is having the means for this to happen."

"Well, it is realistic for others, and I'd like for people who do know me to get behind me and support me. I want people to believe in me, and have confidence in the teachings that they have given me, and show me that now is the time for me to implement them."

There was tension in their conversation, but also a sense that this was neither the first nor last time for this disagreement. Like the endless debate over who started the argument that ruined the family Thanksgiving, there was clearly no resolving these problems. At least not today. Before things got way out of hand, I thanked Betty for her time. Then the reverend and I hurried out to my car. Despite the awkwardness of that last conversation, she seemed to be just fine with it all. Just like Doug Shreffler, her presidential candidacy was something that brought joy into her otherwise troubled life.

"I am blessed! I am happy! Oh, I am blessed! I wouldn't change anything on my journey," the reverend told me. "I wished things would have been different, and I pray that the time I have lost shall be redeemed, and that the things that I have lost will be restored. But I am blessed! I am not even supposed to be alive right now. I am not even supposed to be in my right mind right now. I am not even supposed to be able to talk to you right now about what I have been through. And even what I am going through."

When I dropped her off a few minutes later outside her apartment, she offered up one final blessing. This time, it was for both the book and myself. It had been a long day. However, when she got out of the car, I was sad to see her go, not relieved. Maybe it was my own parental instinct wanting to take care of this woman who seemed to need protection from a very difficult world. Then I realized I hadn't looked at the paper she'd given me back at her daughter's house.

I unfolded it and saw she had written a poem called "I Am."

I am free.
No matter what they have done and are doing to me
I am free.
They perceive me as a slave.
They have even buried me in a grave.
Yet, inside of me
I am still free.
They stripped me of all that I am and have.
This includes my integrity.
But I am still free
I walk in the truth
I live in what is left of me.
I stand on who I am not who they think I should be.
I am blessed.
I am free.

On the back of the paper she'd also written: "Thank you for taking the time to consider me in word and deed. With love, Rev. Pamela M. Pinkney Butts."

I sat back to absorb all this, finally realizing she and I were much more in sync than I originally thought. She was trying to gain the respect of her mother and daughter. I was trying to be a good father. Once again, it was pretty clear that running for president wasn't truly about running for president. As was the case with Usera, it's far more about redemption than leading the country.

Watching someone else's family drama play out in front of me all day had me aching to talk to my kids. As I drove toward my next stop—Buffalo, here I come!—I called my son to tell him I missed him. The conversation went like this:

"How was your day?"

"Good."

"How was baseball?"

"Good."

"What are you doing now?"

"Homework."

"I really miss you!"

"I have to go now."

I told you parenthood was complicated...

Sydneys Voluptuous Buttocks

I wish I could say I've always been a political junkie, that from my earliest memories I deeply cared about this country and who ran it. It would certainly make this book seem a whole lot more authoritative. There's no reason this *shouldn't* be the case. After all, I hit my teens just after 18-year-olds got the right to vote and G. Gordon Liddy's burglary at the Watergate hotel and office complex exponentially increased our awareness of how shifty politicians were. But while the youth of America was busy helping to end the Vietnam War, I sat at home complaining about how the 1972 Republican and Democratic conventions preempted my favorite show, *The Jerry Reed When You're Hot You're Hot Hour.*

Sadly, the only political discourse from that era that had any impact on me came from comedy shows like *Laugh-In* and *The Smothers Brothers Comedy Hour.* (Sort of like my generation's *Daily Show.*) It was far simpler to laugh at Richard Nixon saying "Sock it to me!" or comedian Pat Paulsen, who ran for president with claims of being "just a common, ordinary, simple savior of America's destiny." That preference for political awareness via comedy has stuck with me well into adulthood, making me one of those people who got more of his news from *The Daily Show* than from any allegedly legitimate news organization. At least Jon Stewart's jokes were written on purpose.

I suppose this explains why campaign ads have become indistinguishable from late-night TV comedy parodies. Candidates shoot rifles to prove who's more macho. (Even the women). They mingle with folks growing tomatoes and teaching their dogs not to eat the garbage as proof they know about "everyday Americans." (As opposed to "Wednesday night and every other weekend" Americans.)

Cable news departments handle opinion polls and scandal in the same breathlessly worshipful fashion their sports departments reserve for the NFL playoff chase. At what point do people start presidential campaign fantasy drafts? We now watch debates the same way we watch NASCAR races, hoping to see someone crash and burn, even though it'd be wrong to actually admit that.

Which brings me to Buffalo and Sydneys Voluptuous Buttocks. When I came across that name in the FEC list of candidates, it was like finding a lost $20 bill buried in the pocket of an old jacket. Here was somebody who recognized the foolishness of the presidential race and put a giant comic strip bubble right over the top of it.

Tracking down Syd and her buttocks had been a bit of a challenge. The name naturally cropped up in every story I read about 2016 fringe candidates. Despite the frequent mentions, however, there were no interviews with the candidate to be found. That's why I was probably more excited than I should have been when I got an email from someone named George. He'd received my letter asking for an interview with Sydney and wanted to get more information in order to pass the request on to "her committee." That led to a phone call that was both promising and bewildering.

George was the ultimate quiet talker, whose sentences were as succinct as they were hard to hear. He assured me Syd was indeed a real person, that the campaign was an attempt to "shake things up" and every member of "her committee" grew up, and still lives, in a working-class neighborhood on the west side of Buffalo, New York. The committee decided to grant me an interview, but details of a time and meeting place were TBD.

I was a little wary of traveling all the way to Buffalo simply for the chance to meet Syd and her group. Still, I also needed some comic relief at the halfway point of my trip. So I shuffled off to Buffalo, in search of Sydney and her voluptuous—and mysterious—buttocks. Luckily, George called to say "the committee" would meet me for lunch at a place called Prima Pizza in downtown Buffalo. Even more than my trip with Kitt to the ATM, I felt some suspense as I strolled in the frigid (at least for this Californian) afternoon breeze toward my date with Syd and pizza. Everybody else I dealt with had spilled their guts on the phone. George had barely given up anything. I didn't know *what* to expect this time.

Huddling just inside Prima Pizza were two young guys dressed like they were on their lunch break from the copy center. The first kid—quick FYI, I have aged to the point where anyone under 40 is considered a kid—had his curly hair pulled back in a sizable ponytail, a radical contrast to the standard blue work shirt and khakis he wore. The other kid looked much heavier, although that could have been due to his bulky winter jacket, work pants and boots.

It was nothing personal, but neither of these guys looked like a woman named Syd. And, at first glance anyway, it seemed neither had particularly voluptuous buttocks. Despite every attempt at journalistic integrity, I'm sure my disappointment was obvious.

"I'm George Boria," said the kid with the ponytail. "This is Ricardo Nunez. We're the committee." As we all shook hands, ELO's "Strange Magic" appropriately played in the background. Then Boria delivered the bad news. Syd was a no-show. Apparently, she had to go to the emergency room the night before because she's still recovering from lymphatic cancer. (So much for the comic relief in her campaign...)

"She wanted to be here," Boria assured me with the same soft voice he used on the phone. "But she had to go to the hospital ...[it was] a very last minute kind of issue. I'm sure she'll be fine. And there is an actual Sydney. I could probably get her on the phone eventually."

"So it's just us for now," Nunez chimed in. "Wanna get some pizza and find a place to sit?"

We got in line to grab our slices and then headed to find a table upstairs. I was thinking what I assume you're thinking right now: Syd didn't get on the phone; she didn't show up for the interview; she's never talked to any other media, nor had her picture taken. It wouldn't be wrong to suspect Sydney V. Buttocks was about as real a candidate as SpongeBob SquarePants.

The best I could get out of Boria was that Syd's "about" 36 years old. She's a friend who used to babysit him when he was growing up. Although he claimed not to have noticed back then, Boria admitted when asked about it that he now considered her butt to be quite lovely. The 23-year-old stayed in contact with his former babysitter as he got older, and in 2012 they watched a Republican debate together.

"We made note of how much the people were assholes," he told me as we sat down. "We watched them avoid all of the questions and just bash each other. Politicians are assholes. So we thought it'd be funny to run a campaign about somebody's *actual ass*."

Boria and Syd started emailing each other "humorous ideas around the concept," creating some memes just to amuse themselves. To see how far they could take the gag, Boria discovered the Federal Election Commission website near the end of 2014 and filled out the forms using Syd's first name and (to keep the theme going) *Buttocks* as her last name.

"And we realized that she should have a middle name," Boria continued as Nunez focused on his pizza. "And you wouldn't vote for Sydneys *Ugly* Buttocks. So it had to be Voluptuous."

As the Genesis song "Misunderstanding" played in the background, Boria told me he received an email from the FEC in early 2015 informing him that Sydneys Voluptuous Buttocks was now officially a candidate for President of the United States.

His gag was close to its punch line. But what began as a ruse was turning out to be a task "we started to take more seriously." Boria added, "realizing the fact that the government would accept a form from Sydneys Voluptuous Buttocks says something." And that something wasn't a positive.

"I thought he was joking about it all," Nunez added. "And then he showed me the official email and I thought, 'God, this is real!' I couldn't believe the government would actually allow something like that."

The more Boria explained the origin story of Syds Butt, the more I realized it didn't matter whether or not she actually existed. The *idea* of her was enough to make her candidacy fascinating. It wasn't just the fact that we live in a land where somebody can pretend her last name is "Buttocks" and run for the highest office in the land. It was also evidence of how complete the union of comedy and politics had become.

It was Nunez's turn to weigh in. He and Boria had first met a few months earlier at the Buffalo Housing Authority, where he'd gone to pick something up for a friend. While there, Nunez noticed a janitor belting out Michael Jackson's "Man in the Mirror" as he mopped the floors. A fellow Michael fan, he introduced himself to Boria and within minutes they were both using Boria's mop to duet on "Man in the Mirror."

As it turned out, they had a lot more than their love of Michael Jackson in common. They'd both grown up in poor Buffalo neighborhoods. Family difficulties kept them from staying close to their parents, so both are far more attached to their grandparents. Both participated in high school politics—Boria was class treasurer, Nunez student council vice president. Both had a flair for the unconventional back then, like the time Boria opted to wear an actual dress to Dress-Up Day. Or the time Nunez sold Ritz crackers at an event called "Puttin' on the Ritz."

Perhaps most critical for their current campaign work, though, is the fact that they're both from Hispanic backgrounds and grew up in what Boria considers "a pretty racist town. And real segregated." To back this up, Nunez told me how he believes it's not just Buffalo's infamous blizzards that look all white. So does the city's approach to cleaning up after those storms, which tends to favor Caucasian citizens first. He still burns about a particularly bad snowfall last winter, when FEMA didn't send any help to his drug-riddled neighborhood for two days—while the wealthier streets in town were cleared promptly.

"The water was cut off, there was no power and a guy broke into my house to steal my tools to fix his place," Nunez recalled. "It was scary, because he had a two-year-old baby at his house and his wife was pregnant. The government wasn't helping. But I had enough food to last me and my family for a month, so I gave him two weeks' worth of supplies."

When that's the window through which you view the world, I can see how life would proceed only one of two ways. Option #1—draw the blinds, yell at cable news shows and grow as bitter as the cheap beer you can barely afford. Option #2—start a campaign to be president.

"I do think that growing up with all that kept George and me a little more open to what's going on in the world," Nunez explained. "If I'd grown up in a different area, I wouldn't have thought about things being as much of an issue."

Boria nodded, his volume increasing as he added, "Same thing for me. If I'd lived in a rich neighborhood without trouble, I don't think I would be doing this [presidential campaign]. But I grew up in the ghetto, and I don't think that real upper middle class people think there is a problem in the country. The [mainstream] candidates want to show people what they want to see. They don't want to show you the truth."

Still, nobody was more surprised than Boria to learn that a plan he'd cooked up "in jest has actually become something serious." I guess there is validity to the idea that behind every joke there's a little bit of truth. I have to say, I was now as impressed by the Syds Butt campaign as I was by anyone else I'd met so far. If all that Boria had been after was a quick prank, it would have been entertaining enough. But in the course of just a few months, this experience had helped him grow more in his life than the Santorums and Huckabees of the world seemed to have done after years on the campaign trail. Boria was not the same immature joker he was when he came up with the Syd plan. Meanwhile, most mainstream candidates seem to sound pretty much exactly the same as they did in the last election cycle. Shouldn't there be at least some personal growth along the way?

"The system sucks and I'd like to see a lot of changes," Boria explained, ignoring the final bites of his pizza. "I'd like to see a smaller military. I'd also like to see a time when science becomes more important to this country again. There used to be a Department of Science, [but] it was shut down because the federal government decided there was no real reason to fund science."

Maybe there was a real Syd. Maybe there wasn't. I had no idea if I'd ever find out. However, as I listened to Boria talk, it was clear that this was his campaign. Nunez was on board to help by using the Internet to get the word out to the media. Before he'd come along, the best Boria could come up with were promo videos that Nunez told him "were kind of shitty…excuse my French."

(New note to self: find out later if the French swear, then ask to excuse their English.)

For instance, one of Boria's videos was called "War" and featured pictures of soldiers in combat, accompanied by Simon and Garfunkel's "Sounds of Silence." Another video, entitled "Love," had Joe Cocker singing "You Are So Beautiful" while sappy shots of happy couples flitted past. Toward the end of "Love," Boria explained in voiceover that "every year in the United States, there are over 800,000 divorces. Every year, over a million couples are separated and their love dies. Vote for love that lasts. Vote for Sydneys Butt as president of the United States."

"I told George I could do better," Nunez explained. "I took a class on how to [use] Photoshop in high school. What he was doing was too long, too fast. So we started a Facebook page. I told him to get the advertisement out there for the Facebook page, and how many 'Likes' do we have now, George?"

"Like 130."

"We even had a guy say to us, 'I would so vote for this.' It was surprising. And while I was editing the Facebook page, some guy said to us, 'I will donate $2,000.' As more people started supporting us, supporting Sydneys Butt, I thought, 'This is kind of messed up that people would donate money to us.'"

He seemed to have gotten over that initial shock. As the person in charge of marketing the Buttocks campaign, Nunez knew the importance of media attention. And for him, it came down to one word. A hint: it rhymes with Hope-rah.

"I targeted the big shows I used to watch with my grandparents, and I got an email back from Oprah's people," Nunez proudly explained. "I contacted her office and it took me a month, because they were shuffling me around, trying to sell me tapes of Oprah's show instead of explaining what they could do about us. And I was, like, 'Can I just speak to Oprah?' They said there might be an opening for us somewhere. If that could happen, it could change everything."

He's also got designs on Ellen DeGeneres, Jimmy Kimmel and a Spanish-language show he's been trying to remember—"the name was something *Mongo*." All he needed to get the promotional blitz going, apparently, was the blessing of the woman whose name—and derrière—is the cornerstone of the campaign.

Nunez and Boria seemed very well aware that without having an actual Sydneys V. Buttocks to take on the talk show circuit, they could run into some booking troubles. Still, Boria insisted that the campaign so far has "definitely been something that she seems to be enjoying, and she's glad I found somebody else (Nunez) to work on it. I think she was just surprised that everything we sent in got accepted, but it's also kind of frightening to wonder how far we can go with this before something happens."

Added Nunez, "I find myself thinking, 'Can we make it, if not across the finish line then at least maybe a foot away from it?' To come in even fifth in the race would be amazing!" Nunez added.

It's obvious as they talk with each other that this prank has taken on a life of its own—a life they never expected. Whenever they mentioned fundraising and getting on a ballot or two, they fidgeted with same sort of naïve hope of 10-year-olds setting up their first lemonade stand.

"We were going to do an event like one that was popular when we were in high school," Nunez told me. "It was called Cash for Cars, where you take an old car and give people little bats. For $5 or $10 you go beat up the car. We raised a lot of money back then—$2,000 in two days."

He spoke with such endearing optimism that I decided to refrain from my usual cynical journalistic scoffing. (Although I was sooooo ready to explain that his $2,000 wouldn't buy the shoes to go with Hillary Clinton's new $11,000 Armani jacket.) Instead, as we got up and tossed away our plates and napkins, I accepted an invitation from Boria and Nunez to take a quick walk through the city they hoped would give America its first openly asshole president.

We walked down Pearl Street to Niagara Square, practically yelling at each other because of the sounds of all the construction going on. I was struck by two essential realizations. First, even if it's *May* in Buffalo, wear a jacket. Seriously, I suspect it never gets warmer than a bowl of gazpacho. Second, my paternal feeling that had already kicked in with Rev. Pinkney Butts and Doug Shreffler was rising up once again with Syd's "committee." But I didn't feel empathy as I had with those other Can't-idates. Rather, it was an eagerness to encourage them. These kids were not much older than my son and setting a damn fine example for millennials everywhere.

Speaking as an old guy, which I've done a lot here already, there's overwhelming scientific proof that the youth of today have: a) horrible musical taste and b) the attention span of a dog in a yard full of squirrels. I grew up in an era where we were warned not to trust anyone over 30. These days, it's more like, "Don't trust anyone who has less than 30 Instagram posts."

Boria and Nunez had to be commended for combining the counterculture politics of the hippie era with the jaded sentiment of their generation. Even if it started as a cynical move, the mere fact that they were turning the negative into a positive is worth some recognition. I'm not saying that creating a presidential campaign around a joke that appeals to a six-year-old's sense of humor ranks up there with the Selma-to-Montgomery march. Still, at least these guys were *doing something*.

As we said our goodbyes, I told Boria and Nunez about my next stop: Rockport, Massachusetts, where I'd spend the day with veteran political prankster Vermin Supreme, the godfather of presidential protest runs. In that moment it occurred to me that connecting Syds Butt with Vermin Supreme might not only help my project, but it could be the start of something great. Who wouldn't want to check out a Supreme-Buttocks ticket?

According to my all-seeing, all-knowing Waze navigation app, the headquarters for the *Buffalo News* was just around the corner. So I figured it was worth pitching the local newspaper on the story of Syds Butt.

The ground floor was the perfect metaphor for the state of the newspaper business—gray and empty. A security guard sat at a desk in front of the elevators leading to the newsroom, and I explained to him that I was in town for the day working on a book about real people running for president. He laughed, then grumbled about how he'd be happy to vote for anyone who wasn't one of the usual "bunch of idiots."

He got an even bigger kick when I told him about Boria and Nunez. I did feel strangely proud of those kids when he snickered at "Sydneys Voluptuous Buttocks."

The guard called up to the newsroom and repeated my story, right down to "Sydneys Voluptuous Buttocks." Then he handed me the phone.

"It's the city desk," he explained. "They can help you out."

I repeated everything to the voice on the other end of the

line, racking up yet another chuckle. This editor seemed intrigued, telling me it's the kind of thing their political writer might enjoy. He took my number and said he'd get somebody to call me back as soon as possible. It felt an awful lot like the blow-off I'd gotten back at the Rapid City newspaper, so it hardly seemed worth it to wait around. I got in my car and started heading for Vermin Supreme in Massachusetts.

A few minutes later, as I sat in downtown Buffalo traffic, my phone rang. The caller identified himself as Bob McCarthy, the political writer for the *Buffalo News*. McCarthy had gotten my message about a potential story, so he was dutifully checking in to learn more. I launched in with my brief bio, explaining that I, too, had covered politics back during my newspaper days in the state of Washington. Since then, I'd moved on to writing for outlets like the *New York Times*, *People* magazine and *TV Guide*.

My credentials were enough to get me to second base with McCarthy, and I explained my long month's journey into the off-kilter heart of American democracy. He asked what brought me to Buffalo, so I told him all I could about Syd, Boria and Nunez. I'd spent a few years in the same spot he was currently in: desk-bound in a fluorescent newsroom, sucking in the stench of ink and cigarette smoke while writing about the same people doing the same things. That's why I was sure I understood Bob McCarthy. He had to be yearning for new and different stories that might shake things up a bit, right?

Wrong.

I hadn't even begun to explain what I thought was the most interesting part of Boria and Nunez's story—how the racism they experienced growing up fueled their presidential bid—when McCarthy interrupted me.

"So how many ballots are they on?"

None, I explained, adding that I didn't think that was quite the point.

"So they aren't real candidates?"

They were legally qualified, I told him. Once again, however, not the point. Even if he wasn't interested in the story of how a juvenile prank by some Buffalo kids had taken a serious turn, there was certainly a fascinating tale to be told about a record number of ordinary citizens taking part in the most unique presidential election this country has ever experienced.

"My plate is pretty full right now. Thanks, anyway. And good luck."

And he was gone.

My first thought? Maybe he's right. After all, he's the one who's spent a lifetime covering politics. I'm the guy whose reporting career featured scoops like Jackie Collins' meat loaf recipe. Maybe my Rapid City experience had turned me into the very creature that I'd wanted to mock—someone who used politics just to get media attention in order to shore up a rickety self-esteem. (Here was the one thing Donald Trump and I had in common.)

The further I drove, though, the more McCarthy's reaction bothered me. This was precisely the problem with how the bulk of American journalists cover presidential elections. They complain about do-nothing politicians who repeat the same clichés, but their coverage does nothing to lure back a jaded electorate— of which I'm a reluctant part. It's not that we don't want to care about politics. It's just that the politicians and those who cover them don't seem to care about making the process more honest or compelling. What I'd experienced in my three minutes with Bob McCarthy was what the Can't-idates experienced every day.

I don't think I'm a crazy person. (My love of Patrick Swayze's *Road House* notwithstanding.) I just feel frustrated by media gatekeepers who seem to have forgotten those gates should swing wide open more often than swing shut. There are times when it seems the whole presidential campaign cycle has evolved into a *Mean Girls* sequel. The similarities are uncanny. A handful of self-appointed leaders get to decide who's cool and who's not, based solely on their own subjective judgment, completely shutting out anyone they deem unworthy of the world's time and attention. Meanwhile, the people they put down understand they've got very little shot at becoming prom queen or king. All they wanted was to have somebody pay them a little attention without getting mocked at the lunch table.

The *Buffalo News* just left me feeling like I'd been stuffed inside my own locker again.

Vermin Supreme

Somewhere along the line, probably as a way of downplaying expectations, we've all heard that we shouldn't meet our idols because they'll only disappoint us. After decades of interviewing celebrities, I'd love to say that isn't true at all. (Caution: Dropping Names Ahead!) I'll admit that making Mel Brooks laugh on three separate occasions was a pretty sweet experience. So was cruising the streets of Beverly Hills for hours with a not-yet-famous Will Smith. However, after a few hours with Denny McLain, I left disappointed enough to figure he was the rule for celeb encounters—while Brooks, Smith and the rest were the exceptions.

When I was a kid McLain was my hero. He played for the Detroit Tigers and in 1968 became the last big league pitcher to win 30 games in a season. I liked him because he was a great player, but even more, I was a fan because he wore glasses on the field. I was the kid who got Coke bottle specs in first grade and was not a fan of the subsequent "four eyes" jokes that followed for the next decade. Seeing a fellow geek in glasses become a big-time jock filled me with hope. That hope took a dive in the '90s when an embezzlement conviction landed McLain in federal prison.

Still, I wanted to believe in the guy. That's why I arranged to meet him at the McKean Federal Correctional Institution in Pennsylvania. It had taken two flights, 12 hours and a crappy rental car to get to there, but despite the exhaustion, I was more nervous about meeting this childhood idol than I was that time I got to make up jokes with Bob Newhart. I'd spent more time in my earlier childhood talking to the McLain posters on my wall than I did with any kids in my school. I devoted endless hours pretending to wind up and throw just like he did. This was going to be a dream come true, even if that dream took place in a federal prison.

McLain and I spent an hour together in the visitors room, and almost immediately the disappointment began. This ex-athlete's inflated physique made Chris Christie look like a runway model. Even worse, McLain barely spoke with me until I bought him a vending machine burger and fries. Throughout our conversation, he never owned up to any of his self-destructive life choices. There was an excuse for everything. Later his friends and family would offer up tales of his arrogance and foolishness. I remember flying back to Los Angeles unsure whether I should be more disappointed in my childhood idol for being a dick—or myself for being a fan in the first place.

That probably explained why I felt a little apprehensive as I drove along the narrow Massachusetts road hugging the Atlantic Ocean's rocky shoreline 40 miles north of Boston. I was on my way to meet Vermin Supreme, the one Can't-idate I'd actually heard about long before I'd even *considered* starting this project. He was a veteran political prankster, having run for president with at least some degree of sincerity since 1992. He'd become a folk hero to the crowd that was sick of "politics as usual."

YouTube was filled with videos in which this man—sporting a rubber galosh on his head at every campaign appearance—

promised every voter a pony. He urged passage of a law requiring Americans to brush their teeth. He suggested solving the energy crisis by harnessing the power of zombies. His motto had been the same from the start: He's a "friendly fascist, a tyrant you can trust" and he simply wants you to "vote early, vote often and remember that a vote for Vermin Supreme is a vote totally thrown away."

He promises to never deliver on his promises. Because he's openly untrustworthy, he's the one politician we can actually trust. I won't go so far as to say he was the one Can't-idate on my list I admired most, but I certainly wanted to know more about him. He had brilliantly seized on the same philosophy that clicked for Ronald Reagan 35 years earlier: Make your campaign less about issues and more about personality, and you'll stand out from the crowd.

Supreme had given me an address where I should meet him, but also explained that this wasn't his place. It was the home nearest to the trail leading to his place. I parked alongside a tiny, twisty street a couple blocks up from the rocky beach. The old neighborhood looked the way it probably had for generations, dotted with Cape Cod-style homes that seemed to have sprouted up not unlike the random vegetation on the roadside.

It looked as classic as the man who wandered out of the woods to greet me. Supreme was exactly as advertised. Picture Dumbledore going vegan, losing 100 pounds, moving to the forest and swapping out his robes for an oversized, long-sleeved grey T-shirt and dark work pants, and you've got the idea. In other words, he was what kids under 30 imagine everyone at a Grateful Dead show must have looked like.

"I brought something for you," Supreme explained, his smooth FM DJ voice a surprising contrast to his backwoods appearance. He handed over a pillow-sized bag of taffy and lollipops, already delivering on a campaign promise ("free candy!") before we'd even had time to shake hands. Highly unusual for *any* candidate. He explained that the only thing remaining on his agenda for the day was going to feed his mom that evening. Until then, Supreme was all mine.

With that, we tromped through the thicket of trees and bushes that stood between us and the house Vermin and his wife, Becky, have lived in for 25 years, crossing over some railroad tracks that looked like they hadn't been used in 50 years. Further ahead, there was a smattering of wild orchids, which lured flower collectors here when they were in bloom. He pointed out a small pond where the neighborhood kids sneak out to play hockey during the winter. Then there was the witch house, a rickety old place off in the distance, barely noticeable behind the trees.

"I believe it was Sarah, or maybe Elizabeth," Supreme told me as we trudged along. "According to the legend, one of the Proctor's witches was pregnant. Instead of crushing or hanging her, they decided to let her go. Her brothers helped her build a one-room shack and it sort of turned into what you see there. I just think it's counterintuitive to do something like that. You'd think that if someone was carrying Satan's child, you'd want to kill them both."

Clearly he was a tough-on-crime candidate. Good to know, should he become president and that creepy girl from *The Ring* movies slithers into the White House. I saw signs indicating we were nearing the Supreme compound. The trees and underbrush were now filled with all kinds of random objects: old croquet set, mailbox, skeleton wearing football shoulder pads, Student Driver sign, mannequin leg, multiple Barbie dolls riding plastic toy horses. Some of these items sat by themselves, while others were pieced together like the world's least glamorous modern art exhibit.

"This is where the magic happens!" he said with a laugh. "I tidied up a bit. I thought you might like to see some things."

I thought Doug Shreffler's house was a *Hoarders* producer's wet dream, but the inside of Casa de Vermin Supreme looked like a thrift store had just vomited. There was not a single space in the tiny home that wasn't occupied by some vintage knick-knack or another. The refrigerator door featured everything from a Supergirl Valentine's Day card, to a newspaper headline congratulating the New England Patriots, to a pair of medical scissors. The living room was stacked with all kinds of books, the most prominent being Harlequin Romances with titles like *Beloved Tyrant*. I was knee-deep in a hodgepodge of chaotic randomness, best exemplified by the vintage wooden baby high chair, in which sat four creepy dolls with beady, unblinking dark eyes (including one swaddled in a Patriots sweatshirt).

Noticing my amazement at his collection of tchotchkes, Supreme explained, "Most of these are family heirlooms or things we've collected from various trips around the world. And I just realized looking at all those old brooms, we've collected them from places like Russia and Poland."

As he spoke, he moved to a kitchen counter cluttered with mismatched dishes to pour us each a cup of coffee. Then he led me into the living room, where I tried to be a good reporter by asking for personal details. Like his age.

"Let's just say I'm around 50," he told me with the sort of come-and-get-me grin the Joker gives Batman right before his next prank. "Generally when I'm dealing with the press, I lie to them. I'm always pushing to see how old I can be. And it's easy to lie about most things." So he's a skillful and unrepentant liar, a quality that would work wonders for Donald Trump many months later.

Knowing full well I couldn't trust his answers, I asked about his name. Vermin Supreme freely confessed he was (shockingly) *not* born Vermin Supreme, but there was also no way he would be using his given name today or any other day. The Vermin moniker is all he's used since the '80s, when he was a Baltimore-area music booking agent. At the time, pretty much everyone who booked bands for clubs was viewed as vermin. So he figured he might as well at least be the most *supreme* vermin he could be.

"Let me show you what I just got in the mail," he told me as we settled into his well-worn living room chairs. Vermin grabbed a thick stack of papers, pulling a handmade greeting card off the top. The drawing on the front featured a stick-figure little girl standing next to a stick figure man with a beard on his face and a boot on his head. The message inside read: *"Dear Vermin Supreme, I think you're awesome! I like you a lot. P.S. Nice hat! From Claire."*

"That's from a little girl in North Carolina," Supreme said proudly. "How friggin' cute is that?"

He has become the "Weird Al" Yankovic of politics, a parodist whose juvenile sense of humor strikes a chord with the 14-and-under crowd. If teens and tweens could vote, he'd be President Supreme in a heartbeat. Pulling out his laptop, Supreme scrolled through hundreds of emails that proved the point.

"People keep reaching out," he explained. "Like these kids from Point Loma High School: *'We strongly support your cause and wish to see you elected as president. We'll be graduating soon and Cory has emailed you about a graduation speech from the Almighty Vermin Supreme. We have growing support to fund a flight and payment for you, if you're willing to come speak at our graduation. We believe your wisdom is needed as we enter the real world.'"*

Supreme looked up at me with that Joker grin again.

"That's so true."

Some students want him for their commencement. Others want to send him money. Those who can't afford to give him cash volunteer their time.

As the youth of America hit voting age, more and more

of them are already so disillusioned by our disillusioning system that "they see me as the face of the third-party candidate. I would feel so terrible if that were the case. But for the young people, I became an alternative candidate by just being me. I'm a protest vote, the *Vote None of the Above* candidate."

He's grown up to be the sort of guy he would have wanted to vote for when *he* was a kid. Born and raised in nearby Beverly, and then Gloucester, little Vermin was never one to sit quietly in a corner. His dad owned a shop behind their house and would drive to Florida, pick up motorcycles, then ride them back to his shop to turn them into custom choppers. While the senior Supreme never joined the Hell's Angels, plenty of his friends did. And they all liked to hang out at the shop, teaching Vermin the counterculture hippie ways at an early age.

"You'd see Hell's Angels tearing up and down our driveway," he recalled. "I had this little box with a weasel tail in it. You'd look in the mesh on top and see that tail, then there was a little lever that would make the tail go up and down. You spring the lever and the tail would whip into a person's face. I remember doing that to the Hell's Angels. It was very, very entertaining!"

It should come as no surprise that his household was not exactly strict. The bikers had something to do with that, but it also went back to Supreme's mom's upbringing. She was an orphan, raised as a foster child in a strict Baptist household where the rules were severe. For instance, boys who peed the bed at night had to go to school in a dress the next day. (And I thought *my* childhood was tough...) After enduring that kind of discipline, it's no wonder she vowed to give Supreme, his brother and sister free reign around the house.

The way he saw it, he wasn't so much a free spirit but "just a guy who did sort of geeky shit, really." Case in point: one Christmas while he was in high school, he decided to stir up some spirit by getting other students to join him in singing Christmas carols.

"So I started to sing in the cafeteria and the teacher came up to me. I was like, 'Okay, fine, fuck y'all!' I go out in the hallway—there's the jocks, so I thought, 'Can I get these guys singing?' No. Umm, okay, fuck y'all. So I go to the front where people are smoking cigarettes and shit. They were smoking their weed, so they were more open. I started singing 'Silent Night' as a doo-wop tune. I thought it was simple, that they could do that. And then they start yelling, 'Do it up! Do it up!' And then they started getting loud and rowdy. Then the vice-principal comes out and talks to me. 'Hope you know what you are doing here, boy. And the principal came up and told me, essentially, the same thing. And I was, like, really amping it up. Then someone suggested that we go inside, so we all went inside, piled into the stairs—essentially, this big mob at that point."

The prank was a perfect example of what would later become routine in Supreme's life—start with an innocent gag that may not break any rules, but keep it going to the point where it pisses off those who prefer everything to be orderly. Most of his misbehavior in school wasn't particularly political. But his "main act of infamy" as a teen was definitely a protest with anti-establishment undertones.

It happened after one of his school's hockey players was suspended for taking speed. The police and local newspaper decided a major drug epidemic had hit the school, so they set up raids on the students' main hangouts before and after school. One of the offenders they nabbed was a close friend of Supreme, so he decided to use his drawing skills to create a rallying cry against the unwarranted harassment. Thus was born "Big Pig," a porcine policeman who wore thick glasses while constantly smoking a cigarette.

He sketched the cartoon on a poster, along with the words:

"Big Pig is watching you." A friend who worked at the Gorton's frozen fish factory in town helped him sneak in one night to print up 500 copies, so flyers could be passed out to everyone at school. When the police showed up at a student hangout, unknown vandals secretly crammed their squad cars with Big Pig posters.

"It was my first political statement," Supreme said, grabbing a scrapbook from a pile of papers on a nearby table before pulling out a tattered copy of Big Pig's debut. "Everybody sort of knew that I did it. The principal kind of appreciated that shit, saying it was very creative. So I started selling T-shirts with Big Pig on them. I actually got arrested once while I was wearing one."

As he talked, Supreme accidentally spilled a spot of coffee on his gray shirt. You'd think, given the disheveled state of his home and wardrobe, this would have been no big deal. Like peeing in the ocean. But for the first time since we'd met, Supreme seemed concerned. He may be excellent at playing the fool, but this coffee incident indicated there was something more going on with him. He acted like he didn't care what the world thought of his appearance. Still, watching him worry over a small coffee stain, it was clear he cared more than he let on about presentation and order.

Supreme excused himself to change shirts. When he returned a couple minutes later in a plain shirt, not much different than the one he'd changed out of, he came armed with a new plan.

"How about that game of golf now?"

That had totally slipped my mind. When we'd talked a few weeks earlier, Supreme told me he'd turned some of the woods near his home into an 18-hole putt-putt golf course. Knowing how important golf has been to seemingly every president—from Ike to Obama—I welcomed the offer to play a round with the latest presidential hopeful from Massachusetts. Supreme led me outside to a course that wasn't quite like any I'd ever played before.

There were no giant dinosaurs or windmills or clowns. In fact, there weren't even holes. Instead, it seemed more like a collection of pipes, hoses, cinder blocks and pottery that got lost in the woods. Instead of water hazards, there was some oozing swamp water. Instead of sand traps, there were gnats buzzing everywhere. It wasn't much to look at, but the course had apparently become a hit with all his neighbors, who occasionally pop by for a round or two.

"Grab a club and a ball—maybe a couple balls—and let's get started," Supreme said, happily snagging his own club and golf balls from a pile on the ground. "Everything is par two or three here. After three shots, if you ain't got it, boom!"

Since there were no actual holes to knock one's ball into, the goal was to bang it against the pipe where the holes should have been. His advice: "Imagine the pinball sound...ding ding ding ding!" I suggest that this might not be the fairest way to keep score. It would be almost too easy to simply cheat and tap on the metal when he wasn't looking. It was reassuring to know that Vermin Supreme was that rare politician who had faith in the trustworthiness of the American public.

"You are a very ethical journalist, Craig," he said, hand over his heart. "I trust you."

This was most likely sarcasm, given that we just met. Still... it was nice to hear. A connection between politician and reporter was forming. A ticket to the inauguration ball was all but assured.

I'll admit that golf is not my game. I used to hate the "sport," but apparently there's a law that every suburban white male dad must learn to play upon turning 50. So I taught myself to swing at a driving range near my home, at first bringing my son along so I'd looked more skilled than at least one person there. And then even he was beating me at our local par 3.

I figured the golf course was where the rich kids (and

grownups) hung out, where all their deals are done. So I taught myself how to survive on a course and learned the two most important things about golf. First, the game's a vicious cycle—the more you play, the less you feel like you know. Which is so frustrating that it makes you want to keep playing. Well, that and the 250-yard drive you hit once and are forever trying to replicate. Second, the point of golfing isn't golf. Rather, it's the time to talk at the tee and during the endless walks up the fairway. It's strange how a game that prides itself on silence on television is really all about the talk.

Both of these golf truisms definitely applied to my outing at the Vermin Supreme Country Club and Cultural History Museum. The more my chip shots flew into the swamp or the woods, the more I covered up my embarrassment by belittling my minimal golf skills—and the more I kept moving the topic of our conversation back to Supreme's life, post-Big Pig. Drawing the character had whet his appetite for art, so he opted to study fine arts at Maryland Institute College of Art in Baltimore.

"I generally don't play that up too much because it doesn't let me claim to be a real folk artist," Supreme said absent-mindedly after warning me of a wicked dogleg coming up on the next hole.

MICA may have been a traditional school, but there was never a chance his life in Baltimore would be routine. He moved with a bunch of friends into an eight-bedroom house—"it was a bit of a collective"—and the abode quickly became the place to go for music, alcohol and "just over-the-top shit." They were all eventually kicked out of the house (go figure) and Supreme combed the streets looking for new places to rent.

"I'd call the places and tell them that I was working on set design or building design and had to build something for production, so I needed to rent their place for a couple weeks," he explained as he finished the 8th hole in two strokes to my six. "We'd spend the time getting ready for this big party, have the big party and then move on. It was sort of the prototype for hit-and-run raves before there were raves. We did that successfully for a while, then unsuccessfully when the fire department started shutting us down pretty regularly."

Scrambling for a new party place, Supreme and company ended up at a rock club that had sat vacant for months. He set up a bar, hired some bands and charged admission at the door. It was his most successful venture yet. "When the manager saw that I basically packed the place," Supreme recalled, "dollar signs went off in his head. I was able to broker a deal where I did bookings and promotions for the place. I was making a decent wage, just promoting all these shows. As a result, I was meeting a lot of people, shaking their hands…It was a great job."

Unfortunately, his time being one of Baltimore's premiere "vermin" didn't last particularly long. He squabbled over money with the club's manager. He broke his leg. A love affair went very badly. He lost his job because of the injured leg, which prevented him from working anywhere. He went out drinking with friends one night, eager to figure out a plan to get him out of Baltimore and into a new life somewhere else.

"They had cheap pitchers of beer, so at some point I announced that I was running for Mayor of Baltimore," he recalled, laughing. "It was really out of the blue, just me looking for something to do. And it became sort of my next project."

Some of us get drunk and maybe make an embarrassing call to an ex. Vermin Supreme gets drunk and becomes a politician. There was just one small problem. Actually, four if you add the fact that he had no political experience, no money and no connections: the next mayoral election was still a couple years down the road.

Meanwhile, he'd read an article in *Mother Jones* about the

Great Peace March for Global Disarmament. The movement's plan was to protest nuclear proliferation by getting 5,000 activists to walk from Los Angeles to Washington, D.C. in 1986. That plan collapsed just a few hundred miles into the march, when funding ran out and many of the 1,200 who had actually started the journey quit. Undaunted, several hundred marchers found enough money to keep the walk going, and by November they reached Washington and celebrated with a final ceremony at the Lincoln Memorial.

It was strange hearing Vermin Supreme talk about the '80s and nuclear weapons protests. He might as well have been your drunken uncle complaining about the "Red Menace" over Thanksgiving dinner. Communism stopped being our national *Great White Whale* a few decades ago, and the fact that we'd gotten into more than one war to stop it seemed more like a fable than reality. The occasional Vladimir Putin outburst notwithstanding, it's often hard to believe there was a time not that long ago when people truly feared that the Soviet Union and the United States would get into some kind of global pissing match, unleashing warheads that would destroy us all.

I had just started my reporting career in Seattle at the time, and I covered the kerfuffles that frequently ensued when communities voted to make themselves "Nuclear Free Zones." I'm not saying this wasn't a worthy cause. It's just that, given all the economic and social crises since then, the idea of establishing a nuclear free zone in this day and age has about the same urgency as making sure you take down the Christmas lights. This isn't a crisis that will make most Top 10 lists.

"I guess I liked the issue," Supreme told me as his golf ball dinged against a post and put him another shot under par. "But there was also this amazing sense of all these people motivated to do that walk. So I went to the thrift store, got some fresh clothes and a sleeping bag, and walked to D.C.

to meet up with them. I wanted to be in on it. We were trying to make this political statement about waking people up."

He instantly bonded with some of the marchers, and when a handful of them decided to keep the protest going by forming a new splinter group called Seeds of Peace, Supreme signed on. With a kitchen trailer, a port-a-potty and a water truck, they trekked to Cape Canaveral in Florida to protest the nuclear submarines that had been docked there. Protesting became his life and he would travel wherever marchers gathered. In 1987, Supreme went on a peace walk through Michigan and noticed a woman in the crowd.

"I thought, 'Oh, she looks nice,' and I wanted to meet her. She was a teacher at the time. I was on my way to New England, where another march was in progress. I said, 'I gotta go.' She offered me a ride and we've been together ever since."

Over the next several months, Supreme and Becky wandered from protest to protest. They slept wherever they could and went dumpster diving for their food. They eventually made it to Boston, where Supreme supported himself and Becky by doing human lab testing for money. He volunteered to take experimental anti-depressants. He did drunk driving simulations where "you'd guzzle a pitcher of screwdrivers, then pretend to drive in a video game." He participated in sleep disorder studies. And with the money, he returned to Baltimore to make good on his promise to run for mayor.

He and Becky moved back to Charm City, where they printed up posters with slogans like—"Vermin Supreme as your mayor. Demand a recount!" This was also when he developed one of the key platforms for all of his future presidential campaigns: government-mandated tooth brushing. Inspired by states that required people to wear seat belts, and concerned about the gradual eroding of personal freedoms, Supreme decided "what could be more absurd than a phrase like, 'Brush your teeth! It's the law!'" Thus was born the notion of secret dental police monitoring our bathrooms every night to ensure plaque and gingivitis would not destroy this great nation.

The mayoral campaign failed, to the surprise of nobody. The toothbrush message, however, seemed to stick—and it was particularly popular in Russia. Supreme and Becky started traveling the world as part of the Rainbow Family, a loose organization of peace protestors. At one point, Supreme carried around a giant toothbrush, once even leading a parade of musicians and toothbrush-toting protestors wearing gorilla masks into Red Square to scrub Lenin's molars.

"When we'd travel, I made a point of having certain phrases translated into the local language," Supreme recalled. "I'd say something to the effect of, 'I do not speak your language. I am a lunatic. I am with the secret dental police. Brush your teeth or you will be arrested.'" (I made a note to use his bathroom at some point, just to make sure there were plenty of toothbrushes in there. But when I excused myself to use the facilities later, the only bathroom I found was a tree out back.)

The afternoon sun high in the sky, Supreme and I lined up our next putts. His ball clanged against the 16th pipe, once again cashing in on his home course advantage, while mine skipped over a tree stump and into some primordial ooze from which extraction was impossible. Game over.

We walked back to Supreme's house as he reminisced about his evolution into a presidential candidate. After failing to become Baltimore's mayor, he ran a few other attention-getting campaigns: Mayor of the Eastern Seaboard, Mayor of the Lower 48, Emperor of the Universe. Before the 1992 elections, Supreme and Becky had moved to their Rockport home, leaving the experienced candidate a mere pollster's throw from New Hampshire, location of the nation's first primaries every four years. And so began the Vermin political dynasty.

His first presidential runs were modest—consisting of him driving the few miles north every fourth January with a bullhorn in his hand and a rubber boot on his head. (He'd put one on his head to stay dry during a storm at a Rainbow gathering and found the look became him.) Slowly, though, Supreme's campaigns for the White House actually gathered speed—like in 2004, when he got his name on the District of Columbia presidential primary ballot.

"It was the first time I was in a format where people could easily vote for me," he recalled. "Seeing the words 'Vermin' and 'Supreme' together with all the other candidate names was special, in that people who didn't know me or know the shtick could vote for me."

Unfortunately, that was also the year that a postal error kept most D.C. voters from receiving their voter pamphlets until *after* the primary election. Hence, most eligible voters never knew about the toothbrush police, Supreme's offer of free ponies to all citizens and his recommendation to harness zombie power for good instead of evil.

His 2008 campaign didn't last beyond the New Hampshire primary either. It *did*, however, garner a little national press when he crossed paths with some of the more prominent candidates. For instance, when he showed up at the New Hampshire state capitol to pay his $1,000 filing fee, he saw the parade of news crews shadowing Hillary Clinton. So it was perfectly natural for him to ask her if she supported waterboarding of school children. When Clinton didn't respond, a reporter for the *Salem Observer* newspaper used that anecdote in his story about how Hillary Clinton doesn't answer questions.

Supreme's run-in with John McCain went slightly better. Both men were walking down the same New Hampshire hallway when Vermin asked the Arizona senator for his opinion of the mandatory toothbrushing law.

"He told me, 'As a matter of fact, I have my staff hiding in people's bathrooms late at night, making sure people brush.' He immediately grasped what I was doing and hit a home run. It was all about surveillance, about the government hiding in our homes—and he got that!"

Supreme's approach to his campaign was definitely the opposite of the other candidates I'd visited. They wanted desperately to be taken seriously. The day he's taken seriously, though, is the day his presidential runs become a moot point. There was that scare in 2011, when he came perilously close to legitimacy. He'd developed enough of a following to earn an invite to The Lesser Known Candidates Debate. This event is sponsored by the New Hampshire Institute of Politics and it's Valhalla for any fringe candidate hoping to stage a campaign. For Vermin Supreme, it's just another stage.

The night before the debate, he learned that he'd be sitting next to infamous anti-abortionist Randall Terry, who is probably best known for creating the group Operation Rescue. Supreme's first thought was to liven up the evening by nailing Terry with water from a penis-shaped squirt gun. Then he remembered hearing about protestors pelting serious Republican candidates like Newt Gingrich and Michelle Bachman with piles of glitter. A new plan was formed.

"I went out to the craft shack and filled my pockets with glitter, then—*bingo bango bongo*—I waited for the most opportune moment in the debate. I knew that I was going to end with a chicken dance. But in the moment, I just got up and hit him with the glitter, while telling everyone that Jesus told me to turn Randall Terry gay."

Video of the incident went viral. Before he knew it, Vermin Supreme was so popular on the Internet that the massive upgrade in visibility meant he had to now "wonder what my responsibility is as a *de facto* leader of discontent." It's odd to think that a man who promises ponies and wears a boot on his head has any political power. Slowly and surely, though, Supreme seems to be acquiring enough of it to warrant thinking about finding money for a real campaign.

"There are more expectations now, but because I'm not in it to win it, because I win just by doing it, it doesn't matter," he said, briefly distracted by the sound of someone who'd just entered through the back door. "I've done what I had to do. Point out the absurdity of the system? Check, done. Create an alternative? Check, done. I'm always about making this bigger, better, more of a spectacle. And I have a few tricks up my sleeve with the right level of [financial) support. I told you I'm going for federal matching funds, right?"

This is the $250 per contributor the government will offer official party candidates who have already raised more than $5,000 in at least 20 different states. He hadn't mentioned this at all. I was about to point out that fact when Supreme turned to face the petite, energetic, bespectacled woman who had just entered the room.

"Becky, tell him what you think of me trying to raise the federal matching funds."

This was Mrs. Supreme, who politely shook my hand and smiled broadly as she happily explained, "I have no comment."

"She disagrees with me," said Vermin, while smiling at Becky. "She doesn't want me begging for money."

"Whatever you say, honey! Forget that. I hate that!" She gave her husband a wry smile. This was clearly one of those "never go to bed angry" couples.

"I think [public financing] is there to open the universe up so people can throw money at me."

I could hear more voices chatting outside. While Supreme went out to investigate, I asked Becky if she'd mind talking to me a little about her husband.

"I don't usually talk to people," she explained with the sweetest smile ever used to shut me down.

Supreme apparently was still within earshot, because he shouted, "I can see it now—'Vermin's wife clearly, *clearly* despises him!'"

Becky just kept smiling. She did agree to sit down and chat for a few minutes, but she continued to be the toughest interview of my trip. She confirmed they met at the peace march in Michigan, when she saw him cutting up six-pack rings for environmentally correct disposal. And she admitted that she fell for him as instantly as he fell for her. Beyond that, I had a better chance of drawing military secrets out of her husband than I did of getting a good quote out of her. That's probably why I felt relieved when her phone rang and she left the room to take the call.

"Matt and Jimmy are outside. You should go talk to them," she told me as she exited.

I wandered out near the trail Supreme and I had walked in on. He was there with two men and a woman, all about his age. Matt was the heavier of the two, Jimmy the slighter fellow with a New England accent so thick he could have passed as an extra in a Gorton's fish stick commercial. The middle-aged woman had the disapproving demeanor of a DMV employee as she looked at the guys. They all gathered around the remains of what probably used to be a desk, solo cups of unnamed booze in hand. It felt like I'd wandered into an episode of *Cheers*—if *Cheers* was set outdoors, and the patrons were all in their 50s and didn't own suits and ties. Supreme introduced me to the gang and Jimmy didn't hesitate to launch right in.

"We've all known Vermin since we were all 15 years old. He

was cool, always a hippie at heart. He was the guy a lot of people wanted to run for president of his class back in high school."

"I've only known him 10 years," Kim said, stepping on Jimmy's words.

"Matt! What amazes us about Vermin?" muttered Jimmy.

"He had that beard in the fifth grade," explained Matt. "It started in early puberty."

Jimmy stepped in again, clearly the loudmouth of the group.

"Look at him! He looks like a fuckin' chipmunk! And it took me five years to call him by that new name, Vermin Supreme. But it rolls off the tongue very well. Verrrrrmmiiiiiinnnnn! It was very easy to make that transition to the name."

"It wasn't for me," said Matt, sipping from his cup. "For years, I called him by his given name. Did he tell you he used to be called Vermina?"

"If you've got a better candidate, I'd like to fuckin' see him," Jimmy said. "There ain't one out there, because it's all fuckin' bullshit!"

"Lies for less," added Kim. "That's my favorite line of his. 'I'm gonna give you lies for less!'"

The longer the conversation, the more Jimmy got worked up about his friend's presidential ambitions.

"Vermin says what people don't want to say. It's like the purple elephant in your living room. Our process is so stuffy and fucked up. It's all about money. His best work is in New Hampshire. You haven't seen the real Vermin until you've seen him working the crowds up there."

"Remember when we went to that John McCain victory party, when he won the New Hampshire primary?" Kim asked nobody in particular. "We walk in and there's a bar. A cash bar!"

"First of all, it's the swankiest hotel you can imagine in Nashua," interjected Jimmy. "They're carving meat! It's a regular political meet-and-greet!"

Talk of food and parties now had the group revved up, fondly recalling the appetizers, the roast beef and "all the typical Republican pretty blonde white girls" Jimmy noticed filling the room. Kim jumped back in.

"Remember when Vermin did that Khrushchev 'We Will Bury You!' thing with his boot in slow motion!"

"You really have to see him stump in New Hampshire," Jimmy said, stepping on her words.

"*Hello?* Can I finish my story?" Kim shot back, engaging Jimmy in a debate about how they're not married, but people (like me) assume they are, given the way they behave around each other.

This was clearly a conversation that had played out in this same location on several other occasions, with no consensus ever emerging. Perhaps it was for the best that Supreme came over to tell me he had to go. Ever since his mom had a kidney transplant, he's spent all his evenings checking in on her. This was important for a variety of reasons, not the least of which was the kidney keeping her alive once belonged to him.

As Matt gave Vermin and me a lift to the road where I'd left my car, the only noise came from the clattering of tires bumping along an unpaved path in the woods. I was busy digesting the fact that Vermin Supreme had totally buried the lead. It's easy enough to imagine a candidate donating his/her kidney to a family member—but not alerting CNN and *People* magazine to milk the sympathy vote? That's crazy talk.

Up until this point, I'd totally enjoyed the sitcom that was Supreme's political career. He was Yoda to Syds Buttocks' Luke Skywalker, the sort of sage, yet sarcastic, advisor who could teach the Syd committee how things actually work. However, after discovering a few small details—the coffee stain and his kidney donation—it was clear the Supreme campaign ran far deeper and more serious than he usually let on.

Just as I'd found something unexpectedly sincere with Rev. Pinkney Butts and oddly inspirational with Josh Usera, Supreme's approach to the presidential race was more human and relatable than I ever imagined. While he certainly had a sense of humor, his campaign was no more or less a laughing matter than, say, Ted Cruz's. (Only without the vitriol and racism.) As we exited Matt's car and walked over to mine, I had to ask one last thing: What challenge would Vermin Supreme like to issue to his mainstream rivals?

Without a hesitation or grin, he explained: "The kidney challenge. If you have two kidneys, I challenge you to give one of them up to an individual who needs it. Right now as we speak, tens of thousands of Americans are slowly dying because their kidney has gone bad. You could live on one. I live on one. You regain 90% of your function after the first year. Sure it could be a little scary, but don't be a chicken."

I turned to Supreme with my best Scooby Doo "*zoinks!*" look of surprise, not sure what to make of how our discussion of presidential satire had taken a serious turn at the end. He must have sensed the shock, assumed it was discomfort and did what came naturally—he made things easier by returning to levity.

With a rooster cluck, he blurted out, "C'mon, everyone! What are you, a chicken? Give up a kidney!"

It felt like watching Will Ferrell in *Anchorman* for 90 minutes, but Ron Burgundy goes into rehab and does an anti-drinking PSA. Perhaps I was making too much of the fact that this man who'd devoted his life to lampooning life had literally given up a part of himself to give someone else life. On the other hand, I'd met yet another presidential candidate who wasn't as he at first appeared. Bart Lower was the conservative-looking guy with surprisingly liberal positions. Josh Usera was the tough guy who had tender, familial reasons for his campaign. Vermin Supreme was the social satirist who, at the end of the day, was a mama's boy in the best sense of the term.

Would he actually *want* to be president? He laughed louder than he had all day.

"Look at my life. What could be better than the life that I live? Financial security? That's nice, but I have always been well-respected in my field. And when my obit hits, people are going to say—'Oh, bummer!'"

I said goodbye and headed off for the next interview, turning on the radio to get a quick roundup of the day's news: five international banks had been fined $5.4 billion for currency manipulation; President Obama continued to beat the drum for stopping climate change; an oil spill covered nine square miles of California coastline; ISIS made new inroads in Syria.

Depressed by all the bad news, I searched the dial for anything else to listen to. I finally happened upon yet another conservative local talk show host—or, as I'm sure he's known in hell, "Boss." He and a female guest were going after Mexican immigrants as if *they* were the primary reason America was in serious trouble. I quickly switched to a station that was playing Metallica, which was actually more soothing for my psyche than whoever it was I'd just been listening to.

I'm not saying immigration isn't a problem, but talk about not seeing the forest for the lumberjacks. These two hapless hosts seemed fine with finding emotional issues to sidetrack serious discussion of *actual* issues. And they say a guy promoting peace and ponies with a boot on his head is the clueless one...

Deonia "Dee" Neveu

A week before I started my electoral expedition, my younger brother in Seattle called to wish me good luck on the trip. Toward the end of our conversation, I could tell in his voice how envious he was that I was about to get in a car, drive across the country on my own, sleep in places where I didn't have to make my bed and eat what I wanted, when I wanted.

I totally understood his attitude. While my main memory of our cross-country family treks involved headaches from pipe smoke, there was still something charmingly all-American about them. It's that whole "Born to Be Wild," Jack Kerouac, *National Lampoon's Vacation*, Ram truck commercial notion that there's something liberating and soul enriching about being behind the wheel with no particular timeline holding you down. Two weeks of Wendy's salads and Motel 6 showers, however, and I was starting to reassess that notion.

Let's just say that after nearly 5,000 miles and a couple dozen cans of Kickstart, any romance of the open road was waning. It had become more like that regrettable fling who seemed really hot around closing time, but after a couple of dates where she continually grabbed food off your plate—while complaining about trying to lose weight—you'd had enough. I was right at that tipping point the morning I headed out to Chicopee, Massachusetts to meet up with housewife-turned-presidential-candidate Deonia "Dee" Neveu.

First, I'd used my AARP discount on the room, prompting the night desk guy to assume I was even older than I am. So he stuck me in a handicapped-accessible room, complete with assisted living shower seat. Then I woke up to find a tick crawling in that bathtub—*and another just settling into my left armpit!* Finally —and quite possibly most disturbing—the room phone rang just as I was getting ready to head out. This hadn't happened once during my two weeks on the road, largely because nobody knew where I was staying. I couldn't resist this element of mystery, so I answered it. A cigarette-soaked voice (3:2 odds it was female) asked me, "Do you need room service?"

I explained that I was fine and would be checking out momentarily.

So the voice croaked, "Do you need any condoms?"

Admittedly, it had been a *very* long time since I'd had sex. Mostly by choice. But even a born-again virgin such as myself understood what was *really* being suggested here. It's not unlike going to a sold-out sporting event and having suspicious-looking characters ask if you had any tickets to sell. We all know that really means they're the ones *selling* tickets. I offered a "thanks, but no thanks" that, given the circumstances, was probably far more polite than it should have been. (Then again, I'm the guy who once got an obscene phone call from a man who explained all sorts of things he wanted to do with/to me, and when I said it was not my thing, we ended up having a 10-minute conversation about the Chicago Cubs.)

"Okay, have a good night then," said the oblivious Demi Moore impersonator before hanging up.

During the ensuing 45-minute drive to meet Neveu and her family, two questions nagged at me. First, what kind of person would actually say yes to an offer like that at 10 a.m. on a Saturday morning at a Motel 6 in Hartford, Connecticut? And second, would that voice on the phone also have given me the AARP discount if I'd asked? Eventually, though, I had to focus on my concern about meeting up with Neveu.

This was her second run for the presidency, having also given it a go in 2012. And while talking to her wasn't like talking to a high school civics teacher, she was definitely the most serious of all my Can't-idates. Not necessarily humorless, but someone who was devoutly dedicated to the principle that any of us could grow up to be—or at least *run for*—president. She was active on YouTube, making videos with titles like: "I Want to Give You the White House Keys." There was no messing around with Dee Neveu, and I was happy to connect with someone who understood my project instantly and completely.

I appreciated her intense interest in *The Can't-idates*, but I'd also sensed some tension developing between us over the past few days. She'd been checking out our *Can't-idates* Facebook page to watch the quickie campaign videos I'd shot of everyone. These were never intended to be professional commercials—just Shreffler, Emrit, et al. speaking extemporaneously about their political ambitions.

Neveu emailed me to express concern that these videos seemed to be mocking, rather than legitimizing, everyone. It was a sensitive subject because, while I was trying to let these Can't-idates be themselves, they were anything but smooth talkers on camera, which I knew could be seen as a cruel joke. I was worried she was going to cancel on me. She was the best example so far of a "normal" person with no political background who just wanted to help the country by being its president.

So I took it on faith that all would be well when I pulled up at the yellow tract home underneath a long line of huge electrical transformers in Chicopee, Massachusetts. Neveu, her husband Richard and their daughter Rileyann live in Richmond, Virginia. But, because it was Memorial Day weekend, they'd made their annual 500-mile pilgrimage to see Richard's mother, Dorothy. When Neveu met me at her mother-in-law's front door, it was clear that all would be fine.

It was no surprise that she was ready to take this interview seriously. She'd put on what I assumed was one of her finest going-to-church dresses, a purple outfit that matched the hair ties she'd used to hold the long black locks atop her head. Her thick glasses and helpful smile made her seem librarian-esque. Talking to her had the same sweet, guile-free feel as talking to my mom—if my mom was a 55-year-old African-American presidential candidate.

Neveu politely welcomed me in, clutching a sheet of paper she'd scrawled all over. Even though we wouldn't be doing her Facebook video until the end of our afternoon together, she was already prepared for it.

"I wrote my notes," she explained, "because you know when you do an interview, you don't know how you are going to feel, or what you are going to remember—and you don't want to miss saying what you are going to say. So I wrote what I wanted to say. After I saw the first couple [videos] on your page, they seemed empty. So I prepared."

She introduced me to Dorothy, an equally sweet elderly woman who also seemed to have spent significant time that morning making herself look as presidential as possible. We walked into a back bedroom, where I could hear a young girl squealing. Inside the room, a man in khakis and white polo shirt stood over a computer, as a toothpick-thin girl with long hair and glasses continued to squeal while typing on the keyboard.

This was Richard and Rileyann. They each provided a major complication in Neveu's life, and I was curious about how she handled them. Richard was Caucasian and nine-year-old Riley suffered from autism. I'm not saying that a mixed-race marriage and raising a kid with developmental disabilities are burdens. These situations just don't necessarily make life easier.

Seeing Rileyann fidget and fuss, my mind drifted back to when my son was in the fifth grade. He was having his share of social issues and not mixing well with others at school. His doctor sensed he was depressed. Based on all this, we went to a series of specialists to check and see if there might be some form of autism going on. I barely slept for two weeks, worrying about the diagnosis.

We were sort of damned if it was Asperger Syndrome, because it meant a lot of adjustment ahead—and damned if it *wasn't*, because it meant he was feeling the aftereffects of his parents getting divorced. Any way it landed, I'd feel responsible since it was either my genes or my decision to end a marriage that had messed up my boy. Thankfully, things weren't quite as dire as I'd assumed, as all the tests indicated he was fine. He started doing some social therapy at school and seeing a therapist to talk about the divorce. Eventually he didn't even remember going through all this. The only one clinging to that fear of discovering I might have an autistic child was me, which gave me the extra interest in Neveu and her family.

"Sorry...her computer screen shut down, so we have to wait for it to restart," Richard explained as he put an arm around his increasingly agitated daughter, trying to calm her down.

"She didn't get much sleep either," his wife added, "because we traveled late. It doesn't help her little attitude, but she does good [on] long drives."

It has been a significant week for the Neveus. "The other day she told me, 'Mommy, please help me!' That's the first time she's said 'Mommy!' Usually she'll just say, 'Help me, please.' That got my attention, that's for sure! There was a time where she didn't have any words, where she would just pull you to what she wanted to talk about."

This wasn't how they pictured parenthood going. When their daughter was not even a year old, Richard began to notice quirks in her behavior. While other kids would see planes in the sky and point them out, Rileyann tended to stay in her own world. By the time she was two, her family was having her see specialists. On her fourth birthday, she was officially diagnosed as autistic.

"She's kind of middle-of-the-road—it's not Asperger Syndrome and it's not the non-verbal, unable to be potty-trained stuff," Richard told me. "We feel blessed for what we have. If you spend your life comparing your kid to someone who is normally developing, you're going to be miserable."

Good advice, and yet...that's precisely the opposite of what I was doing. I could see the exhaustion and stress in each line on Richard and Dee's faces. I involuntarily sighed a silent "thank you," knowing I had two healthy kids back home. Neveu walked me into the living room, and as we settled in I mentioned that I had hoped to connect with a friend in Boston whose teenage daughter also suffered from autism. He'd spent years dealing with a school system that never fully understood how to help her.

"Each state is different, the districts and everything," she explained. "Richard says if he's First Man he's going to work on that...special needs, autism, other things like that. He's really into it. That'd be his First Man responsibility for the country."

Although she insisted her daughter's condition ultimately hadn't played into her desire to become president, she had admitted on the phone that she "never paid much attention to politics" until Rileyann was diagnosed. After a lifetime of working as everything from a singer to a typist, staying home to care for her daughter gave her time to pick up newspapers and surf the Internet. Suddenly, the downfall of the United States "was right in front of me." Being someone who considers herself a responsible person, she felt she had no choice but to take charge.

"I care. I try to be helpful. I'm not always appreciated, but I care. Sometimes too much," she said, delivering her words in the sort of deliberate, precise manner of a high school speech teacher. "And that makes me think, 'My goodness! I'd like to help my country!' So looking at life, not just my life but also the lives of others, I'm going, 'There is something wrong with this. It is time to shout out—we need to talk about this and get this awareness. Get people focused. People who are asleep, wake up, look, listen! Be pro-active about your government.'"

That was the sort of thing you'd expect to hear from guys who call into AM radio talk shows or drifters about to sneak into Area 51. It's not what you'd expect from a well-dressed, middle-class woman who grew up convinced only wealthy white men ran for office, so why bother? Politics was a foreign language to her, other than voting straight Democratic when she'd go to the polls because her African-American family taught her "that is what we do." Until now.

"I'll tell people, 'By the way, I'm doing something crazy—I'm running for president.' And they say, 'Good for you! We need that!' We talk more about it after that, and I tell people, 'I actually do think it's crazy to do this too, because you don't get anywhere.' And they're like, 'No, no!' Then they say, 'Everybody has to start somewhere.' People are good like that, even though I hardly know them."

She likes to think of herself as a real "people person." In my experience, people who say that are usually more like "people who want attention from other people" persons. But Neveu seemed genuine in her desire to help everyone with everything. It's been that way pretty much since her mom (a secretary) and dad (a singer with the late '50s doo wop group, The Ladders) split when Neveu was still very young. She spent a lot of time the next several years hanging out with her grandparents in their Harlem housing project.

It was an experience she enjoyed because "in a project, everybody knows everybody. From building to building, it's a community. Even still to this day, they get together every year, and all the generations of us know each other."

Her grandparents were originally from the South and free with their "y'alls" and old-home hospitality. Neveu was particularly fond of her grandma—"my favorite lady...I was raised holding onto her skirt"—so she quickly and happily adopted Southern-speak. Unfortunately, Neveu's mom wasn't pleased.

"I think she was embarrassed by it a little bit and wanted to shy away from it. I used to say *'sault'* for the word *'salt,'* and she'd drill me...'It's not *sault*, it's *salt*. Say 'salt.'"

Growing up poor inspired her mom to make sure Neveu and her younger brothers led better lives. She worked constantly—at a hospital, as a dietician, eventually as an executive secretary and stenographer—and began to make decent money, eventually buying a brownstone in the Bedford-Stuyvesant neighborhood of Brooklyn. The positive: Neveu grew up never wanting for anything. The negative: her mom wasn't around as much as she would have liked, to the point where Neveu remembers getting more nurturing from her grandma (whom she called "Mom") than her mother (whom she called by her nickname, "Bobby").

Bobby was a very protective sort of parent, having her kids go straight to, and straight home from, school. No hanging out with friends. No snacks at the donut shop along the way.

Dinner was to be on the table when Mom got home from work. And because she had a background as a dietician, there were rules, such as eating liver once-a-week and never drinking chocolate milk—although molasses in milk was allowed as a substitute. When dinner was served, Neveu and her younger brothers would eat at the table while their mother went off to eat alone.

"I guess that was her time for her. Now, as an adult, I can understand. She was working very, very hard to make sure that we lived a wealthy kind of lifestyle," Neveu mused quietly, making her comment seem like it was intended to be an *interior* thought. "She is a very, very responsible lady, who always made sure that we had everything we needed. People can come out of good families and come out bad, and people can come out of bad families and wind up good. After a while, you become your own person. Your own experiences become you, despite what you were raised with. Sometimes people just forget whether it was good or bad, and they have their own experiences as they become older in life, and take it from there. So I have seen both worlds, in a sense."

I wasn't sure what to make of this cryptic statement, except to assume that Neveu and her mom (who remarried and moved to Barbados) were not particularly close. Neveu did admit that despite living in relative affluence, she didn't exactly enjoy her teen years the way her mom hoped she would. At school she was picked on for being too skinny, for wearing glasses (she should have discovered Denny McLain) and for "not being black enough."

"I hate to say this, but I always tell people that I have never really, really experienced prejudice," she explained. "People don't like it, but it's the truth. There was a time that I hated the color of my skin, because I wasn't dark enough. I wanted to get darker. I took Hawaiian Tropic, slathered myself all over with it, and got out aluminum foil and laid out in the sun with it."

Even her musical tastes knew no racial boundaries.

Singing was in her blood, courtesy of her father, so she'd spend evenings belting tunes into her hairbrush or lying in bed with her little transistor radio grooving to everyone from James Brown, to Michael Jackson, to Tom Jones, to the Partridge Family. She loved it all, but that wasn't a politically correct thing to do. Friends and family regularly scolded her, especially when she'd visit Harlem and put on a Caucasian artist like the Bee Gees.

"My cousin would say, 'No, no, no! You're not going to play any white music here!' I was like, 'What? This is great music! What are you talking about?'"

Neveu could belt out a prototypical Caucasian anthem like "You Light Up My Life" without a second thought. She was all set to make it as a mainstream songstress when that dream was delayed, courtesy of her marriage to—and the child she had with—a high school boyfriend. Instead of a life spent hanging out in recording studios and concert halls, she was running to secretarial classes while her grandmother babysat her young daughter.

It would have been easy to resent either her husband (with whom she split a year after the wedding) or her child, but she "never felt my kid took anything away from me. I was still able to go to the clubs and parties." She managed to find work in an office typing pool in Manhattan and started to look for bands to sing with in her spare time.

Whether it was sending homemade audition tapes to the Apollo Theater or Oprah Winfrey, or showing up at open mic nights at clubs around Manhattan, Neveu was always hustling to get noticed. But nothing clicked, even after her dad came to listen and told her "that I wasn't singing the right songs." She started working with a vocal coach who got her singing in a higher range than she had before. That didn't feel entirely comfortable, but Neveu was so eager to make it, she went ahead with the plan. It was a decision she'd eventually regret, when she developed vocal polyps. Combine that with the fact she was approaching 30 and it became pretty clear that it was time to change the trajectory of her life.

"I wish I'd had a lot more family support," she said with a sigh that was interrupted by the arrival of Richard's brother, Bob, who walked in the house clutching bags of carryout food. He apologized for the intrusion before wandering off toward the kitchen.

"My mom never paid me any mind, because she was working hard. I guess she looked at me as a kid. And my dad, he got a job as a school security guard, and we didn't have a relationship until I was 17 or 18. So I was fending for myself, learning the world of music."

Well, not *entirely* by herself. She'd remarried and had a son with her second husband. It was time to grow up, so she settled into attending Queens College, then Ramapo College in New Jersey to study education and psychology. The adjustment to adult responsibility wasn't easy.

In particular, there was a second divorce that left her devastated and alone yet again. Her second husband had decided "he wanted to move on, and I was left in a situation that I had to deal with, living from paycheck to paycheck. I cried a lot. People would ask how I was and I'd say, 'Just terrible today!'"

The worst part was how alone she felt, away from the Harlem family and friends she'd hang out with. Once she moved to New Jersey with husband number two, she'd essentially handed her life over to him. They made "couple friends" together, but as soon as the marriage ended, so too did those relationships.

I was surprised to hear her say that, mainly because I thought the whole "couple friend" phenomenon was a guy thing. A month or so after I'd separated from my wife, I remember going to a fundraiser at our kids' elementary school. By this point, word of my impending divorce had become public knowledge, so the moms mostly avoided me—while the dads pulled me aside out on the playground to grill me about how many women I'd already slept with. (Zero, for those keeping score at home.) This wasn't conversation I particularly enjoyed, but I went home that night feeling like I had friends who'd hang out with me as I transitioned back into the single life.

Not so much. I saw some of those guys some of the time, but it turns out even your closest acquaintances view divorce like it's a communicable disease. People who might normally hang out with you for a drink or two suddenly have plans when you call about getting together. If they run into you on the street, their happiness at seeing you quickly gives way to nervousness about seeing you for too long. Ultimately, I'm sure it's not this simple—and maybe I was being a bit too paranoid. But self-confidence isn't exactly a boom market in the months after a marriage ends, so it felt like everyone was simply afraid they'd catch a bad case of divorce.

My solution was staying home, swilling inexpensive scotch and watching *When Harry Met Sally* every night for weeks. Neveu's was somewhat more practical. A roller skating club opened up near her home, and the music she'd hear thumping from inside reminded her of the discotheques where she loved hanging out back in Manhattan. One night she decided to stop by, even though she had no idea how to roller skate.

Neveu began spending more time there, clinging to the railing until a man came over one night to say, "You look like you need a friend." While she really could have used a pal, this guy didn't seem to be it. Still, the more she visited the club, the more he persisted in asking her out. Eventually, she'd made enough friends there that it seemed safe enough to go on a date—which led to her third marriage, and, eventually, twins. Neveu started to regain her confidence. At one point she even launched her own temp agency back in Harlem. Unfortunately, like marriage number three, the business didn't last. (Being divorced, I was interested in delving further into the topic. But the hesitant way Neveu mentioned those previous marriages made it clear details wouldn't be forthcoming.)

The single mother of four was now in her 40s and "beginning to be the jack-of-all-trades, never mastering any. Yet I had all of this knowledge, which no amount of money can buy you, whether it be negative or positive."

All that was missing in her life was a way to channel that knowledge. Her opportunity emerged in 2008, when Barack Obama and Hillary Clinton become the leading Democratic contenders for president, giving her the first real taste of political desire.

"We had people running that we hadn't seen before," she recalled thinking at the time. "It wasn't the average white male candidate who had always been running before."

She even felt inspired by Sarah Palin, whom Neveu saw as the perfect example of "a regular person who could run for office." So, instead of just voting and forgetting about it until the next election, she began to realize "somebody is making these decisions, so maybe we should pay a little bit more attention."

It became much easier for her to do that after Rileyann's condition was diagnosed. Neveu spent her days at home instead of an office, and that allowed her to examine politics in a way she never cared to before.

"I studied and read and read and read for a whole year, until I needed thicker glasses. I needed a new prescription because I read my eyes out. I read about politics, about all of the presidents and about congress people."

Two historical figures inspired her. One was Shirley Chisholm, the first African-American woman ever elected to Congress. She was originally from Brooklyn and the more Neveu read about her, the more she recalled her mom telling her to admire Chisholm when the congresswoman ran for president in 1972.

"[Chisholm] said she ran because she wanted people, even ordinary people, to dare to do this," Neveu said.

The discovery of Chisholm then led her to read about Victoria Woodhull, the leader in the women's suffragette movement of the late 1800s and the first female to run for U.S. president. These women got her thinking about public service for the first time in her life. Once that happened, all Neveu needed was someone who supported her political ambition.

She figured that wouldn't be the family she grew up with, since she never felt they totally backed her past endeavors. Richard was her one hope. So after months of reading and blogging on political websites, she floated the idea of a presidential run to him. At first he wasn't sure what to make of it. From the moment the corporate financial analyst had met his future wife at a Catholic singles group in Richmond, they were about as likely to talk politics as they were, say, the implications of String Theory.

Up to this point in the day Richard had stayed with Rileyann, rather than come out and talk to me. He played with his daughter in the bedroom. He took her out for a walk. He took her to the kitchen for something to eat. Every few minutes, Rileyann would pop her head out to see her mother, but Richard always emerged to apologize for the distraction and take her elsewhere.

After I asked Dee if it was possible to get a few minutes alone with her husband, Richard walked in with Rileyann literally clinging to him. He tried to start a conversation with me, but his daughter began squealing and refused to leave his side. Hearing the fuss, Dee came back and volunteered to take Rileyann for a quick walk. The girl protested for a moment, not wanting to be separated from her daddy. But after some cajoling, mother and daughter left.

Once they'd departed, Richard explained that "when Dee and I met, conversations were all about her kids. And we both liked to travel, so we focused a lot on that. Then I think she just told me [about running for president] one evening. I thought, 'You know what? That's kind of strange.' I thought maybe she should run for a local office; start small and build your way up the way most people do. But she said, 'I have no real interest in anything but *that* office, because it's the only office where I could really affect the people I want to affect."

Shooting for the moon like that seemed quite logical to Neveu, but pragmatic Richard still tried to talk his wife out of her plan—especially when she wanted to spend $5,000 of their money on her 2012 campaign.

"I'm very frugal and I think of $5,000 as ten car payments. But I guess what it is is she's my wife and I love her, and I want to support her. Even if it's ridiculously low odds of something happening, you still want to be there for your partner. And she's passionate about this. It does give her a sense of purpose."

That's why he's occasionally awakened to see her in front of the computer at 2 a.m., sharing her views on Facebook about various social issues such as abortion and gay marriage ("We have to learn to co-exist with our differences, with respect") and illegal immigration. ("It makes no sense to send them back to places they don't even know anymore…that's not right.") If any of her thousand or so contacts have a question for her, Neveu is waiting there to answer as quickly as possible.

Richard talked about his wife's ideas and ambitions with the same sort of reserved reverence parents use to describe their child's finger-painted self-portraits. There was genuine pride there, but it was a pride outsiders most likely could not fully see or appreciate. I never met any of Dee Neveu's previous three husbands

—she was very careful to avoid giving me their names—but as I sat there listening to Richard, his serenity made me feel glad that these two had found each other. It's pretty safe to assume her ambitions wouldn't take her to the White House. Nonetheless, the process of trying had clearly proven she'd found something she needed just as much—a man she was sure would always stand by her.

The front door swung open again, but instead of Dee and Rileyann, it was another one of Richard's siblings, sister Sandra. Dorothy reemerged from the back of the house, and as I watched the Neveu family greet each other, I felt like an intruder. Apparently their annual family Memorial Day picnic was under way—and I was the one thing keeping it from starting.

I got up and began thanking everyone for their hospitality. I'd wanted to have one last word with Dee, but there was no way of knowing exactly when she and Rileyann would be back. Richard offered to go find them, while Dorothy insisted that I share some of their lunch before I hit the road. She walked me into the kitchen, where Robert stood proudly by the food he'd brought earlier.

"You have to at least have some spaghetti," she told me, serving up a plateful without waiting for me to say no. "It's from our favorite place in town. It's really great! Oh, and you have to try the pie. We got it from the best bakery here."

I sat down at the kitchen table while Dorothy, Robert and Sandra watched me chew every bite. To be honest, the pasta quality was Boyardee-esque at best, but I didn't want to be a bad guest and criticize their favorite meal. So I shifted the conversation to Dee's quest, a plan that lasted all of about 30 seconds. They much preferred hearing tales of other people I'd interviewed, getting particular kicks out of my descriptions of the night at The Busted Shovel and my 10 minutes with Josh Usera's probation officer.

Before I could determine whether this reaction was amusement or simply relief that theirs wasn't the only family with a citizen candidate, Dee returned. I told her that it was time to hit the road, but it would be nice to get that video message from her first. Was she ready to tell voters why they should at least listen to what she has to say?

"No one starts this out thinking, 'I just want to be a voice,' and *my* initiative is to *win*," she insisted. "I mean, if you believe you have a great idea for this country and you love this country then, darn it, you're going to make people listen to you. It's going to come to this. Get to the finish line with whatever I have. I might be in 200th place, but getting to the finish line…that's what counts. It comes down to that. Keep trying and don't give up."

Neveu seemed more and more like the first Can't-idate I'd encountered who considered the quest to be as natural a part of our political process as voting itself.

"I've heard people say that they would vote for me if I was on the ballot," she told me. "I would tell them, 'Don't vote for me unless I *am* on the ballot, because I don't want you to waste your vote. If you know anybody on the ballot, and they are the lesser of two evils, go ahead and pick that one. But if you really don't care, if you throw away that voice and you are the type of person that will not go out and vote—and you don't like *anybody*—then write my name in. Please come out and at least write my name in.'"

Finally, it was time to get to what I'd been so nervous about: her Facebook video. She grabbed that handwritten speech I'd observed when I'd arrived, mouthing the words as she went over it in her head one more time. I got my phone ready and, after a few warnings to the Neveus in the kitchen to keep their volume down, she nervously began to read her speech. I was a bit surprised at how tentative she was, especially given a) how comfortable she'd been when we talked, and b) how concerned she was about the poor, unprofessional nature of the other campaign videos.

In her speech, she urged Democrats and Republicans to get in touch with party leaders and ask that outsiders (such as herself) be included in upcoming debates. I could appreciate her sentiment, but by the time she hit a minute and a half, there was no indication she was about to finish up, despite earlier assurances that she'd go no longer than the minute I was giving everyone. Even worse, my phone was so full of videos and photos that it kept shutting down.

For the next several minutes, I felt increasingly bad as I kept insisting Neveu trim her speech—and then trim it some more. I could tell she'd labored over every word, figuring our Facebook page for *The Can't-idates* may well be the biggest break her campaign had thus far received. All I kept thinking was—*If this goes over 60 seconds, nobody's going to watch.* We eventually made it through, and I made sure Neveu was happy with the final product before posting it.

I headed out for my car, feeling as awkward about these videos as I had felt when I'd arrived. Maybe Neveu had been right earlier about how unprofessional they were. They might actually be doing more harm than good, despite my efforts to keep them as straightforward as possible. They were definitely "unfiltered," as opposed to the mainstream candidates. Guys like Ben Carson and Bernie Sanders were scoring points with voters because they also spoke off the cuff. However, I find it hard to believe what they say hadn't been vetted through an advisor or two first. The Can't-idates just had me, my iPhone and 60 seconds.

As I drove to my next interview to see a boxer in Brooklyn, I was feeling guilty about how I might be doing precisely what I'd hoped to avoid—making everyone look like a joke. I really began to feel the weight of everyone's hopes and dreams. As if it wasn't bad enough that Harley Brown had already pinned his divine destiny on me.

I stopped for the night in Bridgeport, Connecticut. Eager to unload some of these burdens I'd decided to strap on my back, I did something I hadn't done for two weeks. I treated myself to a real dinner, walking a couple blocks from my motel to a Thai restaurant. As I waited for a table, I noticed an attractive middle-aged woman standing by the door, studying her cell phone intently, then using it to call someone. At the same time, a cell phone rang at the bar. A bearded, paunchy guy in a rumpled sport coat answered it. They both scanned the restaurant until their eyes met. They gave each other a slight wave.

She walked over to the bar to greet him and their awkward handshake-kiss made it clear—this was an online date about to happen. At first, they traded furtive glances to size each other up. Then it was just him looking at her, while she pulled her phone out every couple of minutes. It didn't take long for him to pick up on her lack of interest, so he began staring blankly at a basketball game on the big screen above the bar.

The woman excused herself and walked to the restroom. Five minutes later, she still hadn't returned. So the guy ordered himself another drink and continued to study the ballgame. Given the dozens of failed dates I'd been on in the past nine years, I could relate. I know how soul-numbing it can be to keep putting yourself out there, hoping each online date will be *The One*. Instead, they usually become *The One Who Remembers An Early Morning Appointment*, so the evening had to end abruptly. I should have felt sad for the couple, I suppose, as they slipped back into the safety of their own personal bubbles. Instead, I felt strangely satisfied by their failure to connect. For me, it was justification for why I'd stopped even trying to date. All I could see was the hole the process left in my heart, not the plug it *could* offer to fill that hole.

I thought back on what I'd learned from Richard and Dee Neveu. To the rest of the world, she looked like a lunatic because of her presidential ambitions and he looked like a pushover for supporting her. From what *I* could see, though, Dee was looking for a partner who understood her and Richard wanted someone he could take care of. They kept each other going no matter what anyone else thought, and what could be better than that?

I glanced back over at the bar. Online Date Man was raising his glass to toast Online Date Woman, and they shared a laugh about something. The waitress told them their table was ready, and they smiled and stood side by side as they walked over to have their dinner. I'd given up on them too soon, projecting onto them my own bitter feelings about relationships. Clearly they hadn't quit on one another. These two strangers were pretty much like every Can't-idate I'd met with. It all comes down to a desire to be understood and appreciated. And never quitting, no matter how impossible the odds.

As I looked at the empty chair across from my plate of General Tso's Chicken, I ordered a double scotch and felt like a quitter.

Craig Tomashoff

Luis Ramos

When my son was 11 years old, I thought it'd be fun to take him with me to Comic-Con. I was two years into divorce and still felt I needed to go overboard in spoiling him rotten. I'd been going to that annual pop culture orgy in San Diego for years, moderating panels and letting the geek times roll. So it seemed perfectly natural to take my sci-fi-loving son, letting him meet some of his favorite stars and wear his favorite anime character mask without shame.

He got to pose for pictures with some of the actors. He got to play lots of *Star Wars* video games. He had a front row seat at my panel and I got everyone in the hall to applaud for him. Then, on the drive back to Los Angeles, we stopped at a fast food place to get some dinner and he asked to get the extra-large French fries. I said no, he'd eaten enough crappy food all day. He promptly turned to me, looking ready to cry, and said, "You're the worst dad ever!"

Anyone looking objectively at our day would agree that he pretty much had a dream experience for an 11-year-old. Yet the only thing he was taking away from it all at this moment was being stuck with fewer fries than he wanted. He swears he has no memory of this, but I still cling to the valuable lesson I took away from the day: When people complain about how tough their lives are, it's entirely subjective.

That's why I was interested in Luis Ramos. He'd called me shortly after getting my letter and it was immediately clear that this 50-year-old presidential hopeful spoke with the vocabulary and elocution of a child. Initially, he seemed like another crazy Can't-idate stereotype and I'd simply be another media bully by putting him on my list. Then, right before we were about to hang up, he mentioned what his life was like growing up.

Ramos' dad was a career criminal. His mom had so many kids that she left Luis to be a ward of the state—and then she was murdered. He didn't get out of high school until most of his peers were leaving college. The guy lived through enough traumatic events by the time he was 21 to fill a season's worth of soap operas. And yet, as we finished that initial call, he told me he saw himself as "the Rocky Balboa of candidates...a million-to-one shot. But let's see what happens once I get on the ballot."

"I was always very interested in being president, and I told my mom I was going to run someday," Ramos said with the same innocent earnestness my son used to display when talking about growing up to be a ballplayer. "And now I am! I want to do this because I want to feel like I can make a difference. I wasn't born with a gold spoon sticking out of my mouth. So I know what it is like for all those struggling Americans out there who were losing their jobs and still can't find jobs, still can't afford to pay the rent. I can relate to that."

Despite a childhood that makes Oliver Twist seem like a Jolie-Pitt offspring, Ramos still clung to that dream of working in the Oval Office. He stood a better chance of being declared emperor of Unicorn Town than he did of moving into the White House in 2016, but I could fully appreciate his gutsiness. He was hesitant when it came to setting up a location for our meeting, leading me to suspect he might be homeless. That suspicion got stronger when he finally left me a voicemail as I was saying goodbye to the Neveus, telling me we couldn't meet where he lived. But we could connect at one of his favorite hangouts: Gleason's Gym in Brooklyn.

The gym was located between the Brooklyn Bridge and the Manhattan Bridge, two blocks from the East River. I hadn't been to this area in at least 20 years, and it had certainly changed during that time. These days it's filled with overpriced cupcake shops and parents pushing expensive baby strollers. The entrance to Gleason's was practically invisible in this neighborhood filled with West Elms, Starbucks and the like. I finally noticed a small sign with the Gleason's logo and walked inside, up the empty stairway to the front door. Underneath the gym's logo was its unofficial motto, courtesy of the philosopher Virgil: "Now, whoever has courage, and a strong and collected spirit in his breast, let him come forward, lace on the gloves and put up his hands." Good advice for boxers—as well as presidential wannabes.

The walls were painted the color of blood, which I'm assuming was no accident. There were four full-size boxing rings on this giant slab of concrete, along with several heavy boxing bags, small speed bags and free-weight racks. Because it was Sunday afternoon on a holiday weekend, there were only half a dozen or so people working out. I told the woman behind the front desk that I was looking for Luis Ramos. For a moment, she stared at me blankly.

"He's a quiet guy, running for president?" I said.

"Oh, you mean Pinky? He's not here."

I had no idea if Pinky was the guy I was looking for.

Luckily, it all became clear moments later when a painfully thin bald man walked in and the woman greeted him with a happy, "Hey, Pinky!" He was clutching tightly to a plastic shopping bag and a blue banker's envelope that were both bulging to capacity. He stood about my height (5'10"), but couldn't have weighed more than 140 pounds, even after Thanksgiving dinner.

"I'm Luis Ramos," he said, his New York accent so over-the-top it reminded me of the one my daughter used to play Nicely Niclely Johnson in her fifth grade production of *Guys and Dolls*. "They call me Pinky because I wear pink shorts and use pink gloves! I just like the color. People get funny ideas when I wear pink. They used to call me names, slurs for gay, and I'm straight. Now those people who used those slurs are the same ones who wear pink shorts."

There was no pink on him today, although his neon green athletic shoes and crimson shorts more than made up for it. A plain white T-shirt hung like a boat sail off his Taylor Swift-skinny shoulders as he eagerly led me over to a far corner of the gym. There was something almost adorable in the contrast between this sweet man's intensely polite, child-like demeanor and the violent sounds of boxers bouncing around the gym smacking punching bags. He looked like someone I could take in a fight, and I scream in pain if my cat swats at me.

"That ring over there…that's where Mike Tyson, the former heavyweight champion of the world, watched me fight once," he said, pointing to one of the rings on the other side of the room. "So I thought, I'm going to dedicate my boxing to Mike Tyson, and I did. He was cheering for me. I said, 'Mike Tyson, this fight is for you.' After that, he was cheering for me. And after the fight, he came up and shook hands with me. It was mind boggling, a Hall of Famer cheering for me! I don't want to sound like I'm bragging…"

I could see how excited he was telling this story, but he

stopped short as he spoke and never finished the Tyson tale. Apparently, pride is like underwear for Ramos: neither is to be displayed in public. He disappeared to snag us a couple of metal folding chairs, then returned to set them in front of one of the boxing rings. As we sat down, he gently placed his bag and envelope on the ground next to him. I wasn't sure what the contents were, but he watched over them as if they contained his life savings.

"Most politicians today, it's all about them—money, power and fame," he said. "What makes me different from any other candidate is: number one, I do what I think is right for the American people. People have to stop playing the blame game and start working with each other as a team, so that this way we can get the economy back together."

His words weren't unusual for someone running for public office. They all want to prove how compassionate they are. What was different, though, was the fact that this sentiment was coming from a man whose life had given him no reason to feel compassion for anyone. His dad was sent to jail before Ramos even hit puberty ("I don't know what he did...maybe he murdered somebody"), and he has no idea what happened to him after that. His mom had at least a dozen children that he knew about. She couldn't take care of them all, so she sent Ramos to live in group homes. He bounced around from Westchester County to Peekskill to the Bronx, "never letting it get to me. Because I figured if I am weak, I'm not going to survive. It's life. Things happen."

He had plenty of reasons to maintain a tough mindset. However, since he was built like a Pixie Stick, keeping physically tough was more difficult. So in his early teens, Ramos took up boxing and it seemed to help. He kept himself alive and relatively safe. Then, when he was 14, he got called into his room at a South Bronx group home.

"I am a little bit psychic and I sensed that something was

not right. I would say, 'Mommy, I think something is going to happen to you' and she didn't like what I had to say. Then they brought me into my room and said, 'You are old enough now and we have to bring you this news that your mother is dead.' I was like, 'Holy damn!' They could see it on my face that I was shocked. The last time I had seen her was about six months prior."

Ramos lost interest in boxing and developed a taste for partying. Even though he was nearing 18 at that point, he was reading at a second grade level ("that's if I was lucky") and hadn't learned his ABCs. His school did nothing to help, sticking him in Special Ed classes that left him feeling "like I was a straight A student, a scholar."

Then he was moved to a new home out on Long Island. He was Hispanic in a largely white high school, which meant getting used to regular abuse from his fellow students. "I was called the 'S' word…The girls looked at me funny because I didn't have the money that their parents had. I didn't have their fancy cars. I felt like I didn't fit in."

Instead of making life better, leaving the inner city for a middle-class suburb only made things tougher. It certainly didn't help when a guidance counselor explained that the new school didn't accept his previous credits. So if he was going to graduate, Ramos basically had to start over again. That's tough news at any age. But when you're 18 and hear it's going to take at least three more years to finish high school, it's very hard to stick with the program.

Being the sort of person who sighs passive-aggressively at such life misfortunes as the guy in front of me in the express checkout line having 12 items instead of 10 (and yes, I *do* always count), I kept looking at Ramos' baby face for some sign of anger or malice. It just didn't seem possible to go through all this and not be at least a *little* bitter. If anyone had a right to feel the world owed him something, it was Luis Ramos.

Instead, he just kept finding silver linings in every Category Four storm cloud. For instance, just as he was preparing to quit school, he learned that someone wanted to take him in as a foster child. After nearly 18 years of bouncing around the system, never having a real home, "a miracle happened and this beautiful woman named Marie Boschen took me in."

He knew very little about this Russian immigrant, but they quickly bonded and he decided to stay in school. As she pushed him to learn, Ramos started studying seven days a week. The school system didn't make it easy on him. Although he was 18 and six feet tall, he remembers being put in classes with fifth and sixth graders.

"I looked like I was 14, but the kids would stare at me funny, like, 'What's *he* doing here?' I just told them I got left behind and that I was there to learn like everyone else."

The plan worked...to a degree, anyway. He didn't get A's. He didn't even get C's. His final GPA was more like a D+. Still, at the age of 21, Luis Ramos could call himself a high school graduate. While most other grads just walked across the stage to grab their diploma and move on with life, Ramos "jumped up and danced in front of thousands of people. Everybody looked at me like I was crazy, but I didn't care! I'd made it!"

It's not everyone who can take pride in getting a D+ average to become a high school graduate at 21, but few people I'd ever met were as innocent as Ramos. When he talked about his difficult life, he seemed like a grown-up version of one of those starving kids from a foreign land you want to hug when you see them on late-night cable TV ads. Then he started talking about his plans to run for New York City mayor if he isn't elected president in 2016, and you want to hide him from a world that would eat him alive.

Either way, I suppose, the end result is the same: You feel sorry for him. The truth is, though, Ramos is 140 pounds of

American dream—a poor kid who struggled to survive within the liberal social welfare system, yet continued to cling to the belief that hard work and ambition would carry him to where he wanted to be.

Case in point: after graduating from high school, Ramos learned very quickly that his degree didn't mean as much to the rest of the world. The only work he could find was for $3.50 an hour at Wendy's, Burger King, McDonald's, et al. He continued to live with Boschen, until he argued with her adult son and was shown the door. With no other options, since rentals hovered around $1,000 a month, he ended up living in a Flushing Meadows park where "being homeless was the least of my worries. I had to worry about the crackheads and the dopers."

He kept enough hope alive, and set enough money aside, to eventually get a bed at the local YMCA for $150 a month.

"Most people get the impression that people who live at the Y are gay, blah, blah, blah. That's not true," he said smiling happily, with no apparent awareness that this might be just a bit offensive. "I will never forget when a taxi driver told me, 'You're clean for someone who lives in the YMCA.' I thought, why would he say that?"

Ramos continued to live at the Y even after his career took a step up in 1990, when he took the Civil Service Exam and ended up with a job in the food services division at the Department of Veteran Affairs. And suddenly, "I wasn't going nowhere anymore." He'd graduated to earning $8.13 an hour, serving food to veterans and eventually becoming a cook. For most of the next two decades, his life revolved around the VA, where he became what he considered to be "the LeBron James, Larry Bird, Michael Jordan and Magic Johnson of food service." Ramos was finally starting to feel appreciated by the world, like the time he won the Outstanding Performance Award and the $500 prize that came with it.

"It was in 1993, and I was on the second floor. There was a patient and I was just about ready to pass his tray to eat, [when] I saw his face was turning blue. I'm not a doctor, so I went to the office and nurses weren't there. At the time, the government put a freeze on hiring, so everyone was working extra hours and under pressure. I found a nurse, and a doctor came in and they saved his life."

The job also afforded him his first chance to explore a world beyond the poor side of New York. He would spend his money traveling with tour groups to places like Paris, Amsterdam and London.

"I met people. They liked me. They wanted me to sit at their table with them. They *wanted* to hang out with me."

If you ever doubt the healing power of simply talking to strangers, just look up Ramos and have him discuss his experiences while traveling through Europe. He was finally fitting in, to the point where he started to boast about achieving his childhood goal and dedicating it to his mom and Marie Boschen: "I told people I was probably going to run for president."

If we've learned anything over the years about trying to be Commander in Chief, it's that having a military past—even if that simply means you used to go to air shows when you were a kid—will sound very impressive. It's a lesson Ramos had certainly taken to heart. He'd thought about joining the military years earlier, rather than finish high school. In 2010, he signed up to become a civilian mariner—a regular citizen who provides services on military ships.

He went through the basic training and as soon as he passed, "things started getting better and better." He worked as a laundry man ("That doesn't mean I'm washing people's drawers and socks...I wash sheets and blankets and things like that"), never figuring he'd last four months on the gig. Now he's made it more than four years and lives on a Navy ship that docks in New Jersey when not traveling the world to "supply bombs, gas, missiles, guns, machinery, food to people who are starving."

"A lot of people doubted that I would make it, and here I am winning awards for my work—I feel like I'm living in a dream," he said. "Let me read some of these letters, because seeing is believing."

He reached down and grabbed the overstuffed banker's envelope, pulling out a pile of papers. After a long search, he pulled out a couple of commendation letters from superior officers. He began to read them...slowly...painfully. It was clear that he was still learning to read as he stumbled over one word after another, explaining every sentence to me upon completing it.

"'He is self-motivated and always gives his all to get the job done,'" Ramos read haltingly. "'He is constantly at work during his tour of duty and can always be found helping his fellow co-workers with their assignments.'" He looked up to elaborate. "In other words, I worked on my own time. I worked on my lunch breaks and I stayed late, too."

Ramos grabbed the second letter, a note he received upon winning the "On the Spot Award." It was written by a medical officer on his ship after Ramos was called in to assist a sailor who took ill. He studied the paper for a very long moment.

"I have a little trouble pronouncing..." he told me before drawing in and letting out a huge sigh. Then, under his breath, he said to himself, "Okay...'Supply Utility Ramos distinguished himself for outstanding achievement while selflessly providing hospitality and care that greatly enhanced a crew member's life while admitted to the ship's hospital.'"

The process of poring over the letters seemed to take a little out of Ramos. He leaned back in his chair, drawing another long breath before adding, "I feel really good, because when I joined,

I had people saying, 'Don't do it. You're too old. You can't follow orders. You'll never make it.' But I did follow orders—military orders—and here I am winning awards. Wow, I feel like I am living in a dream world!"

For a brief moment, I tried to picture Ramos at the podium in a presidential debate. It'd be like putting Mother Teresa on the dais for one of those celebrity roasts—everyone else is battling to out-asshole each other, while he just keeps talking about how blessed everyone is to be there.

"Researching running for president helped me with my pronunciation and my English. It has forced me to educate myself. That's why I read every day and want to get better. If I become president, I want to speak to people, to communicate, to learn."

That Forrest Gump-ish quality was certainly charming. But as Ramos told me about his plans to get his name on the New York primary ballot, I could also see a significant drawback to his naïve nature. He'd done his research and discovered that he'd need signatures from 15,000 registered voters. His solution? Hire a media company that promised to get him those signatures—for a not-so-cool $3,750.

There's nothing illegal about this…most of the time, anyway. Companies that solicit signatures are called "paid circulators." While the laws about who can do it and how they get paid vary from state to state, savvy entrepreneurs have been making cash this way since the early 1900s. It's just that the idea of a guy who makes almost nothing spending his savings to *possibly* get on the ballot in an election he's never going to win seemed so wrong.

My parental instincts kicked in once again, as they had with Rev. Pinkney Butts and the Syds Butt guys, and I felt the urge to inject some reality into our conversation. I didn't want to see a nice guy like Ramos taken advantage of. Yet his presidential bid also seemed to be something that truly helped him get out of bed in the morning. So I opted to go with kindness, rather than cold hard facts. I kept quiet while he reached down to grab the worn-out brown plastic bag that looked ready to rip apart at the seams.

Most people these days keep the information that defines their lives on their smartphones. Sometimes you'll come across old school folks, like me, who also keep a wallet full of pictures. Ramos was the only person I'd ever met who apparently put all of his memories into a bag. (His cell phone was of the flip variety, circa 2002, so no help there.) He was like a kid grabbing presents from under the Christmas tree as he pulled out one tattered photo after another. Because family was something that eluded him for most of his life, most of the pictures were of him meeting celebrities: Paris Hilton, the Spice Girls, Connie Chung, Willard Scott, Sugar Ray Leonard. Ramos had somehow mastered the very important presidential skill of finding photo ops.

"That's me with Howard Stern at the Grammy Awards in 2003," he said proudly, pointing to a decade-old shot in which he looked pretty much the same as he did today. "I was a voting member of the Grammy Awards. I wrote songs like 'Revenge of the Rejects,' which is about people being rejected. I wrote other songs called 'Millennium Girl,' 'City of Amsterdam' and...I could go on and on and on. The record company provided the music. I wrote the lyrics. I paid them the $400, so I don't know if my songs have been recorded. But I think that's how I became a voting member."

Here we went again. Just as with the ballot signatures, this was another situation where he was happy to hand over his money *and* his hopes to strangers who may not treat him the way he wanted to be treated. I was just hoping he wouldn't tell me he had an upcoming meeting with a Nigerian prince.

After a few more moments of stargazing, Ramos mentioned that he had to get back to his ship soon, so we should probably wrap up. As he began to stuff everything back into his envelope and bag, I noticed a fresh lottery ticket in the mix. He smiled broadly when he saw me looking at it.

"Do you play the lottery?"

I explained that I didn't, without telling him that was largely because I resented governments trying to pay for things by convincing poor people to gamble away what little they did have on the astronomical chance they might win millions. Well, that and the fact that I never win anything.

He looked at me cheerfully.

"You should play. You might win. All it takes is one dollar. You could get your own publishing company and put your book out yourself."

We walked outside to the gourmet cupcake-buying, ergonomic stroller-pushing, selfie stick-toting crowd, where Ramos gave me a firm handshake.

"Some people are supportive of my candidacy, and some people think I'm crazy," he said without prompting. "But they're all just regular people, and I take the good with the negative. It makes me stronger. And I think this book is really going to work for you, man! I got a good feeling about it!"

He disappeared into the sunny Brooklyn afternoon as I headed off for my next interview. Instead of immediately turning on the radio, though, I headed along the New Jersey Turnpike while mulling over my Luis Ramos experience. He was the sort of innocent soul who makes used car dealers gleeful and mothers nervous. He had what all politicians claim to possess, but clearly don't—absolute faith in humanity.

Ramos will never be president. He'll probably never be more than he is right now, as a matter of fact. But the amazing thing was, he didn't seem to mind. For me and most people I know, the circumstances of his life are the sort of story we see end tragically in an art house movie, after a really nice Italian dinner.

For Ramos, though, it was just life. And life was enough.

Knowing that I was in for my longest drive between Can't-idates yet—all the way down to Florida—I stopped for the night in Richmond, Virginia. I chose this particular location for one specific reason: While passing through Lansing, Michigan after meeting Bart Lower, it dawned on me that I had yet to buy any souvenirs for my kids. Years ago, especially once I became a divorced dad, buying souvenirs became pretty routine. I'd go out of town for work and come back with some item from the trip to prove I was thinking of them while I was gone. This, I believe, is why God made snow globes.

My daughter liked fun T-shirts. My son liked baseball. I liked both. So I decided to stop in every city that had an unusually-named minor league baseball team and buy souvenir shirts. So far I'd collected shirts from the Lansing Lugnuts, the Akron Rubber Ducks, the Erie Seawolves, the Vermont Lake Monsters and the New Hampshire Fisher Cats. When I learned there was a Richmond Flying Squirrels how could I not stop?

I drove by the stadium and learned that game time was still hours away, so the souvenir shop wasn't yet open. Thinking of my long trek ahead to Florida, I wandered around the entire stadium to see if there was anyone who could help. Sitting in the shade alongside the parking lot, I came across a young African-American woman and man smoking a cigarette. Neither of them could have been older than 18, and both were wearing Flying Squirrel red shirts and khaki pants.

When I explained what I was doing, the woman told me that the shop didn't open for another hour. When I told her I couldn't wait that long, she promised to help. She walked through the gate and up some stairs to the top of the stadium, heading for God knows where. While she was gone, I asked the man who stayed behind if he was a big Squirrels fan.

"Nah," he said, taking a long final drag from his cigarette before flicking it into the parking lot. "I'm starting work here today. Just got a job working concessions. I'm kinda nervous, man! I need this job to pay my rent and in this town...shit, it ain't easy when you're a black man trying to make money and survive in this town. Why don't you see if one of your people can do something about that!"

He shrugged and wandered inside the gate. As he left, I saw his friend motioning to me from the top of the stairs. I headed up to her and she led me past the other Squirrel staff setting up for the game. We walked to the souvenir store door, where she waved to the staff inside.

"I told them about your presidents," she said to me. "They aren't open yet, but you can go in."

I thanked her and hurriedly picked out three shirts. As I paid, the young guy behind the counter started volunteering his own views on the crop of presidential candidates.

"To be honest, they all seem like a bunch of assholes," he explained. "I hope you're finding some good people, because everyone I've heard about so far sucks. Except that one guy...that guy who wears a boot on his head and has that crazy beard. He seems cool! I'd consider voting for him."

Pretty much every convenience store clerk, every motel night shift manager, every baseball souvenir shop customer I'd spoken to—they all had a similar opinion about the 2016 campaign. However, this was the first time anyone had referenced someone I'd interviewed. Not exactly a groundswell, but still...it was definitely an indication that I might be on to something.

Before hitting the road for Florida, I decided to stop for gas...and a lottery ticket.

Tom Menier

If you think about it, the last people in the world we should hate are politicians. After all, we're the ones who give *them* their jobs—essentially, to take care of us when times are tough and leave us alone when times are great. Yet even politicians spend much of their time bad-mouthing politicians. They're kind of like the rectal thermometers of society: nobody likes them, but there are times when you need to have them around.

So why *do* we hate these public servants so much?

After zero scientific research or intense surveying, I can sum it up in two words: Joseph Morrissey. In a nutshell, Morrissey started out as a Virginia attorney who was eventually disbarred after being cited for contempt of court 10 times and jailed or arrested five times. Despite this, he ended up getting elected as a Democrat to the Virginia House of Delegates, where he served until being indicted on felony charges that involved allegedly taking indecent liberties with a minor, possession and distribution of child pornography, and electronic solicitation of a minor.

Morrissey resigned his seat, only to run in a special election for the Senate as an independent. Meanwhile, he's the father of four children with four different women, the youngest of whom was a boy Morrissey at first denied spawning. Much later, he admitted having the child with a 17-year-old girl who once worked as a secretary in his office.

I don't know Joe Morrissey. The first time I'd ever even heard of him was on the radio as I left the Richmond Flying Squirrels parking lot and headed for an evening date with another minor league baseball team, the Savannah Sand Gnats. Maybe he's a great buddy to go have a beer and catch a ballgame with. But as I listened to him speak with a local talk show host that morning, it took about 37 seconds to realize he was the personification of everything we can't stand about public officials.

The 57-year-old was in the studio with his now 19-year-old former secretary, talking about how much he loved her and how proud he was that she was going to college. Morrissey happily rambled about changing his young son's diaper, before a female caller ripped into him for his lack of ethics and morals. He responded by explaining that she was his baby mama's sister, and that she was just bitter because she'd had a baby at an early age too. (I would love to have seen him try to get this sexist logic past Rev. Pinkney Butts' daughter.)

All of that would be reason enough to despise Morrissey, but here's what had me screaming: Whenever the host or a caller challenged him on a point, his response began with—"Let's be clear..." It's one of those phrases used right before saying something to deliberately obscure what had just been said. I don't know whether self-absorbed egomaniacs are the culprits corrupting politics, or if it's the political system itself that inspires self-absorption. Either way, Joe Morrissey's complete and total inability to step outside himself and realize how foolish he seemed astounded me. If this guy was a co-worker or in-law, you'd talk trash about him. But since he's a politician, voters apparently shrug it off as normal behavior.

I guess the one good thing about the way Joe Morrissey had me cursing was that it reminded me of why I was out on the road in the first place. I had high hopes that Tom Menier would be a good example of an alternative candidate. When we spoke on the phone, he came across as the exact opposite of Joe Morrissey. Menier seemed like the real deal, a Vietnam vet who'd seen friends die—first in the jungle during combat, then decades later from illnesses that the government never helped treat. Inspired by the causes of forgotten veterans, Menier was drawing attention to their plight by running for president.

Now 66, he had long ago left the military, although he was still mighty proud to have served. He lived a couple hours south of Tampa, in Cape Coral, Florida. This was one of those south Florida towns where the average age hovered somewhere between *"Get off my lawn!"* and *"Matlock's on!"* His apartment was a mustard-yellow duplex just off a main drag filled with plenty of strip mall stores selling beer and cigarettes, and he greeted me at the door in a way nobody on the trip had: Shirtless. With no apologies and no explanation whatsoever.

The lanky, grey-haired Army vet looked to be a couple Big Macs short of Luis Ramos' fighting weight. On the plus side, he *was* wearing pants. And the no-shirt look allowed me to get a good look at his tattoos, particularly the large dragon that appeared to be clawing its way up his arm and chest. Menier explained that he used to have a tattoo with his ex-wife's initials.

"I kept saying, 'I'm gonna fix that.' So when I was in Thailand, I covered the old tattoo up and put something unique on. Now everybody says, 'What the hell is that?' It's a dragon, done by this Thai guy who created it himself. I didn't want it really gaudy. I said, 'Small! Small!'—and there it is. Everybody who saw it said, 'Wow! You must have paid a fortune for that!' It was $75!"

He led me into the living room of his cramped two-bedroom apartment, minimally furnished with a dining table, some chairs, a couch and TV. In the far corner, alongside a sliding glass doorway leading to an empty field, was his "office"—a small desk, chair and computer—and window to the world. On the other side of the room, a folded wheelchair and a circular saw sat next to each other. The chair belonged to his ailing 88-year-old mother, who he told me was napping in another room. The saw was left over from when he was trying to help his 36-year-old daughter renovate her house.

"My mom's had two strokes and is struggling along," he told me as we sat down at the dining table. "She didn't get paralyzed, but her mind isn't quite there. I take care of her. She'll get up to meet you when she wants to. I had a wife...Hey, hon! You getting beautified, is that it?"

He cackled and pointed toward his bedroom door, which opened to reveal Connie, who was as tiny as he was tall.

"Connie is my little sweetie from the Philippines. She's special," he told me as she shook my hand, before quietly settling down in another dining chair. They'd been introduced via email by a mutual friend in 2012, when he was working as a private contractor in Afghanistan and she was cleaning houses in the Philippines. They went to eat at a McDonald's in Manila, when Connie realized for the first time the kind of man she was dealing with. As they were eating breakfast and getting to know each other, a little girl started tapping on the window to get their attention.

"I looked and looked again," Menier recalled, "and Connie said, 'Don't look at her!' And I was like, 'This ain't gonna work.' So what did I do?"

"You said, 'Come inside,' and you bought her some food,

along with two other kids," she said deferentially. "And when we came out of the McDonald's, two more guys were there to get their food."

"I'd feed upwards of 20 or 30 kids when I'd walk from my hotel. I'd walk down to Kentucky Fried Chicken and buy buckets of chicken to feed them, because the Kentucky Fried Chicken wouldn't let the kids in to get their food and sit to eat it."

Not only was this act of kindness enough to charm Connie —who moved to the United States to marry Menier in late 2014— it also got him thinking about a new career direction.

"Kids shouldn't be hungry," said Menier. "That's probably when I first thought maybe I should get involved in politics and run for president, because there's no reason for children to starve."

There was some degree of irony in this, considering the relationship Menier had with his own kids. His daughter was in Tampa and there was a time not too long ago when he thought he and Connie would move into the house he was helping her and his son-in-law renovate. However, non-drinker Menier wasn't exactly happy with what he considered to be their excessive lifestyle. So he, his mom and Connie moved into this tiny Cape Coral apartment instead and haven't contacted his daughter since. Then there's his 41-year-old son, whom Menier claimed has been in legal hot water since he was around 16.

"I think that the last I heard from him was about two months ago. I said, 'I'm in the middle of something, can I call you back?' Then when I called him back, he said, 'Well, I know you are busy and you can't really talk, but I just wanted to say thanks for talking with me.' It had been about 38 years since I had talked to him, and *that* is what he said."

It always makes me anxious hearing about parents and children who don't get along, because I worry that might happen to me and my kids. Parent-child relationships are a lifetime commitment. And even though Menier wasn't the sort of guy to indulge in self-pity, I could sense that the anger he displayed talking about his kids was masking something more. Something sadder. It went back to his relationship with his own father. And after hearing his story, I could really get behind that whole "you reap what you sow" theory.

Menier grew up "kind of a hell-raiser" in Burlington, Wisconsin. "Some of the friends I hung around with did some incredibly stupid stuff. I didn't really do the drugs, none of that crap. My thing was racing cars and raising a fuss! I had my '57 Chevy with a V-8 engine. I'm quite sure that everybody knew me."

His father ran a local company that made bug spray and rat poison. Menier worked there from age six to 14, loading trucks, labeling packages and stacking boxes. For some people, helping your dad with his business might be a good bonding experience. Judging by the way his right leg started fidgeting and his hands began motioning independently whenever his dad was mentioned, this was definitely not the case with Tom Menier.

"He had his little animals—that was us, working animals, little mules. We were the employees, my mother, my sister and myself. And then my dad would go out; that was the happy moment. It was always good for him to go on the road."

Menier's father came from a long line of military men and taught his boy to shoot, hunt and play army by the time he was seven. While Christmas for his friends meant unwrapping toys, the holiday meant something entirely different for young Tom.

"Dad didn't do toys. I'd get pants. If I did get a toy, it was from a relative—and I cherished that, hid it. Because if my dad got mad, he would break it or throw it away."

Life was pretty bleak—going home and getting beaten by his dad, then going to school and getting beaten up because he was a skinny kid. His dad would warn him, "If you don't fight them, *I'll* beat your ass." Menier learned how to fight back—at school, anyway—but teachers and principals started telling him, "You're just crazy."

The more he spoke, the faster Menier's words poured out. All the decades he'd survived hadn't taken away the anxiety. I completely understood. I imagine a lot of people from my generation have similar memories of feeling like it was vacation during the occasional weeks when dad would go out of town on business. The house was remarkably free of eggshells to step on. No yelling. No tension. No fear. It's easy to learn to love being alone when that's what you grew up with. But Menier didn't seem like a guy who could take too much solo time. He kept gazing lovingly at quiet Connie.

With this kind of home life growing up, he ultimately "didn't give a rat's butt about school" and dropped out in the 10th grade—which, not coincidentally, was around the time when his father left his mother. Menier now had to help earn money for his mom, sister and brothers, so he found work wherever he could—milking cows on dairy farms, saddling and brushing horses at a local stable, anything.

His goal was to join the Army, but he was too young. Even when he turned 17 and tried to sign up, Menier was rejected because he wasn't big enough. Three months and several pounds later, he was crushed when he was still four pounds away from the minimum weight. Finally, after taking on gigs setting up circus equipment and stacking beer bottles at a bottle company, he found the four pounds to make his life's dream come true. He enlisted in the Army with no other goal than maybe being a platoon sergeant someday. After several months of training, he was shipped off at 18 to Long Binh Post near Saigon. Menier found himself in a unit sent to replace soldiers who'd been blown up just as he arrived. On one of his evening patrols, Menier went out with a medic known only as "Doc."

"We were probably 200 meters out and damned if they didn't hit us. They ambushed us with grenades. I saw one go by, and [as] I was hitting the ground there was an explosion. I saw one of my gunners walk past me, and he said, 'Sarg, I'm hit.' He hit the ground and I am trying to yell for a medic, [as] I am trying to plug the holes in this guy. I saw the medic lying on his back, with his legs all blown up. I thought, 'Shit!' I am looking around and everybody is out, and down, and leaning up against trees—we had three or four guys wounded. I thought, 'This is not going to work,' and told the radio guy, 'Relax, calm down. Can you tell them on the radio that we need help?'

"About that time, a couple of tanks pulled up and I said, 'Be careful. There are booby traps!' I am bandaging up the guy. I'm looking at him, wrapped up his legs and everything else, and said, 'They're going to medevac you in a little bit. Just relax.' And he said, 'What am I going to tell my wife?' And I said, 'I don't know. You had a bad day? You're fine. You are going home.' His legs were a mess. Only to find out later he played professional baseball—and had volunteered.

"Later, I thought that was kind of a dumb thing to say. Here's a guy that was serving his country. He could have stayed where he was. But instead, here he is on the ground, wounded, and nobody really gives a shit. There I was patching everybody up, and that was the first time that I cried."

This tale spilled out of him, almost without a single breath. He wasn't so much telling me the story as he was purging it. It was pretty apparent that Menier was a cautious guy who needed to spill his stories—but didn't feel he could trust others with those memories.

"Those of us from the Vietnam era...we didn't have close friends, because they may not be around later, and you don't want to stay close," he told me. "When you get too close, it bothers you. For whatever reason, I have acquaintances. I don't have friends."

His ability to make friends wasn't the only thing Menier left behind in Vietnam. His faith in his own government also never made it home. That happened courtesy of Agent Orange, the defoliant the U.S. military sprayed on the jungles to eliminate vegetation that provided cover and food to the North Vietnamese. At the time, Menier was reassured by the military brass that the chemicals were safe for troops to be around.

"I thought it was incredible stuff," he recalled. "I even wrote my mom, saying, 'Man, this is neat!' The helicopters would spray, and five or 10 minutes later, the leaves started dropping off the trees. I never questioned what it was. Why would you think the government would spray something on your ass that would hurt you later?"

Once or twice a week, the choppers dumped their load while soldiers like Menier were out on reconnaissance missions. They would get so wet it was like they'd been rained on. Then Menier and his fellow vets got home, only to learn that herbicides like Agent Orange might cause everything from various cancers to nerve, digestive, skin and respiratory problems.

"You didn't really think about it until crap started growing on you, like open sores," he told me. "You didn't think about it until your body starts falling apart. And the government did it to us. They wouldn't admit it—and nobody cares."

By the time I started college in the late '70s, the horrors of Vietnam had gone mainstream in movies like *The Deer Hunter* and *Coming Home*. I remember thinking that since Hollywood was now giving the country sympathetic portraits of Vietnam vets and their struggles to re-enter civilian life, things must be okay. Love or hate the war, at least Americans seemed to be accepting the returning soldiers.

This was very easy for me to assume, considering that by the time I hit 18, there was no more draft. War was something I only had to experience from the cushy comfort of my cineplex seat or on a video game screen. It was all just one big theory to debate in political science classes before going out and getting drunk. For Menier, though, it was *Catch-22*—only non-fiction. It would all be funny, except for the fact that it's not. Take, for instance, his post-Vietnam experience getting orders to head to both Fort Dix, New Jersey and Fort Polk, Louisiana. A few calls to the military brass didn't straighten the situation out. So with a 50/50 chance at being right, Menier headed to Fort Dix—only to be reported AWOL because he hadn't gone to Fort Polk.

While that confusion was being sorted out, Menier heard he was being shipped out to a base in Germany. The problem was, it was wintertime and he had only been issued his "summer greens"—cotton socks, thin shirts, etc.—with the assurances that more appropriate outfits would be waiting when he got overseas. Not surprisingly, that didn't happen. Instead of warmer clothing, all he got was a hotheaded sergeant as his superior.

"He was angry about race issues. He was angry about the drug crap going on. I heard about five minutes of it—and I was freezing, standing in about six inches of snow—and I said to myself, 'I don't think he's talking to me, because I just got here.' So I got out of formation and started walking up to the barracks [when] he said to me, 'Get your ass back into formation! I didn't release you, and you will stand at attention!' I walked back and stood at attention, and was there for 45 minutes to an hour, in weather that was way below freezing. When he finally got done, they carried me off the field because I had frostbitten hands and feet."

Doctors were able to avoid amputation, but he'd lost feeling in his feet. Add this to his Agent Orange experience and hearing loss from being near explosions, and Menier was neither physically nor emotionally the same man when he left the military and returned to the states in 1983. His first marriage ended. He remarried. He worked constantly at a variety of jobs, at one point even raising Arabian horses. Already in his 30s, he opted to study marketing at Virginia Commonwealth University and then Averett University, where got a Masters Degree.

Meanwhile, the war continued to rage on in his body. Trips to the Veterans Administration didn't help. "It was hell going there," he said, shaking his head. "I tried to avoid it as much as possible." Menier says he had a brain tumor removed, survived heart surgery and saw fellow soldiers die from cancer while waiting to be treated at VA hospitals.

"People go in there for their appointments and are told, 'You missed your appointment. You were supposed to be here last week.' They have a tendency to call you that morning to tell you that you don't have an appointment, and if you don't have a phone with you, which many don't, you wouldn't know. I was going to my cardiac appointment and I was on my way in when I got the call canceling it."

I have no problem with the military philosophy of fighting them over there so we don't have to fight them over here. It's like texting a break-up: war is tolerable as long as you don't have to actually see the enemy. What I don't understand is how elected leaders continually urge us all to support the troops, but then hesitate when they have the chance to offer government-funded assistance. And it wasn't just his health care that Menier struggled with.

"Know that when I was going through school, my professors told me, 'Why are you doing this? There are no jobs for you.' Because of my age. 'Why would they hire you?' I thought they were joking. 'Who needs experience and work ethics, when they can hire a younger person for half the price?' They are not going to hire you."

With a professor's help, he managed to find some work as a human resources consultant, which he squeezed in during the hours he wasn't working his part-time job for the State of Virginia's Corrections Department. Menier worked in a prison infirmary with juvenile offenders, keeping peace between the doctors and nurses and the young inmates. The place would cycle youths back out into the world, only to have them return on other charges a few months later.

Menier quickly grew frustrated with teens who learned "the magic words—'I found Jesus!' Six months later, they'd be back again. I'd say, 'How'd Jesus work out for you?'" He'd grown up a hell-raiser because his dad just didn't understand him, and now he was an adult baffled by a bunch of hell-raising kids. This continuum seemed a bit lost on Menier.

"You can feel bad for [the inmates], but I can tell you their thinking and it comes from their parents. You can't have a mom that is a crackhead, or on heroin or coke, with a child, because what the child ends up doing is joining [gangs], selling drugs, so mom can get her drugs."

I can't imagine seeing troubled and violent youth every day without it softening you at least a little inside. However, the experience seemed to *harden* Menier. That was clear when he leapt into an unprompted 15-minute soliloquy about a young kid— probably 13 or so—who came into the infirmary one day and was "sicker than a dog." The boy didn't speak, but Menier was fully aware that the kid was in prison for one murder and a suspect in about 20 more. They would encounter each other a couple more times, including the time when Menier stopped an older prisoner from harassing this boy.

Then came a night when Menier ran into trouble with another inmate who refused to turn his TV off and his lights out.

Menier was finally able to push the TV out of the kid's room and lock the door. His next stop was the room of that murder suspect he'd encountered a few times before, yet never spoken to. The teen remembered when Menier stopped him from getting picked on, and said, "I think I like you." Menier responded with, "Okay, I don't have any feelings one way or another about you, my man. But I hope you get better."

Later in the evening, Menier stopped by the boy's room again and noticed he was lying quietly on his bed. "I said, 'Are you okay? Do you need the nurse or anything?' And he said, 'No, I was just thinking.' I said, 'What were you thinking about?' And he said, 'I will probably live for a week before I'm dead, when I get back on the street.' I told him, 'Go somewhere else. You don't have to go back there.' He said, 'I don't know where to go. I have no one.' I said, 'I don't know what to tell you. Did you talk to your counselor? Maybe they could find you a home.' And he said, 'Nah, I guess I better just go home and deal with it.'"

Menier offered to let the kid watch TV, but the boy said no and just rolled over. As he exited, there was a commotion in the hallway. The inmate Menier had problems with earlier ran past and tossed a large table at him. Pushing a nurse out of the way, Menier took the full brunt of the table on his back. Unable to move, he looked up to see the quiet kid step from his room, pick the table-tosser up, put him back in his room and calmly say, "I will kill you if you move."

About that time, guards came running and assumed that the peacemaker was the kid trying to escape. "I said, 'No! No! No! This kid did nothing wrong. As a matter of fact, he saved my ass.'" The boy was taken back to his room, while Menier was taken to the ER without ever getting to say thanks. Four days later, he was back at work and another corrections officer asked, "Remember that kid that saved you? He's dead. Got back on the streets and they killed him. Didn't even make it 24 hours."

It's the kind of story that you'd think would bring out a couple of tears, or at least choke him up a little. After all, just like in Vietnam, people were dying around Tom Menier. Instead of making him more sensitive to the heartbreaks of this world, though, he just got tougher.

"So what do you do to change? I don't know anymore," he said, palms now pressed on the table rather than waving wildly. "The judges put them in there, over and over again. After a while, it just seems hopeless. Like one inmate said to me, 'I make more money in a day than you make in two years. So what are you going to tell me? And if I die, who cares?' Their perception is, in their situation, where they live, their life doesn't matter. Nobody cares."

Having seen repeatedly how the system can let people down, Menier began to pay more attention to the politics he figured were messing everything up. He wasn't Republican or Democrat, just a guy who wanted change—without being entirely sure what to change *to*. Still, the idea of running for office took a back seat to his need to make a living. Through acquaintances, Menier found work as a freelance human resources manager for American companies in Qatar, Kuwait and Afghanistan.

Since returning to the U.S. and marrying Connie, though, work has been scarce. Even the local McDonald's wouldn't hire him—"They said I was too educated." As he told me about how he's living off his veteran's disability checks, I heard bumping from behind one of the bedroom doors. Connie got up and went in, emerging a few minutes later to help Menier's elderly mother slowly step past us and over to the couch on the far side of the room.

"Ma, do you know who that is?" he asked as she fell into her seat, Connie by her side. "He's the writer who came over to write about me running for president."

Breathing heavily and looking not at all well, his mother

turned to me with as much of a smile as she had the energy for, and said, "Oh, yes! Does he get my vote? Yeah!"

This seemed to please Menier, who smiled and said he had something important to show me. We walked over to his computer, where he pulled up dozens of Tea Party emails with subject headings that featured the same sort of conservative, borderline racist, spam I occasionally get from relatives. Menier apparently formed a lot of his political opinions based on these messages, and hearing that kind of crushed me.

I really was trying to approach all these Can't-idates without judging their personal politics—but Menier's views were starting to seem very close-minded. The same guy who wanted to feed the starving kids of Manila had started sprinkling our conversation with the occasional racial epithet or demeaning comment about poor people. I was hoping this selfish bluster was just his way of processing information through the prism of his own sad experiences. Menier clearly did not agree.

"I don't see it as I have had a tough life," he explained when I asked if his life had indeed informed his politics. "I think I am more in touch with the American people than any politician that's out there, because they have never had any downs. They talk about how rough their life was, but I would like to have one of their rough days as a good day. I don't think they really give a rat's butt about America.

"Maybe I am not as educated as they may be, or as good at the bull crap that they pass out. But I bet you $10 that I can fix what they screwed up over the last 50 years—and it's not that hard. I will embarrass [Congress] to do the right thing, and convince the voting population that the people that they think are taking care of them are selling them down the river. At some point, they have got to see it."

He certainly had the spirit I was looking for. However, for

the first time since Doug Shreffler (although for very different reasons), I was seriously regretting an interview. It took several more minutes to convince Menier to let me go—he followed me out to my car, still without shoes, but now wearing a shirt he'd put on to shoot our Facebook video. As I drove away, I felt like I'd failed by including him in my trip. I assumed the hardships he'd lived through should have made him more understanding of those leading less fortunate lives. Instead, they seemed to just make him angry about everyone and everything, with no avenue other than running for president to channel that bitterness.

One minute he'd complain about Marxist leadership dumbing America down, the next minute he'd do a philosophical 180 and rail against corporate greed. "How much money do you need?" he griped. "You don't give a shit about the people that work for you. You don't care about whether we got jobs here in America—because I got my job, I don't give a shit about you."

Menier was angry about taxpayers footing the bill for entitlement programs—then warned politicians to keep their hands off his Social Security. "If they touch it," he warned, "they don't have to wait for me to become president to change that. They will have a battle on their front door step."

He sidetracked with disparaging racial comments and worries that America is being flooded by immigrants—and he's married to a woman from the Philippines. It would have been pretty easy to have just eliminated Menier's chapter, since he was all over the map with his views. After all, it's not like the country would be hurting if it didn't hear from another older, conservative white male candidate. But the more I thought about dropping him, the more I realized I actually need him in this collection. He's the perfect embodiment of the American electorate these days—mostly well-intentioned people who are suckered into fear and loathing by cable news hotheads, Internet cowards and pandering politicians looking to find someone else to blame for everything that's gone wrong; It all leads to political beliefs that seem to be lacking one key ingredient—logic.

I've heard conservatives complain that this country is soft on crime. The little guy (and gal) isn't being heard by his (or her) elected representatives. The media is totally biased against the Right. Meanwhile, liberals believe that corporate criminals are getting off too easy. The powerful are simply adding to their already large fortunes. The media is totally biased against the Left. Opposite sides of the coin belittle each other without ever realizing they're both still on the same damn coin. Menier personified this contradiction, and he'd been through some pretty horrible things to get him to that point. No way was I going to drop him now.

I settled in for another long drive and turned on the radio to keep me company on a stormy Florida night. The pouring rain and booming thunder provided the perfect soundtrack to the show I stumbled across, something called *Ground Zero with Clyde Lewis*. I'm a sucker for supernatural reality shows—the ones where just before the commercial break, our ghostbusters see something that makes them gasp. But when they return from the break, it turns out they just saw a spider.

We all know that if they had really found something from beyond the grave, we would surely have heard about it long before we watched the episode. *Ground Zero* was sort of like that, only Lewis didn't seem to feel the need to pander to his audience the way those TV shows do. He was a believer. And if you weren't? Well, that's *your* problem. With his booming *Voice of God*, Lewis sucked me in by talking about the latest spooky Internet fad. Apparently, teens everywhere were playing the *Charlie, Charlie* game, wherein they balance one pencil on top of another, then try to contact a demon named Charlie. If the pencils move, he's come to play with them—and, according to legend, steal their souls.

For a few hours, I powered through a pitch black night punctuated by frequent flashes of lightening, as Lewis himself contacted Charlie and swore the spirit was in his studio. This eventually segued into a discussion of past spooky fads—like the Ouija board, Bloody Mary and Europe's child-snatching Emul Negru. Listening to all this, I realized three important things: First, I had to call my own teen to see if he'd ever heard of Charlie (he hadn't); second, I had to listen to *Ground Zero* every night for the rest of the trip, because Lewis' stories of conspiracies—both governmental and supernatural—were vintage campfire tale-telling; and third, despite all the spine-tingling horror that Charlie and Mary and Emul Negru were responsible for, Joe Morrissey was still the scariest creature I'd encountered on the radio all week.

Lori Fleming

The trip to Lori Fleming's place was just one disturbing hitchhiker short of being the first 15 minutes of *The Texas Chainsaw Massacre*. She lived in Melbourne, Arkansas, about two hours north of Little Rock. This town of 1,800 people was in the thick of the Ozark Mountains, and I felt more and more isolated with each passing mile.

The roads got narrower, the potholes more plentiful. The trees and underbrush grew thicker, to the point where they may well have been concealing an entire army of the dead. I drove past houses, which gradually looked more and more derelict. In one field, there was a sign offering both barber and handyman services—presumably performed separately. A little further up the road was a beat-up Airstream trailer with a sign outside reading: "Medical Clinic."

The Baptist churches on these back roads were as plentiful as the check-cashing places in Vegas and pawn shops in Cleveland. And just to make it clear where in the country I was, the few local radio stations I could find showcased angry ministers warning that the day gay men and women get to marry will indeed be the day before we are sent to a pit of hellfire for all eternity. (Although, given the choice between living in hell or the desolate Ozark countryside, it was kind of a coin flip.)

Fleming had told me to meet her in the parking lot of Melbourne's lone grocery store, where I'd follow her into the woods to get to her home. I saw her beat-up minivan, gave a quick nod of acknowledgement, then followed her through the only traffic light I could see in Melbourne. Very soon, we were bumping along a path in the woods that had dreams of someday being a *real* road.

Fleming pulled into a clearing alongside a large garden and three tiny shacks. A guy in baggy shorts and an Oakland Raiders T-shirt stood nearby, digging into a giant hole. Fleming emerged from her van, a large woman in a gray T-shirt, Dickies-style work pants and hiking boots. She was 40, but could easily have passed for a decade younger. She held a slight wad of tobacco in her cheek and a red Solo cup in her right hand for the ensuing spit. She'd ended up on this 10-acre plot of land a few years earlier because it was almost exactly halfway between her daughter's home in Ohio and her mom's place in Texas.

"Let me show you around," she said, offering the most crushing handshake since Harley Brown. "This September, I'll have been here four years. Right, Mark?" She looked over at Digging Man, who just shrugged and went back to work. "Your smokes are in my door here. They're a different flavor. They had a new one for $1.19."

I assumed this was her significant other.

"He's my other half some days," Fleming said, laughing and spitting out a gob of liquid brown into the cup. "Some days I just want to bury him here in one of these holes." She turned to him and shouted, "Hey, are you Mark or Marcus?" He just smiled and kept digging away. "He doesn't listen to me. No man listens to a woman. You guys hear us, but you don't listen to us."

He'd moved here earlier in the year, after Fleming met him in Ohio while visiting her daughter. They went to play pool at a nearby bar, where Mark worked cleaning up the place. After a few games, he and Fleming became friends and spent the next few weeks hanging out a lot. Fleming was concerned that the owners of the bar were taking advantage of him. So when it was time to head back to Arkansas, she invited him to come along.

"They wanted $5,000 to set up the electricity here," Fleming explained as she pointed out the large electrical pole, with cords extending to the nearest of the three buildings. "So I've been working on building the inside of this [shack] because it only cost me $500 to get it here. This is pretty much where we stay. Except it's not big enough for guests, so we're going to the main house."

Back in my *People* magazine days, I discovered one of the most effective reporting tricks was to excuse yourself to use the bathroom. That's often where you can get the best clues to who people are and what they might be hiding. So I asked Fleming if I could use the facilities inside this back shack, which couldn't have been much larger than an old garden shed.

The cramped quarters were divided into three sections. On the far side was a room separated from the rest of the space by a long curtain. On the other side was a counter upon which sat a pie dish full of what I assumed used to be pickles and roast beef. The bathroom was on my right, complete with strands of flypaper thick with bugs hanging from the makeshift ceiling. The space inside was barely big enough to accommodate a few brooms, but it contained a shower, toilet, water heater and some shelves overflowing with toilet paper, mouthwash, wipes and assorted bug and cleaning sprays (neither of which, to be honest, were doing their job very well).

These were living conditions that might inspire a $20 donation to Save the Children after seeing them in an infomercial. It's not like I live a life of luxury, but I was Bill Gates compared to Fleming. She was waiting for me as soon as I walked out of the bathroom. I wanted to tell her how sorry I was that this is how she lived. At the same time, though, I knew that would make me sound like an a-hole. She didn't show any sign of feeling bad about her current economic status, so it would be pretty condescending for me to express condolences. She did express concern for one aspect of her country living though.

"Not to be gross, but do a tick test from head to toe when you leave," she said, casually hocking another lump of brown stuff into her cup. "Arkansas is really bad with ticks this year."

Then it was down to business. We sat on her porch couch and Fleming immediately began venting.

"Hey, did you hear about Hillary's big faux pas last night?" she asked, shaking her head. "I just heard it on the radio when we were driving here. She was in South Carolina last night. She was trying to pull off a Southern accent, and all she did was offend a bunch of people."

The day before, Fleming's fellow Arkansan presidential rival had spoken to the South Carolina Democratic Women's Council using a distinct Southern twang. The press had a field day with her political pandering and Fleming couldn't help but pile on. It wasn't so much Hillary trying to act hillbilly that annoyed her. It was more the idea that the media was spending its time on these ridiculous details about big-name candidates, rather than good ideas from unknown candidates.

"We're not billionaires, so what we say doesn't matter," she explained. "The best outcome for me would be that there would be enough people who actually heard me—who listened and actually took time to think before going to the polls. Instead of going, 'The only name I know on here is Hillary, so I'll vote for her.'"

It's not like Fleming hasn't tried to get some press of her own. She went to a local newspaper to pitch a story on her campaign and the editor happily agreed to write about her—for a fee of $600. Since that was a non-starter, she was using the Internet to get the word out—until about six weeks ago. Unfortunately, she'd "spent too much on a meet-and-greet and not enough on the bills," so now the only computer access she has is either at the local library or her daughter's house. She's handed out flyers and held fund-raising bake sales in Melbourne. But when people ask, "You want to be president of *what?*" her answer—"of the United States"—is frequently greeted with laughter.

As she spoke, I could see her jaw clench.

"They say I'm not old enough, that I'm not rich enough, that I'm too honest, I'm too small-town, I'm single, I can't scratch nobody's back in Congress—so why should they even waste their time listening to me? Everybody tells me, 'Why are you even trying? Because an honest person is never going to win.' Well, *why?* Why won't an honest person win? Because we have conditioned ourselves to follow the crowd?"

It figures that she was born in a town called Defiance, tucked away in the northwestern corner of Ohio. Life was pretty much a battle right from the start. Her dad was a machine operator whose company moved him around a lot. The Flemings eventually found themselves in Clintwood, Virginia, living so far back in the woods that they had to ride horses along dirt roads to get to the local schoolhouse.

There were some good times during those days, most notably hanging out with her Uncle Jack, who "taught me to care about the planet and my surroundings. He is the one that made me an environmentalist. You could drop me off in the middle of nowhere and I could make it back home—and [I'd] be wearing a bearskin coat."

Fleming's dad taught her how to wire a house and rebuild an engine, but that wisdom came at a price. "He always made it hell, because if you weren't quick enough, you had a screwdriver thrown at you, a wrench. That hurt. You learned to pay attention and to be fast."

Things weren't much better away from home. She hadn't learned to read by the time she entered the third grade, so she was tucked away in Special Ed classes just like Luis Ramos. And, just like his schooling, there was nothing special about that education.

"When it came to assignments, the teacher read them. And when it came to test time, she would read the question, read the answers, and say it was either A or B. And then, if somebody said, 'It's A,' she'd say, 'No, but it's either A or B.'"

The school held her back in the first grade, the second grade, the third grade. It became clear that at the rate she was going, she'd also be a 21-year-old high school graduate like Ramos. The only help came from one teacher who spent her own money to buy Fleming a set of *Hooked on Phonics* tapes, which helped her learn her ABCs. Then that teacher was let go because, Fleming recalled, the district felt "it was inappropriate for her to spend as many hours as she did with us."

Her family moved again—this time to Texas. School was no better there. Fleming has memories of teachers throwing pizza parties and showing *Nightmare on Elm Street* videos instead of actually teaching. (Several years later, her special needs son, Travis, would attend school in the same area, and she'd find things hadn't improved.)

Fleming had mentioned Travis on the phone. Raising him has not been easy. He seemed perfectly fine until the day of his second birthday, when she walked into his room and he didn't respond. When she went to touch him, he screamed in agony. Travis was rushed to the hospital, where doctors gave Fleming the bad news: he had a neurological disorder that caused pain any time he came in contact with pretty much anything. Then Travis stopped speaking. By the time he turned three, doctors confirmed he was autistic. Since then, he's also been diagnosed with Cushing's Disease, high blood pressure, insomnia and incontinence. Chronologically he's 19, but mentally he's only five and requires full-time attention.

I asked what "Mr. Travis," as she referred to him, was up to today. Rather than just tell me, Fleming called out for him. He'd been watching DVDs in the back shack. It's one of the few things that keeps him company, since he no longer attends school. A minute later, Travis came lumbering around the corner and onto the porch. My first reaction was pretty much the same mixture of pity and relief I'd had listening to Shreffler's disillusionment or observing Rileyanne Neveu's autism—pity for those afflicted and relief it wasn't me. But seeing Travis added a whole new emotion: fear.

The kid was enormous. He stood well over six feet tall and was at least 300 pounds. Travis suffers from a genetic disorder that keeps him growing and he'll probably be at least seven feet tall before it stops. He already wears a size 16 shoe and extra-extra-extra-extra-large shirts.

"He's shattered every one of my ribs," Fleming told me. "He head-banged quite often as a little child, so we would wrap him in a cocoon blanket full of beads that made it heavy. I would hold him against my chest and he would head-bang backwards. Now my ribs are like a spider web."

Travis was carrying a stack of books and a bag with a few rocks. He seemed excited to find some new company. He has no friends and even his nearest therapist is two hours away. He sat right next to me with an expectant look, as I held tight in my seat, wanting to be nice to this kid. I couldn't help but worry about what to expect, when he shoved a piece of paper in my hands.

"Is Field Museum," he said, with the halting speech of someone who is deaf (which he is, in one ear). I thanked him, and he was very quick with a "Welcome!"

It was a map of the Field Museum in Chicago, where Fleming had taken her son several times whenever they could afford the trip.

"Travis loves it there. We've never seen anything but the third floor, where they have all their fossils. He loves dinosaurs, don't you, Travis? We have more dinosaur books than all of our county libraries together."

Travis reached down again, this time to grab a brick-sized rock from his collection.

"That's heavy, Travis! I don't want you to hand it to him," his mother pleaded.

Too late. He dropped it in my lap.

"Okay, Travis, tell him what it is and then put it back."

"You have time portal?" he asked me, ignoring his mother.

"No, baby, he doesn't have a time portal," she answered politely.

The response didn't seem to faze him. He smiled and reached back down to his collection, grabbing an eraser-sized stone he'd taken from his grandma's farm in Texas. Apparently her land was home to dinosaurs 10 million years earlier, and when she started plowing it, the family found all these artifacts.

"Travis, tell him what dinosaur that is," Fleming said, pointing to the fossil in his hand.

"T. Rex," he said proudly.

"No, not a T. Rex. Remember, those are Ammonite, like prehistoric shrimp." He looked down at the rock and stumbled, awkwardly trying to pronounce "Ammonite."

"Okay, Travis," she finally said. "Why don't you go put

them back up now?"

For the first time, he looked angry.

"Why?"

With that same trying-to-not-lose-it tone I used when my kids would ask "Why?" for the fifth time in two minutes, she explained that it was "Mommy's turn to talk now." Her endless patience was not only inspirational, it was also something I'd love to see in a president. If she can calm a severely autistic 19-year-old who could lose it at any time, just imagine how well she'd deal with a petulant Putin.

"Why don't you go back to watch *Space Jam* for a few minutes? We'll eat in a bit," she told him. Travis instantly complied. Other than a quick sigh, there was no indication this had exhausted her. I suppose that's what happens after years of around-the-clock attending to her son. She hasn't been able to even accept temp work. To do so would mean leaving Travis with Mark, who she doesn't believe is quite ready for that responsibility. And besides, even when she's tried, nobody is hiring.

"He has Medicaid, thank God. But without my mom's [financial] help, I wouldn't get by," Fleming explained as Travis left. "We have to drive to Batesville when work is available, or we have to drive to Mountain Home when it's available. That's an hour each way. And there is no way to do that in the winter, because you get snowed in here for three months out of the year. You have to make sure that you have stuff stocked up and have enough money saved."

She's worked pretty much every kind of job imaginable: nursing home aide, paper route, manufacturing breast implants, airport maintenance, telemarketer, hotel security. She'd even be happy to work at McDonald's, if there was an opening. The way Fleming sees it, there's no point in "looking down your nose at people who do that, because there are CEOs right now that would kill to work there, because companies are closing down."

That might be a bit of an exaggeration. I'm not convinced that, should the market go south again, Warren Buffet will be spotted flipping burgers. Still, I understood the point she was getting at. Times are tough for a lot of people, and that means making occasional compromises within your life so you can at least survive.

Not working a steady gig seemed as stressful for her as dealing with Travis. Fleming insisted she's never really been unemployed before and would love to work in the field in which she got her community college degree: construction technology. However, it's been a struggle to find that type of work since the day she graduated. She insists her college even declined to let her walk out for her diploma because it wasn't "an appropriate field for a female."

"I actually had to see a psychiatrist once-a-week at this college," she explained with a last angry tobacco spit into her cup. "They couldn't understand back in 1996 why a female would want to do construction."

The sting of that gender rejection will probably never leave her. It's a reminder of a battle Fleming has been fighting as long as she can remember.

"If it were up to me, young girls could play with the boy toys, boys could play with the girl toys. There shouldn't even be a boy toy or girl toy, because it would teach boys to be better fathers, better husbands. It would teach girls that they do not have to rely on a man when they are stuck on the road for three hours with a flat tire."

Growing up, Fleming was so committed to the idea of gender equality that she went out for the football team in high school because "I wanted to prove that a girl could play." Maybe she wasn't great at the game, but she did have enough skill to become one of the team's quarterbacks. The school responded by giving her "the worst pads and stuff." A rough tackle tore up her knee to the point where she needed surgery. And that was it for football.

That pain was nothing, though, compared to the other matter she was dealing with. Never one for keeping secrets, Fleming was happy to walk into the school cafeteria back then hand-in-hand with her girlfriend. No matter how often people would scrawl "gay and lesbian stuff on our lockers," she insisted on being who she was without hiding—right up until it all became too much for her girlfriend, who broke off their romance.

There was a pause that hung as heavy as the early afternoon humidity.

"I tried to commit suicide."

At 14, Fleming's sexuality made her a pariah. The girl she loved left her. Someone at school planted a stolen stereo in her locker, then alerted the authorities that she'd taken it. Couple that with her struggles at home with her father—plus constantly being held back at school—and Fleming decided she'd had enough.

"It was just a really bad year and I got tired of it all. I took a bottle of about 200 aspirin out of my mom's medicine cabinet. I went to the park, climbed to the top of the ladder and took every damned one of them. I don't know what happened. I woke up in the hospital. They pumped my stomach and then I had charges pressed against me—because it's illegal to commit suicide. If you don't die, you go to jail."

She ended up being sent to a counselor. That didn't go well. "You don't tell your counselor that you are a lesbian or a dyke or bisexual. You don't tell your counselor that your dad is physically abusive to your mom. Or that your brother will beat the hell out of you over spilled beer or a joint going missing. So you just sit there and listen to her tell you how good life is and [how] you shouldn't throw it away. And you promise to bring your grades up, [but] all the time you are thinking—'Witch, walk a mile in my shoes.' That's the biggest problem. Everybody is so judgmental, but nobody has been where you have been. And if they have, they sure as hell ain't going to admit it."

And to think I used to cry on my walk home from school because somebody called me "Beak" or "Four Eyes." Fleming dealt with her pain the only way she could—walking back into the closet. She decided to "find out what all the girls were talking about" and proceeded to get drunk at a party. The night would eventually end with her pregnant at 17 with daughter Robin. "I used a condom and was on birth control," insisted Fleming. "So the Lord wanted her on this planet for some reason."

She was kicked out of school for being "a bad influence on other girls," even though she now reads about Texas high schools where girls can bring their babies to class. At that time, however, Fleming had to get her G.E.D. after giving birth to Robin. She found work as an airport mechanic, repairing the carts that cruised the tarmac, when she met and started dating Kenneth.

"I figured, fine...I'll make my mom happy, I'll make my dad happy, I'll get my brother and sister off my damn back. I'll date this guy. We figured, 'What the hell, we'll get married.' Even though his mother really hated me and my family didn't really like him."

The tension got worse after Fleming, Kenneth and Robin were nearly killed in a car accident. She found out while recovering in the hospital that she was pregnant with Travis. When Fleming was finally able to go home and recuperate from taking a steering wheel to the chest, Kenneth said he was going to go fishing with some of his buddies—and he never came home. She tried calling him. She looked everywhere. Finally, two years later, she got an envelope from California. The only thing inside was a Polaroid of Kenneth on the beach with another man. Although they never spoke again, she and Kenneth divorced. Travis' father was not around when his son began to exhibit signs of autism.

Speaking of which, as Fleming was talking, Travis wandered over to us again and sat down next to me. This time he was holding one of his dinosaur books.

"Look at this," he said, showing me the first few pages of a thick picture book about prehistoric life. "And this...and this..."

I tried hard to be polite and not nervous as he struggled to read the words about the birth and extinction of dinosaurs.

"We journey back in time!" he declared, suddenly and loudly.

Fleming tried to ignore her boy's enthusiasm and kept talking, complaining about our educational system and detailing how she'd entirely revamp things if she got to be president.

"We spend so much time worrying about her purple hair, his pink hair, her shirt, the length of the shorts, the fact that a kid has spiked hair, or that child is playing with rubber bands, that we are not teaching the children. And you have got one teacher, one aide—and 35 kids."

"We journey back in time!" Travis repeated, more forcefully.

Once more, his mom tried to stay on topic.

"Not all kids learn the same. If some children learn better by seeing things, make this side of the room more visual for them. If these children learn better by having things read to them, give them headphones with a book on cassette. If these children learn better by being left alone, leave them alone. If the children cannot learn the way we are teaching them, we need to teach them the way they learn."

"We journey back in time!" Travis said once again, making it sound more like a command this time. Fleming had mentioned his temper tantrums. So while I like to think I'm as empathetic as the next journalist, I tensed up and scooted back.

"Yes, as soon as we get a time machine," she calmly told him.

"Do you have a time machine?" Travis asked her, a bit more relaxed.

"I do not!" Lori snapped.

Now Travis seemed angrier than ever. "Now I'll never get to go to prehistoric past!"

For the first time today, it looked like Travis was getting under her skin. She inched forward and said very firmly, "Travis, go watch cartoons then!"

He quieted down immediately, stood up and walked back to his DVDs. Fleming eased back in her chair, as if this sort of sudden confrontation and resolution was a daily occurrence. Which I'm guessing it was. She can't remember the last time she went to "a grown-up movie." She doesn't attend church functions anymore because she felt the parishioners were not particularly welcoming of Travis.

"Having my son has redefined the world for me. People are not as tolerant as they like to say they are. I have met very few true Christians. The ones that claim they are are the worst. The ones that say, 'I believe in God,' but don't go to church—[they're] the ones that I will hang out with any day of the week. The Bible says, 'I stand upon this rock to talk to my Lord, this rock is my church.' So here's my church. And *this* church allows my son to interrupt me while I am reading my Bible or communing with God. *This* church is not judgmental."

Her one escape, other than going to Ohio to visit her daughter and grandkids, is poring over the books she's taught herself to read.

"I get them from the library. Or we have a little store run by the church, and on Wednesdays everything is 10 for a dollar. So I'll buy 30 or 40 books to get me through the month. I love Harry Potter. My mom actually stood in line when *Deathly*

Hallows came out, even though she was working overnight, just to get it for me."

I'd grown so used to hearing nearly everyone on this trip rip into a parent at some point (including me), it was inspiring to hear about a parent and child who get along. Fleming's mother has always stood by her—whether it was threatening to sue the schools that weren't teaching her to read, defending her when she came out in her teens, or taking her to a Mötley Crüe concert. In fact, it was her 62-year-old mom's troubles with Obamacare that first got her thinking about running for president.

Two years ago, Mom was working three hospice care jobs and struggling to pay $379 a month for her health insurance. Once Obamacare became the law of the land, the cheapest coverage she could find was $425 a month—for fewer benefits than before.

"She had to choose between buying her insulin and heart medication, or paying her bills and having insurance," Fleming recalled. "And somebody who is 62 should not have to worry about paying for their meds, or not being able to pay for their insurance."

A little more than a week before I arrived, her mom's insurance issues stopped being theoretical and got very real. She had a stroke and ended up in intensive care for three days, which meant losing two of her three jobs. Her speech had only just returned a day ago.

Fleming figured the least *she* could do after a blow like this was continue her campaign—because "my mama says that I'm one of the strongest people she knows. But to be honest, I'm not half as strong as my mama. And I figured if she can be like that, there's no reason I can't."

They don't necessarily agree on everything. Her mom has warned her a few times that she doesn't have enough money to run for president. (Even though Fleming is certain that the mystery donation of a few thousand dollars that was recently given to her campaign was from her mother.) And when she mentioned she was going to talk to me, her mom warned her to be very discreet.

"She told me not to let anybody know that I'm a dyke. And I said, 'Why?' It is not like this was 20 years ago, when I could have actually lost my children."

Fleming paused. While she didn't exactly choke up, I sensed a sadness in her that hadn't been present even when discussing Travis. She quickly glanced at Mark, who had moved over to watch something wrapped in foil on their small, rusty barbecue grill.

"I would love to be able to have a female partner hold my hand and walk with my children, without having to worry about if someone was going to call Child Protective Services. It has happened for me. That's why I had to go back into the closet."

Neither of us knew that in a month, gay marriage would essentially become the law of the land, courtesy of the Supreme Court. Even if we had that knowledge, though, I don't think it would have lessened her fearful wince as we talked about the possibility of Fleming finally being able to be herself. After all, she was still going to be in Arkansas, a state where most of the radio stations I'd listened to that morning considered gay marriage slightly more reprehensible than a zombie apocalypse.

It's also a state that not only produced the Clintons, but former governor and current presidential candidate, Mike Huckabee. This is a man who once said that "there's never been a civilization that has rewritten what marriage and family means and survived." The mere mention of Huckabee's name draws the sort of quick, instinctual response Travis had upon learning he wouldn't be visiting the prehistoric past.

"Why don't you call him and see if *he'll* take your call? Ask if he's ever actually been out here talking to real people. If you can't afford $500-a-plate dinners, then they really don't care about you."

She stared again at Mark, who was still sweating over the tiny barbecue grill, and asked if the chicken looked ready. He nodded. Mark was not much of a talker. Fleming turned back to me.

"My plates aren't worth $500—more like five cents. But we made some lunch for you."

After calling out for Travis, Fleming got up and we walked over to the card table that had been set up on the porch before I'd arrived. It held a half dozen foil-covered bowls, along with some paper plates, napkins, plastic forks and knives. While Travis ambled over to sit down on the patio couch, Fleming gently pushed Mark out of the way so she could take the foil-wrapped meat from the grill.

"Help yourself to some salad. I grow it all myself," she said, gesturing with her shoulder toward the garden I'd noticed while driving in. It felt kind of wrong taking her food. She'd already told me a few times how her monthly income—courtesy of family gifts, odd jobs and some government assistance—rarely ends up more than $700. I should have been the one bringing *her* food and regretted I hadn't thought of that until now.

I insisted I wasn't hungry and she seemed hurt that I wasn't accepting her hospitality. "C'mon, I grow all my own vegetables and they're really good. Not like what you'd get in any store. Try some. And you *have* to try my chicken."

There aren't many advantages her life has over mine. However, the presence of fresh lettuce, cucumbers, tomatoes and peppers was certainly one of them. She carefully opened up the hot foil from the grill, serving up some of the free-range chicken that wanders her property, before making a plate of her own.

"Did you hear that Pataki announced today he's running for president?" she asked. "And he talked about how he understands what regular people want…"

I could understand the reasoning behind her cynical tone. Out in New Hampshire, billionaire and former New York governor George Pataki told the world that he was just a regular fellow who deserved to be president *because* he was so normal. I'd caught a little of his announcement, wherein he boasted to a crowd of enthusiastic supporters—would a candidate ever have the guts to announce in front of a crowd that *isn't* stacked with friends and family?—all about his humble upbringing. His parents were poor. He grew up on a farm. And therefore, he knows all about the middle class.

Pataki was using that time-honored tactic both Democrats and Republicans rely on: trotting out any non-privileged part of their background so all the world can see s/he is one of them. This approach pushes the unspoken notion that because they made it the way they did, everyone else should therefore be capable of doing the same thing. If not, what's wrong with *you?*

Meanwhile, the formerly illiterate gay woman who battled with her blue-collar dad and once tried to kill herself is now raising a severely autistic child on (at best) $700 a month, while living off her own land. And at the end of the day, she and Pataki both had about the same chance of becoming president: zero. It's not like Fleming doesn't care about winning. It's just that, looking around at her three shacks and troubled son, she seemed a lot more believable than Pataki when she talked about why she's even attempting to do something crazy like run for president.

"There could be that one couple in the audience that wants a bank loan, but was too scared to go to the bank and ask for it," Fleming told me. "They could say, 'Well, this crazy lady is running for president. If she's willing to do that, we could easily ask for a bank loan.' There could be that young lady that thinks she deserves that raise or that new job, and seeing me out here embarrassing myself could give her the courage to risk it all for what she deserves.

"Or there could be that little girl or that little boy whose mom dragged them out there to see the working class woman running for president. And this little girl could remember this, in high school, college, and go—'You know what? Lori Fleming ran for president in 2016; in 2044, *I'm* running for president. I'm gonna do this. A woman can do this. A working class girl can do this.' The world is out there. The sky is our limit. That is what I want people to realize."

This was exactly what I was hoping to accomplish by talking to her and everyone else on this trip. So I was eager to get going and let the world know her story. We finished up lunch and, after a last look at some of Travis' fossils, I said goodbye. Before I drove off, I was left with these important parting words from Fleming: "Remember, do a tick check when you stop tonight. Those things are pretty nasty."

She seemed like she knew what she was talking about. So when I got to my motel that night, I gave myself the once-over. Sure enough, there was a tiny black bump on my right shin. I grabbed some tweezers and cautiously pulled the insect from my skin with only a slight five-year-old girl squeal, then washed it down the bathroom sink.

A creepy, blood-sucking creature had gotten under my skin. Only by paying careful attention was I able to identify it, purge it from my system and wash it away. Welcome to Political Metaphors 101.

John Green Ferguson/ Ruby Mei

Maybe this is a bit of an overstatement, but as I woke up to my last day on the road, I kind of felt like God was upset the end was in sight. I was in Dallas, Texas, which happened to be in the middle of a rainstorm approaching Biblical proportions. A week of downpours had left so much flooding around the state, I figured I should keep an eye out for travelers escorting pairs of animals along the road as I headed to meet up with the last two Can't-idates: John Green Ferguson and Ruby Mei.

The apocalyptic weather wasn't the only indication of some divine intervention. There was something prophetic about ending this journey with these two people. On one hand, they seemed to be at exact opposite ends of the political spectrum—Ferguson was a free-spirited guy in his 60s with a *"Screw 'em all"* sense of politics, while Mei was a straight-laced 30-something woman who parsed out her words the way Willie Wonka hands out golden tickets.

On the other hand, when I'd spoken to them a few weeks earlier, I also sensed there was something deeper that tied them together more than anyone else on my list. Ferguson mentioned several times how he didn't have many friends and spent most of his time alone out on his 13-acre ranch. Mei, meanwhile, offered up very few details about her personal life. Each time I tried to find out if she had a significant other, she explained that having a partner at this point in her life would be "illogical."

These two people approached politics entirely differently, but it felt like the reason they had gotten involved was surprisingly similar: They were smart people, but people who apparently like the idea of going it alone. Which made me identify with them in a more personal way than I had with the others throughout the trip. Sure, I could relate to the perils of parenting that people like Bart Lower and Dee Neveu faced. I could absorb some of Josh Usera's energy, and Vermin Supreme's sense of humor, and Harley Brown's attitude. However, it was the isolation that resonated from both Ferguson and Mei that felt intensely familiar.

Surviving solo is something at which I had become pretty adept for as long as I could remember. Maybe it was the crew cut, braces and mom-picked wardrobe I sported for years. Maybe it was that whole *going to three high schools in four years* thing. Whatever the cause, developing real, close, adult relationships— romantic or otherwise—felt uncomfortable at best, and excruciating at worst. The whole process seemed slightly more daunting and less dangerous than, say, firewalking.

I did manage to get married. I did have kids. I ate hundreds of lunches and brunches with acquaintances. Still, even with the children, I always felt a bit disconnected from the world. I would eventually learn some of that came courtesy of the chronic depression I'd ignored for decades, but not before I paid the price via divorce and subsequent dates/friendships that failed because it was so much easier to slip back into a cocoon and not try anymore. I got more rest that way. There was probably a lot I was missing out on by being an island. Then again, there wasn't much

I was losing either.

Hearing Mei insist that her life was too full for a relationship—as opposed to the majority who seem to think life isn't full *until* there's a relationship—seemed sensible to me. Listening to Ferguson describe the tranquility of wandering his ranch alone amongst his pigs, dogs, chickens and donkeys left me envious of that isolation. However, while I was happily burying myself at home alone, they decided to put themselves out into the world in a big way by running for president.

Ferguson lived about an hour or so west of Dallas, near a tiny town called Azle, so he was first on my list. After a series of wrong turns past lakes that had been fields a week earlier, I finally found his property. Appropriately enough, given the weather, about half a dozen old boats were piled up alongside the entrance road. A dozen yards further up, there was a large barn and a pen holding a bunch of muddy pigs on the left—and a junk pile of decrepit refrigerators, water heaters and bicycles to the right.

Past all of this, I saw an enormous, relatively modern tract home partially hidden in a thicket of trees. Standing in the driveway, surrounded by a couple lawnmowers, a big pickup truck and a beat-up ATV, was a gentleman who looked like Col. Sanders' hippie cousin. He had the bushy white goatee, and his giant shock of white hair hung down near his shoulders. His shirt was a picnic tablecloth patchwork of pinks, blues and grays. Dark blue work shorts and hole-filled tennis shoes completed the outfit.

"I am quite out of the norm and I know that," he'd explained earlier. "I'm very eccentric and I'm very abnormal. Even though I am as normal as can possibly be. I don't live in an apartment. I don't live in a trailer. I don't live in a cardboard box. But I could, essentially, be a street person if I didn't have so much stuff."

As soon as I stepped out of my car and into one of the dozens of mud puddles dotting his property, Ferguson began talking.

I don't think he drew more than a couple dozen breaths for the next three hours as he spoke nearly non-stop about…well, everything.

He views silence the way Cookie Monster views anything with chocolate chips—it must be swallowed whole. You could start out talking about, say, where he was from (Phoenix). Within three minutes, he's reminiscing about his days as a private investigator, or truck driver, or restaurateur. Stick around another 90 seconds and he'll be explaining how he designed a power system so efficient that the energy costs for his entire 13-acre spread is $50 a month.

He wasn't used to having company, explaining that "I spend a lot of time by myself. So when I have an audience all to myself, I will talk your damn ear off. I get lonely. I have been here four years by myself…me, my dog and my animals."

Before starting my tour of his home for the past seven years, he paused to light a cigarette.

"I smoke too much, because my hands and my mouth have got to be doing something all of the time."

Oral fixation set, he led me over to the massive shipwreck near the entrance to his property. He's a self-confessed "boat whore" and has close to a dozen water vessels piled up nearby in various states of disrepair. Whenever Ferguson sees one for sale, no matter how battered it might be, he'll buy it and dump it here until he has the chance to work on it. Which, judging by this mess, is practically never.

Walking over from the boats, we passed a gigantic stack of red bricks, which Ferguson snagged when a house up the road was torn down. Next up was a Home Depot massacre of neglect—bits of old air conditioner, toilets and heating duct. He'll fix up and sell what he can, when he can, to make a little money.

"Ever see one of these?" he asked, stepping over to a hunk

of junk in the thick of it all. "It's a 1948 Speed Queen Ringer Washer. I bought that for $20 bucks. Took it apart, lubed it up and it works perfect. Kinda rusty, but it works."

Next stop on our show-and-tell trip: the barn and pig-pen I'd driven by earlier. Ferguson scooped a small shovel into a big barrel next to the pen, tossing the contents to the dozen or so mud-covered wild boars.

"A treat for my pigs!" he laughed.

Twice-a-week three nearby restaurants will bag up their salad bar leftovers for him, and he puts the mélange of vegetables, French fries and fish parts to good use.

All in all, Ferguson figured, there were at least 35 animals roaming his property. He sells the pigs he doesn't eat himself to deep pit barbecue spots, and he's got enough chickens and ducks to earn spare cash selling their eggs. And I thought Lori Fleming's place was isolated. The deeper we wandered into the woods behind Ferguson's house, the more I understood how he could go for a walk in his personal "Garden of Eden" and lose all track of time.

"I haven't celebrated a holiday in four years," Ferguson randomly explained, and I couldn't tell if that was meant for me. After all, he was used to talking to himself out here. "I get really bad around the holidays. I mean, I've gone to people's houses. They have invited me cordially, just because they knew that I was poor and alone." He laughed.

We kept walking, but the further along we went, the larger the pits of rainwater became. The combination of flies and Texas humidity was getting so dense, Ferguson suggested we head back to the cooler, bug-free confines of his house. Entering through a garage jammed with boxes and tools, we squeezed past piles of pots and pans and toasters, which were apparently holdovers from his days operating restaurants in the Southwest.

The interior of Ferguson's 3,000-square-foot house was so

filled with broken computers, old electronic devices and furniture, that his crowded front yard seemed as orderly as a museum exhibit by comparison. In his dining room was an ornate set of table and chairs that would have been at home in most old English castles; but instead of hosting dinner parties, it hosted the insides of an old gutted computer Ferguson had yet to get around fixing.

"I have that six-portion table and have never had a dinner here but once in seven years," he said, noticing my stare. "That's why it's my computer fix desk."

It's not that he's lazy. His problem is exactly the opposite. During a quick trip around his house, I noticed little Post-It notes stuck on walls and door jambs and coffee tables, each with hard-to-read fragments of sentences. They contained the germ of a business plan or a recommendation for running the country, scribbled at all hours by night owl Ferguson.

"See all those pads and stuff? They're full of ideas!" He nodded his head in the direction of a stack of unused Post-its on the coffee table, next to an easy chair with a permanent butt indentation. "I've got them everywhere. I just jump up and start writing stuff down. And then it's a three-hour project. Next thing I know, the sun is coming up and I haven't slept. I don't sleep much, never have. I have that 24-hour-a-day deficit thing that blind people have, where I can be really super tired and lay down, but just can't go to sleep."

Considering how words fly from him the way water flows from a sprinkler, this news came as no surprise. This is someone whose mind has always moved about 15 miles an hour faster than the rest of him. Born in Pennsylvania, he never knew his real dad and had to deal with a frenetic home life, which included three stepdads and a move to the "dirt poor" neighborhood of Phoenix. Ferguson would run home from school every day so he wouldn't get beaten up by the girls—"the boys were huffing dope and airplane glue...they were docile." Since he had no real adult supervision, he was forced to make his own way early on.

"I could have been a dope sniffer or an acid freak, but I never went that way," he told me as we settled into old, over-stuffed chairs in his living room. "I've never been addicted to anything, other than surviving. To make money, I picked up newspapers. I picked up everybody's pop bottles. I'd take them over to buy candy. I bought books. I bought clothes. I literally made a business out of it."

He started earning a steady paycheck when he was 14, doing everything from being a paperboy, to a boat repairman, to an assistant manager at Jack in the Box. Ferguson continued to career hop after graduating. He could probably fill 10 more pages with his resumé (and trust me, he tried to as we spoke). He worked his way into the Cement Masons Union and eventually ran his own general contracting business, as well as a janitorial service, in Arizona. He designed and built self-sustaining houses. He created wind turbines and water recycling systems, becoming so involved in green technology that he opted to use it as part of his name.

"Did I tell you I read your story about your dad?"

As is his way, Ferguson abruptly did a 180 turn on the subject at hand. He was talking about a piece I'd written two decades earlier, when I'd learned my genetic dad died before I was born, then went back to Kansas to learn more about him.

"I tracked *my* dad down and talked to him on the phone for, like, 10 minutes before he died. Turns out he was a disc jockey when he was married to my mom, and then the radio station converted him to more like a man-on-the-street reporter."

Ferguson seemed very matter-of-fact as he told me about this, which I suppose might seem inappropriate given the circumstances. He'd lived his whole life never knowing his dad. Then, right at the end, he found the guy who gave him life and they got just a few minutes together. I could excuse his lack of tears as he told me his tragic tale. After all, I'd been there myself.

When I've told people *my* story, they almost always apologize for my circumstance in the same well-intentioned, yet guilty, way you'd tell the homeless guy you're sorry you don't have any spare change—while fingering quarters in your pocket. For those who grew up with their biological moms and dads, I'm sure it seems depressing to think there are those of us who didn't have that same safety net to fall back on. It must be reassuring knowing that no matter how bad things get in your life, there's somebody in the world with a blood bond you can rely on.

The thing is, though, I never knew what it was like to have that connection with a dad. I couldn't miss what I didn't have, and I got by well enough with the parenting I did get. The whole thing is more about closure—learning about your roots and then growing away from them. I got my closure traveling back to Kansas to learn who my dad was. Ferguson got his with a 10-minute call to the guy he'd never know. And sometimes, that's enough.

He did find other familial connections to replace the son-father bond. He got married when he was 18 and had a daughter a couple years later. He and his wife were hitched for 23 years before things started going south. Eager to find somebody he could care for, he decided to look up the families of the men and women his parents married after they split. That led him to a half sister, who died in a house fire shortly after they'd connected. There was a half brother who turned out to be a drug addict and drank himself to death. To top it all off, one stepdad was apparently accused of child molestation and ended up spending 10 years in prison.

Meanwhile, back at home he fared no better. His marriage ended, which meant looking once again for someone special. For a while he did date "a few high maintenance women. They were like Marilyn Monroe types—had money, great jobs and I helped them along in their world. Then they would dump me for a loser. I was taking them on trips to Hawaii on their birthday and paying for $50 meals every night. Driving them around in a brand new $85,000 Cadillac Escalade every day. And I'm going, like, 'What the hell? What is *wrong* with me?'"

There was at least one woman remaining in his life—his daughter. But parenting proved to be as much of a challenge for him as it had been for the multiple parents who raised him. Ferguson was close to his daughter throughout her childhood, when she had been a cheerleader and the top student in her high school class. Then came a day when she was 17, and he claims to have found her with "her tongue down the throat of one of her girlfriends."

It's not that he was opposed to what he saw. "You have the right to marry who you want in the United States...that's *why* it's the United States." It's more that he was disappointed because, from his point of view, she was giving up on his dream of seeing her go into medicine in favor of...well...nothing in particular. He says it's been four years since he last saw her. So with no family or friends around, most of his companionship comes from cable news.

It wasn't supposed to be this way when he moved from Arizona to Texas. He made the trek not because he was particularly fond of the Lone Star State ("It's a Third World country in the United States"), but because he'd hoped to retire and live off the grid on his 13 isolated acres with a very special someone.

She was a 63-year-old Phoenix flight attendant who "looked better than her 36-year-old daughter." They'd run into each other while he was working as a country and western dance instructor, and he realized early on she was the real deal. To the point where he eased away from his businesses to simply be alone with her. Everything went according to plan, until about five years ago when his world collapsed.

"She died," he said slowly, thoughtfully. "Essentially… she had cancer."

For the first (and last) time in our conversation, Ferguson had nothing to say.

Finally, he spoke. "Maybe you should leave all this stuff out. You could just say that she died. We were together. We bought the ranch. We tried. We were going to retire here."

I'd loved to have accommodated him and simply removed these details of his loss. Then again, I wanted to know the turning point in everyone's political life—when they decided that *talking* about what's wrong with America wasn't enough; they had to get involved in the biggest way possible. And Ferguson's motivation certainly seemed to be the empty days after losing the love of his life.

He'd already gone from being "a millionaire on paper" to being broke, courtesy of the 2008 stock market collapse. After she passed, he lived on odd jobs and food stamps, spending endless sleepless nights sitting in the same easy chair, "throwing myself into the news…local, state, national. I'd get one hour of sleep to get up and watch *Face the Nation* and all that stuff. Where most people are watching *General Hospital* and *As the World Turns*, I'm on cable watching BBC news from the UK. I am watching Japanese news. I am watching stuff all night long, I'm reading stuff. And I'm feeding on that."

In particular, he started following stories about the Occupy Movement. The protest against income inequality got its biggest media boost in the fall of 2011, when followers set up camp near Wall Street. It didn't take long for the movement to spread to nearly 1,000 cities around the world, and although the Wall Street protest was broken up after a couple months, Ferguson found purpose in Occupy's ideals.

"It was for my sanity, after being by myself in a prison," he explained. "[Losing my fiancée] was really a kick in the balls. I was left alone to fend for myself. It wasn't the surviving part; it is just that when you haven't got anybody, no friends—I mean, I am away from anybody that I ever knew here."

The best solution to save the country (and himself) seemed simple: Go to the FEC website and file to run for the presidency. He felt confident he could save the nation with his ideas about everything from legalizing marijuana—"Tax it…They're getting a lot of money off of it in Colorado"—to protecting the Second Amendment. "It's a proven fact that in World War II Japan would have come straight to Los Angeles, but everybody in the United States had guns…they'd lose coming here, so they weren't going to do it."

Ferguson is pro-gun *and* pro-choice. It's hard to pin down his politics. All he'd say is, "You have to be a blanket neutralist. I might say, 'Those ideas are Republican' or 'Those ideas are liberal' or whatever. I think the best strategy is *whatever the best strategy is*. The best person for the job is *the best person for the job*. It doesn't matter what color they are. I don't give a rat's ass if they come from Mars. Elect the best officials to take your concerns to Congress and [the] Senate, and to run the government."

There is some downside to attempting to be chief executive. Even your closest friends are going to think you've lost it. That's fine with Ferguson, since he's used to people thinking he's a flake. The only time it's an issue is when he's tried to find a new love.

"I have been looking for six months, but I haven't found anybody," he said, shaking his head with a wry laugh. "It's not really the presidential thing that's the drawback, although that has probably hindered it. I dated a woman once and said, 'I have to tell you that I am running for President of the United States.' And then she just kind of bowed out of the deal."

He still has hopes to find someone, to escape what he refers to as his "prison without walls."

Part of that plan is following through on his recurring dream where he writes a book "about a lonely person with a string attached to his heart, which is attached to the world. That delegates down to the way I am now…I live by myself and am attached to a lot of things, but totally separated from it—which is heart-wrenching."

So much of what Ferguson was telling me about his life was heart-wrenching. Still, he remained pretty upbeat about it all. Right until he began to reflect on what his life has meant to those around him. Then his energy vanished and he sunk into his chair, tears in his eyes.

"Everyone, if it wasn't for me, they probably would be dead or worse. They would be addicts, whores on the streets, drunks or dope addicts. Who knows what would have happened to them? That's where they were. Now they are sustaining. They are good people. They got married. They've got kids. They got good relationships. I have never had a great relationship."

Rather than let his loss cement him to the easy chair, though, Ferguson had been able to rally in a way I'm not sure I could have. He started looking at life outside of himself and decided giving back to the universe as a presidential candidate was the best way to go. It may be a bit self-aggrandizing. But then again, what mainstream politician doesn't display similar ego at some point? At least he is more thoughtful about all this than I'd ever be. I end a marriage, so I get drunk watching rom-coms alone all weekend. He has hard times, so he decides to save the world as the American president. Nothing wrong with that.

It took another hour, but I was finally able to ease my way out of the conversation and back to my car. I liked Ferguson, but I had places to be, and talking to him was turning into a marathon more than a series of sprints. He trailed me outside and even up the driveway as I drove out, leaving open the possibility that he might grab onto the bumper and tag along to meet Ruby Mei.

Mei lived just outside of Austin, about a three-hour trip from John Green Ferguson's ranch—or about two stories away, in John Green Ferguson time. The record-setting rainstorms had hit Austin hardest and Mei's sunroom roof had collapsed. Her air conditioner had also been flooded out, so visiting her home was out, as was going to any of her favorite neighborhood hangouts, thanks to the buckets of water gathering in everyone's homes and restaurants. That's how we ended up a few miles south of Austin at a strip mall Starbucks, which was nearly deserted, given the weather conditions outside.

Although I'd never seen a picture of her, I could easily spot Ruby Mei. Everything about her on the phone seemed very proper, very business-like, very to-the-point. So she had to be the slight woman in the back with very little makeup, hair pulled back bank clerk-style, wearing a sensible brown dress and sweater. She sat with a woman and man whose exuberance when I walked in balanced her polite and respectful demeanor.

Mei had brought along her sister, An, and a friend, Leonard, to talk about her campaign. An lived with Mei— along with their mother. Leonard was a dancer/teacher Mei befriended when they met at a local studio. As soon as we all shook hands and sat down, Mei and company insisted I tell them all about everyone else I'd interviewed.

"What do the other candidates you've talked to think about what you're doing?" An asked.

I was surprised at how automatic it was for me to remember and categorize everyone. There were the good people who seemed to be running for president as a way of filling a hole in their lives—Doug Shreffler, Ronald Satish Emrit, Luis Ramos, Tom Menier and John Green Ferguson. I told them about the crusaders rebounding from trauma—Rev. Pamela Pinkney Butts,

Josh Usera, Dee Neveu, Bart Lower and Doris Walker. I told them about the clown princes of politics, who saw the dysfunction in our electoral system and gave it right back to us—Vermin Supreme and Sydneys Voluptuous Buttocks. And I told them about people who had led fascinating lives and I could talk to for hours—Harley Brown and Lori Fleming.

To my surprise, nobody seemed inclined to ask where Ruby Mei would fit on this chart. One thing became very clear, very quickly, though: She was more dedicated and determined than even Dee Neveu. She was the sort you always wanted with you on every school project or every reunion committee. Once she decided to do…well, pretty much anything, you can bet it's going to get done.

"It's like when you want to skydive," Leonard said of his friend. "She just goes after things. She says, 'I'm going to prove this person wrong.' Say, 'You're not going to jump' and she'll say, 'Oh, yes I will!'"

This was not a hypothetical. It was one of the countless examples of Mei accomplishing whatever she'd been told couldn't be accomplished throughout the course of her 35-plus years on the planet. (All she'll say about her age is that she's legally old enough to run for president.)

While making intense eye contact—one of the very few Can't-idates to do so—she told me, "It gets done. Whatever it is, it gets done. It's like when I was young and wanted a haircut. My mother repeatedly tells it: I wanted a haircut and my favorite cousin was Jacob, so I wanted to look like him."

"She didn't understand the difference between boys and girls," An laughed.

"I went through the house to look for scissors and gave myself the ugliest haircut," Mei explained, cool and detached, like she still wasn't entirely sure she trusted me. There was even a

Craig Tomashoff

hint of proper English accent to her speech, like that posh style Madonna, Johnny Depp and Gwyneth Paltrow use when they want to sound more important. "My mother tried to keep the scissors from me, but that was the first time I remember that I attacked something people told me not to do."

She's been on the attack plenty since then. When she took a job at a sign shop she learned how to weld, after co-workers figured it wasn't a job for a girl. When An was playing violin at an opera and the director realized they needed help designing and making the actors' costumes, Mei got it all done in a week. When she wanted to become a massage therapist and learned that all the hours of "hand time" she'd put in at school didn't count toward her license, she tried to become a member of the health department to change that rule.

From that perspective, running for president isn't crazy. It's simply turning to the next page.

"I don't see my decision as extreme. I'm looking into other things, like the Board of Education, mayor...I'm seeing what they can do. And, honestly, don't get me wrong, but it's just not big enough. It's not fixing some of the issues that could be easily fixed. Running for president is the biggest solution for what I want to do."

And what exactly is it that she wants to do? Hard to tell. Mei's political leanings were not overly transparent. I learned from An that her sister doesn't like fracking (a controversial drilling process that injects a high-pressure water mixture into solid rock to extract natural gas) and the influx of money that has made independent campaigns like hers seem like a joke. But there weren't many issue statements forthcoming.

Despite the lack of specifics—or perhaps because of it— Mei doesn't worry much about others laughing at her candidacy. She was uniquely realistic, more so than most of the other Can't-idates I'd spoken to. It's not as if she expects to be packing for the White House in a year. But for her, running for president is just another demonstration of living life without limits. That's what she's been like all the way back to her childhood near Las Cruces, New Mexico. When I was five, my grandest ambition was to stay up late enough to watch *The Man from U.N.C.L.E.* When Mei was five, she decided she wanted to be president.

It's almost like destiny. Her grandmother had wanted to go after the top job too—to the point where she even named her son George Washington. But grandma's wasn't an era when women had much success in politics. So she passed her drive onto Mei's mother, who in turn "tried to get us to do everything—music, farming, business, accounting. Anything we could imagine. And that's what I've been doing."

Her dad was a civil engineer, while her mom had a degree in theology and ran a construction business. The family also sold chilies, corn and cotton they grew on their land. They did as well as any local supermarket chain "because there was nothing else around," Mei recalled. Her family's heritage was Sicilian, but Mei's grandfather insisted his family speak only English so they wouldn't stand out.

Her family elders did cling to some customs from the old country. Like the belief that women were second-class citizens. Which meant a childhood that, at least to outsiders, sounds like the plot from *Footloose*. Her father said, "Dancing is for whores"— and her mom tacitly went along with the notion. Despite discovering the beauty of ballet at an early age, Mei avoided pursuing dance for years because she knew her father wouldn't allow it. Eventually her mother secretly arranged for her daughter to have private dance lessons. That secrecy ended, along with her parents' marriage, and Mei and her sisters followed their mother into a whole new world. It was a major change in Mei's young life, but it was not to be the only one.

For instance, she never liked going to school, not because she didn't enjoy studying, but because she seemed to like it *more* than her classmates did.

Public school, she felt, was "too slow." So when it was time for high school, "that was something else I attacked. I came home one day and said, 'Mom, I un-enrolled myself from school.' I was home-schooled for the rest of high school, and I saw the difference within the first two months. I actually went through an entire textbook. I went through a whole class. I went through the whole biology curriculum in a month."

She finished her high school requirements by 16 and enrolled at the University of Texas in Austin. Mei struck me as somebody who is not easily surprised, but An remembers her sister sounding shocked when she called home to say "the people here are *happy*." The laidback Austin attitude had enveloped her. She finally felt comfortable exploring many different paths in life rather than simply walking the straight and narrow toward her future. A few weeks into her new life, Mei decided she "was interested in quantum physics. I wanted to study dimensions. I really wanted to study time."

"So she called to say she was going to be a physics major," An remembered. "I don't know how many months later, she calls to tell me, 'I'm a prima ballerina.' I was like, 'How did that *happen?*' But I think by then we were used to it."

"All I wanted to do was dance," Mei happily chimed in. "This was my logic. You can dance professionally maybe until you're 30, but you really have to be established in a company. Most people want to get someone on stage that is between 17 and 21. They don't want older."

The more she explained her resumé, the more I realized how much she and Ferguson had in common. They had both run through more life changes by their 20s than I had into my 50s.

This is not necessarily a bad thing. Forever reinventing oneself is a sign of creativity. (Unless you're Madonna, in which case, *enough already!*) It's just that, as she rolled out one life course correction after another, at a certain point it became almost comical.

Leonard has known Mei since she was an 18-year-old trying to make it as a ballet dancer. Even back then, "it was more like, 'Okay, I'm going to start this job for this amount of time and see if this seems to be my main goal.' She'd start off small, but then there was this idea of *how is what she's doing going to touch the world?* And if it doesn't, what does she need to add to it? There are always building blocks that she is putting together, it is just finding which one will get her to the top."

Those blocks have been building for quite some time. There was her stint welding and working in a sign shop. ("I was so good at it that I wanted to be an underwater welder.") She and Leonard once had jobs at a pool company. She took care of horses at an equestrian center. She ran her own business making designer doggie beds. She's helped people organize offices. Mei, along with her mom and sister, operated a storage business for a dozen years. Mei even spent a very brief time dressing up at Disney World. ("I was waiting to be Jasmine, but they asked me to be Pocahontas. Then I went to *Lion King* and then Chip of *Chip and Dale*.")

"A lot of people will use the phrase 'go through' careers —as in, 'How many careers have you gone through,?'" Mei said, her speech perfectly measured as always. "These aren't things I've gone through. They're things that I still hold. Everything I've done, I still hold onto. I still do it, so it doesn't stop. I am just one of those people who are fascinated with everything."

Dance is the one constant. In her 20s, Mei remembers performing ballet for 18 hours a day at venues around the Southwest. As her 30s approached, she moved into teaching dance, something she still loves to do whenever possible—when she's not performing ballet, or teaching, or welding, or learning a new language (Macedonian and Chinese are just two in her repertoire) or riding motorcycles.

Hearing all this, I realized I'd made a huge mistake that first time I spoke with Mei. She'd talked about how "illogical" it would be for her to find a husband and settle down to have kids. Because she was so adamant about this, I had projected onto her my own love of solitude. I just assumed she was like me, that there was a deeper issue going on. Maybe something happened in her past that kept her from wanting to create significant human attachment in her present?

As it turns out, I think I was just hoping to find someone as emotionally frozen as I was, so I didn't feel like such a freak. We'd both chosen to live life solo. But Mei was honest about her reasons for that decision—her life was too full already—while I was not. Dating and marriage? For me, it all sounds great on paper and in the eHarmony ads. But my cynical reality holds that the odds of winning at that game are about the same as the odds of winning on that lottery ticket I bought after meeting Luis Ramos. I wished again I could have that kind of blind faith in things I can't control, whether it was a person or politics. Love and Lotto— the optimists say *"You can't win if you don't play."* I say, *"Yeah, but you can't lose either."*

For Ruby Mei, though, being single was no more or less a goal than finding a great end table for the dining room. She seemed to have mastered the Gordon Liddy approach to being single. The Watergate co-conspirator once held his hand over a candle until his flesh started to burn. When someone asked him what the trick was, he said, "The trick is not minding." The same goes for relationships. They can be painful. The trick is not minding when they start to hurt.

Besides, it's not like Mei hadn't at least put herself out

there at times. Who hasn't? Friends and family have tried to set her up, with no success.

"They do it inconspicuously. I didn't even know [Leonard] was trying to set me up, I just thought I made a new friend. 'Oh, let's watch the Super Bowl together!'" she laughed.

"He was a good guy," shot back a slightly defensive Leonard.

"He got married right after that Super Bowl!"

There have been a few marriage proposals over the years, like the man from Finland—who was now married and living in London. Eventually friends and family realized they were wasting their time trying to hook her up.

"I think she's better [being single]," Leonard told me. "There's a lot more stability this way. Her mind isn't going, 'Oh, I have to take care of someone else at home.'"

"To me, I didn't see it as an option to have a dating life," Mei told me. "It's not something that I am looking for. In the first place, why do it? There are so many other things that I want to do. I'm never really alone, so I'm not lacking companionship. I'm not lonely. In fact, my sister can confirm, I always try to be alone and it's impossible."

I looked at An, who was smiling and nodding. "It's impossible!"

She should know. An and Ruby share an Austin-area home with their mom—plus a duck, dogs and a cockatoo. They've all been together since An went through what she called "a dark year," and Ruby decided it was best for them to be together under one roof. An's husband was paralyzed in an accident, and she had to devote herself to his full-time care. Ruby moved in to help, while her brother-in-law tried to recover in a San Antonio hospital. Then the darkness arrived.

An's husband was a military veteran. After his accident, he began experiencing the sort of violent, post-traumatic stress disorder symptoms luckier vets like Tom Menier hadn't suffered through. His doctors told her he was unstable and she should hide his extensive collection of historic weaponry. But when An brought him home and he noticed it missing, he flipped out and started throwing things at her.

"He wasn't the same after that," An explained. "I told him it was doctor's orders. [But] he didn't want to hear it, because he was already being violent before then. The following day, he threatened to shoot us all. We didn't know that he had hidden a gun." She took a long pause, fighting back tears, until she looked over at her sister smiling back at her. "After all that, he now lives by the hospital."

Following that incident, An believed it wasn't just her life that turned black. She felt that "everything went bonkers" around the country. Perhaps it's their old school Sicilian heritage, but both An and Ruby grew up reluctant believers in things like evil eyes and omens. And in hindsight, it did seem like An's husband's breakdown was the harbinger for all hell to break loose. There was the Boston Marathon bombing. There was the explosion at the fertilizer company in nearby Waco, which killed 15 people. There were the Moore, Oklahoma tornadoes that killed two dozen people. Race riots ripped through Ferguson, Missouri, while mass shootings became weekly occurrences. As tragedies piled up, An got mad. And "when I get mad, that makes Ruby mad."

"You don't have to be a genius to know something is wrong, and I think that's the feeling of many other people as well," Mei said. "I told An to run for president originally."

"I was like, 'Nooooo! I'm too angry.' But Ruby said, 'Well, we don't need a politician. We need a person.' And then she turns to me and says, 'I'm running for president.' That was the moment!"

Mei smiled and nodded. "That was the moment. And at that moment, that decision wasn't even extreme for me."